CHANGING PATTERN OF CAPITAL MARKETS IN INDIA —AN ANALYTICAL STUDY

Changing Pattern of Capital Markets in India

An Analytical Study

GADDAM NARESH REDDY

2007

CYBER TECH PUBLICATIONS
4264/3 Ansari Road, Daryaganj, New Delhi - 110 002

Changing Pattern of Capital Markets in India
—An Analytical Study

First Edition 2007

Published by G.S. Rawat
For Cyber Tech Publications
4264/3, Ansari Road, Daryaganj, New Delhi - 110 002
E-mail : cybertechpublishers@yahoo.com
Phone : 011-23244078,
Fax : 011-23280028

Printed at
Tanwar Offset Press, Moujpur, # 9810878184

PREFACE

The external sector reforms in India during the 1990s included a market based exchange rate system, introduction of convertibility of rupee for external transactions on the current account and compositional shift in cross-boarder capital inflows from debt creating to non-debt creating flows. The overall approach of prudence was integrated into the process of growing openness and financial liberalization which were basic elements of the package of structural reforms instituted in the wake of the balance of payments crisis of 1991. In order to strengthen the external sector reforms and to benefit from these measures, complementary reforms were introduced in other segments of the economy as well. As a part of the reform process, the Government of India opened up the Indian capital market to global competition and took measures to initiate structural reforms by putting in place the requisite regulatory and supervisory structure in the form of SEBI. In a move towards current account convertibility and to increase foreign exchange inflows, Foreign Institutional Investors (FIIs) were permitted to invest in the tradable Indian securities such as shares, debentures, bonds, mutual fund units etc. through primary and secondary markets as per guidelines issued by Government of India in September 1992.

Change has become a ubiquitous phenomenon. Indeed, the intensity and speed of change in the market place is rendering all veterans, conventional and orthodox organizations and people redundant at an amazing speed. Unambiguously, markets have become merciless without any respect for the long standing and accumulated expertise. Amidst such choppy waves, market participants are virtually left with two choices - either change or perish. Apparently, nothing but change is stable in the world, which interestingly offers both - opportunities and challenges. The changes have been taken place in the administration of stock exchange, securities trading, settlement, delivery versus payment, securities transfer, ownership mode, trading in derivatives, risk containment measures, screen based trading, investor protection fund, introduction of financial derivatives, introduction of commodity futures trading and many more.

In view of that the Indian stock market has been witnessing the most spectacular rise in its history, scaling new heights in the recent past. The last two years have proved to be the most phenomenal for the Indian stock market as equity prices have gained sharply. Increased liquidity on account of record inflows from FIIs supported well by inflows from domestic investors such as mutual funds among others has driven the market to new heights. There is absolutely no doubt that the current rally reaffirms the emergence of the Indian stock market on the global investment radar as reflected in the record FII inflows during the last two years or so. Volatility is an important indicator of the dynamic fluctuation of stock market prices. Sometimes, wide fluctuations in prices of stock can scarce away the investor from the market place. However, they have to know the variations in the stock market from time to time in order to understand the changing pattern of the capital market prices for their decisions to buy/sell the securities.

The present study has been carried out by taking into account the various aspects of the changing pattern of capital markets in India. It covers the primary issues (sector-wise, industry-wise, size-wise, region-wise, euro and book-building), threats and opportunities of regional stock exchanges, investor protection, stock market volatility, liquidity, and its relationship, the impact of FIIs investment on stock market liquidity and volatility, trends and pattern of financial and commodity derivatives on the Indian stock market.

Necessary data and information of the study have been collected from the Government Officials, Reports at national and international levels, and Websites. Various statistical techniques namely Regression Analysis, Co-efficient of Correlation, t-test etc., have been used in this study to analyze and interpret the data. The entire work has been presented in eight chapters including the summary of findings, conclusions and suggestions.

Gaddam Naresh Reddy

ACKNOWLEDGEMENTS

I extend my deep sense of gratitude to my teacher and Research Supervisor, Professor V. Gangadhar for the scholarly guidance, meticulous and discreet care, constructive suggestions, and above all his warm, tender, personal affection, without which this thesis would not have seen the light of the day. I am fortunate to have begun and completed this thesis while Prof. Gangadhar has been the Convener, ICET. He has been kindly and readily continued to evince keen interest in my research even after his busy schedule. Words will not measure to express my heartfelt gratitude to him.

I am grateful to Prof. V. Gopal Reddy, Vice-Chancellor, Prof. R. Sudarshan, Controller of Examinations, Prof. B. Venkat Rathnam, Head of the Department, Prof. K. Krishna Reddy, Dean, Prof. P. Krishnama Chary, Chairman, Board of Studies (Commerce & Business Management), for their moral support and encouragement.

I express my sincere thanks to Prof. G. Srinivas Reddy, Principal, University Arts & Science College (Accredited with "A" Grade by the NAAC), Dr. D. Sakriya, Vice-Principal for their continuous encouragement.

I also thank Prof. O. Ghanshyam Das, Incharge Department, Prof. S. Ravi Prakash, Prof. M. S. Sarma, Prof. K. Sayulu, Prof. G. Narasimha Murthy, Prof. N. Hanumantha Rao, Prof. V.V. S. Sarma, Prof. K. Raji Reddy, Prof. P. Indraseena Reddy, Prof. Ch. Bhagwan Rao, Prof. S. Kamaleshwar Rao, Prof. N. Kusma, Dr. T. Balaraju, Dr. P. Amara Veni, Dr. S. Narasimha Chary, Dr. K. Rajeder, Dr. P. Karunakar Rao, and other friends for their kind cooperation and help during the course of the study.

I am thankful to the Kakatiya University authorities for providing the research facilities.

I am extremely indebted to my parents Sri. G. Bhoom Reddy and Smt. Mallamma, brothers Manohar Reddy, Ashok Reddy, Ravinder Reddy, Thirupathi Reddy, Rajesh Reddy, Anil Reddy, sisters and brother-in-laws and my well wisher Dr. A. Malla Reddy and other friends, my beloved wife Mrs. Vijaya Laxmi and my son Ruthvik Reddy (Bobby), my uncle and aunt Mr. & Mrs. S. Lachi Reddy and brother-in-laws S. Sathyanarayana Reddy and S. Thirupathi Reddy, and all my relatives for their patience and co-operation throughout the research period.

Finally, I thank M/s. Sri Krishna Binding Works, Warangal for their Secretarial work.

Gaddam Naresh Reddy

LIST OF ABBREVATIONS

ADRs : American Depository Receipts
BOD : Bought Out Deal Method
BSE : Bombay Stock Exchange
CCI : Controller of Capital Issues
CFTC : Commodity Futures Trading Commission
CIS : Collective Investment Schemes
CLA : Central Listing Authority
CMIE : Centre for Monitoring Indian Economy
CSO : Central Statistical Organization
DIP : Disclosure and Investor Protection
ECB : External Commercial Borrowing
EDIFAR : Electronic Data Information Filing and Retrieval
ESOP : Employee Stock Option Method
FCCBS : Foreign Currency Convertible Bonds
FIIs : Foreign Institutional Investors
FMC : Forward Markets Commission
GDP : Gross Domestic Product
GDRs : Global Depository Receipts
GDS : Gross Domestic Savings
IMSS : Integrated Market Surveillance System
IPOs : Initial Public Offers
IRDA : Insurance Regulatory & Development Authority
ISM : Indian Stock Market
MAPIN : Market Participants and Investors Identification Number
MC : Market Capitalization
MCX : Multi-Commodity Exchange

MoU	: Memorandum of Understanding
MTM	: Mark to Market Settlement
NAVs	: Net Asset Values
NBOT	: National Board of Trade, Indore
NCDEX	: National Commodity & Derivatives Exchange
NIM	: New Issue Market
NMCE	: National Multi-Commodity Exchange
NNL	: Number of New Listings
NSCCL	: National Securities Clearing Corporation Limited
NSDL	: National Securities Depository Limited
NSE	: National Stock Exchange
OCTEI	: Over the Counter Exchange of India
QUIBs	: Qualified Institutional Buyers
SAT	: Securities Appellate Tribunal
SEBI	: Securities and Exchange Board of India
SEFT	: Special Electronic Fund Transfer
SMILE	: Securities Markets Infrastructure Leveraging Expert Task Force
STP	: Straight Through Processing
STT	: Securities Transaction Tax
TCS	: Trading on Cash Segment
TDS	: Trading on Derivatives Segment
TOR	: Turnover Ratio
TVR	: Traded Value Ratio
UCC	: Unique Client Code
UIN	: Unique Identification Number
ZCYC	: Zero Coupon Yield Curve

LIST OF TABLES

LIST OF FIGURES AND GRAPHS

CONTENTS

CHAPTER-I

INTRODUCTION TO CAPITAL MARKET

1.1: INTRODUCTION

Capital Market is the barometer of the economy. This statement truly brings out the importance of the capital market in the macro economic angle of any country. There is an age old saying that "the capital market discounts the future". The state of the capital market does not reflect the past or present but it reflects the future of the economy of any country. In the long run it is a true measure of the health of any economy. In the recent years, worldwide the countries are moving towards capitalism. In fact the core Socialist and Communist Countries like Russia and China have embraced capitalism. In any capitalist economy, capital markets play a pivotal role in the economy. On removal of the shackles of protectionism and with the liberalization and globalization of economies, the world is becoming a global village and role of capital markets is assuming greater importance. However, larger the role of capital markets greater the responsibility on the regulators, participants, investors for the smooth functioning of the capital markets[1].

Indian economy for over three decades after independence was dominated by the public sector, which was considered as the major vehicle for economic and industrial development. The trend has however, changed since the mid 80's with liberalization of government policies and greater freedom given to the private sector. The policy of progressively deregulating the economy has led to the emergence of stock markets as a major instrument of finance for industry and trade. The Indian economy during

80's had grown at a much faster rate and the average annual growth rate was 5.5 percent as against the almost stagnant annual growth rate of 3.5 percent[2] which was witnessed for earlier three decades. In the 90's, the economy touched a growth rate of 6.5 percent[3]. Equally important is of the fact that the savings ratio in the economy has been high. Gross domestic savings as a percentage of gross domestic products zoomed more or less progressively from a low level of 10.2 percent in 1950-51 to 23.2 percent in 1978-79[4] and has been around 20-22 percent there after[5]. India is thus blessed with a growing pool of savings.

Industry has been growing at a significant rate of about 8 percent in eighties and about 10 percent in nineties as against 5 percent[6] in earlier decades. The driving force for industrial growth is a large and growing domestic market accounting for about 94 percent of the aggregate demand basically emanating from a thriving class of about 150-200 million people[7] with standards of living comparable with their counter parts in developed economies.

The agriculture sector which dominated the economy for a long term, no more does so. The over all dominance of the primary sector comprising agriculture and mining has come down, while secondary and tertiary sectors are having a greater share of economic activity. While the shares of primary sector in the net domestic product declined from 50.1 percent in 1970-71 to 36.15 percent towards the end of eighties[8], and the tertiary sector rose from 30.2 percent to 38.31 percent[9] during the same period. Service sector has also assumed a greater importance and is expected to grow faster.

The reason for which we have been discussing the changing economic scenario is that, we would like to seek answer for the question "whether the changes in the economy have affected the capital and stock market price trends and pattern in India?" For this purpose we have to analyze and discuss at length "Changing Pattern of Capital Markets in India".

1.2: MEANING

The capital market is the market for relatively long-term

financial instruments.[10] It is having a complex of institutions investment and practices with established links between the demand for and supply of different types of capital gains".[11] Capital market may be defined as an organized mechanism for effective and efficient transfer of money capital or financial resources from the investing parties, i.e., individuals or institutional savers to the entrepreneurs (individuals / institutions) engaged in industry or commerce in the business either is in the private or public sectors of an economy[12]. It also refers to the facilities and the institutional arrangements for borrowing and lending term funds (medium-term and long-term funds)[13].

Furthermore, the capital market in a developing economy has to facilitate the main stream of command over capital to the point of the highest yield. By doing so it enables control over resources to pass into hands of those who can employ them most effectively thereby increasing productive capacity and swelling the national dividend.14 The capital market is composed of those who will demand the funds (borrowers) and those who will supply the funds (lenders). An ideal capital market attempts to provide adequate capital at reasonable rate of return for any business or industrial proposition which offers a prospective high yield, enough to make investment worth while. The rapid expansion of the corporate and public enterprises since 1951 has necessitated the development of the capital market in India.15 The major players in the capital market are Corporate Sector, Banks, Financial Institutions and Mutual Funds etc.

1.3: OBJECTIVES

An efficient capital market is a pre-requisite of economic development. An organized and well developed capital market operating in a free market economy must (i) ensure best possible co-ordination and balancing between the flows of savings on the one hand and the flow of investment leading to capital formation on the other; (ii) direct the flow of savings into most profitable channels and thereby ensures optimum utilization of financial resources.

Thus, an ideal capital market is one where finance is used as a hand-maid to serve the needs of industry. Finance is available at a reasonable rate of return for any proposition which offers a prospective yield sufficient to make borrowings worthwhile. The increased rate of savings, proper organization of intermediary institutions, the entrepreneurial qualities of the people and the developed capital market must facilitate the movement of capital to the point of highest yield. Thus, a capital market strives for (i) the mobilization or concentration of national savings for economic development, and (ii) the mobilization and import of foreign capital and investment to augment the deficit in the required financial resources so as maintain the expected rate of economic growth.

1.4: STRUCTURE

Broadly speaking, the capital market can be divided into two constituents: (A) The Financial Institutions and (B) The Securities Market. The financial institutions, e.g., IFCI, IDBI, SFCs, LIC, UTI, etc., provide long-term and medium-term loan facilities. These are also playing prominent role in the capital market operations such as managing and under writing of public issues, participating actively in trading through their mutual fund schemes, etc. The securities market is divided into (I) the gilt- edged market (or the market for government securities) and (II) the corporate securities market. The gilt-edged market is the market for government securities or the securities guaranteed (as to both principal and interest) by the government. Since, the government cannot default on its payment obligations, the government securities are risk free and hence are known as gilt-edged (which means 'of the best quality'). In the corporate securities market securities issued by firms (i.e. shares, bonds and debentures) can be bought and sold freely. It consists of (1) the new issues market (the primary market) and (2) the stock exchange (the secondary market).[16]

1.4.1: Primary Capital Market

The primary capital market deals with new issues of common stock, bonds and preferred stock which are issued by companies to the investing public. The proceeds raised in this market are the new capital or initial capital. The capital can be raised through prospectus, offer for sale, private placement or by offering rights issue.

1.4.2: Secondary Capital Market

The secondary capital market is also called 'Stock Market'. In the secondary markets, the outstanding issues are permitted to trade. In this market, a stock or bond issue which has already been sold to the public and it is traded between current and potential owners. The proceeds from a sale in the secondary market do not go to the issuing organization but to the current owner of the security.

1.5: CAPITAL MARKET INSTRUMENTS

Capital market instruments as long-term sources of finance. They fall into two broad categories (A) Direct and (B) Derivatives. The first category includes (1) Equity Shares, (2) Preference Shares, (3) Deferred Shares, (4) No Par Stock / Shares, (5) Sweat Equity and (6) Debentures / Bonds. The second category includes (1) Forwards, (2) Futures and (3) Options.[17]

1.5. A: Direct Securities

These are the major primary market securities in the financial markets of any country. They differ in their investment characteristics and as such satisfy different preferences of various investors and enjoy differing degrees of popularity. It is necessary to note the major characteristics and the variants of these security types as they prevail in India.

1.5. A.1: Equity Shares

According to Section 2 (46) of the Companies Act, 1956 a share can be defined as "the capital of a company and includes stock except where a distinction between stock and share is expressed or implied". These shares are also called ordinary shares or common shares; represent the owners' capital in a company. The holders of these shares are the real owners of the company. They have a control over the working of the company. Equity shareholders are paid dividend after paying it to the preference shareholders. The rate of dividend on these shares depends upon the profits of the company. Equity share capital cannot be redeemed during the life time of the company. However the Companies (Amendment) Ordinance (October 31, 1998 and January 7, 1999) has allowed companies to buy back their own shares subject to regulations lay down by SEBI. Equity shares have a number of features which distinguish them from other shares and securities. These features generally relate to the rights and position of equity shareholders.

1.5. A.2: Preference Shares

These are complex financial instruments with a number of modifications to its general characteristics. Strictly speaking, it is an ownership security like an ordinary share, but carries a fixed rate of return (dividend) like a debenture. The holders of preference shares are entitled to income after the claims of creditors of the company have been met, but before ordinary shareholders receive any income. Because of these modifications, one comes across the following types of preference shares in the market: (a) cumulative and non-cumulative, (b) convertible and non-convertible, (c) redeemable and non-redeemable, (d) participating and non-participating.

1.5. A.3: Deferred Shares

These shares were earlier issued to promoters or founders for services rendered to the company. Deferred shares were generally of a small denomination and the management of the company remained in their hands by virtue of their voting rights. These shareholders tried to manage the company with efficiency and economy because they got dividend only at last.

1.5. A.4: No Par Stock/Shares

No par stock means shares having no face value. The capital of a company issuing such shares is divided into a number of specified shares without any specific denomination. The share certificate of the company simply states the number of shares held can be determined by dividing the real net worth of the company with the total number of shares of the company. Such shares are issued in certain countries like U.K., U.S.A. and Canada and are gaining popularity there. But in India, no such shares can be issued as the Companies Act, 1956 provides for the issue of only two types shares (i) equity and (ii) preference.

1.5. A.5: Sweat Equity

The term 'sweat equity' means equity shares issued by a company to its employees or directors at a discount or for consideration other than cash for providing know-how or making available rights in the nature of intellectual property rights (say, patents or copyright) or value additions, by whatever name called. The idea behind the issue of sweat equity is that an employee or director works best when he has 'sense of belongingness' and is amply rewarded. Section 79A of the Companies Act, 1956 (inserted w.e.f. 31st October, 1998) allows companies to issue sweat equity shares subject to certain conditions.

1.5. A.6: Debentures/Bonds

A debenture or a bond is an acknowledgement of a debt. It is a certificate issued by a company under its seal acknowledging a debt due by to its holders. In the U.S.A., bonds are secured by tangible physical assets of the company and debentures are secured only the general creditworthiness of the company. In the words of Thomas Evelyn, "a debenture is a document under the company's seal which provides for the payment of a principal sum and interest thereon at regular intervals, which is usually secured by a fixed or floating charge on the company's property or undertaking and which acknowledges a loan to the company's property or undertaking and which acknowledges a loan to the company". There are different kinds of debentures: (a) registered, (b) bearer, (c) perpetual, (d) redeemable, (e) convertible, (f) right, (g) non-convertible, (h) partially convertible, and (i) callable, etc.

1.5. B. Derivatives

The derivatives are most modern financial instruments for hedging risk. The individuals and firms who wish to avoid or reduce risk can deal with the others who are willing to accept the risk for a price.18 Derivative instruments are defined by the Securities Contracts (Regulation) Act to include (a) A security derived from a debt instrument, share, secured/unsecured loan, risk instrument or contract for differences, or any other form of security and (b) a contract that derives its value from the prices/ index of prices of underlying securities. A common place where such transactions take place is called the 'derivative market'. Derivative contracts have several variants. The most common variants are:

1.5. B.1: Forward Contracts

A forward contract is an agreement to buy or sell an asset on a specified date for a specified price in the future. Forward contracts are normally traded outside stock exchanges. They have become popular in all the stock exchanges. The salient features of forward contracts are: (a) They are bilateral contracts and, hence, exposed to counter party risk; (b) Each contract is customer designed, and, hence, is unique in terms of contract size, expiration date and the asset type and quality; (c) The contract price is generally not available in public domain; (d) On the expiration date, the contract has to be settled by delivery of the asset and (e) If a party wishes to reverse the contract, it has to compulsorily go to the same counterparty, which often result in a high price charged.

1.5. B.2: Futures Contracts

A futures contract is an agreement between two parties to buy or sell an asset at a certain time in the future, at a certain price. But unlike forward contracts, futures contracts are standardized and stock exchange traded. The standardized items in a futures contract are: (a) Quantity of the underlying, (b) Quality of the underlying, (c) The date/month of delivery, (d) The units of price quotation and minimum price change and (e) Location of settlement.

1.5. B.3: Options contracts

The growth in organized options markets has resulted with the developments in Options Pricing. The options market is not only extended to stock dealings but also to foreign currencies, commodities, etc. "An option is a contractual agreement that gives the option buyer the right, but not the obligation, to purchase (in the case of a call option) or to sell (in the case of a put option) a specified instrument at a specified price at any time of the option buyer's choosing by or before a fixed date in the future. Upon exercise of the right by the option holder, an option seller is obliged to deliver the specified instrument at the specified price".

1.6: PLAYERS IN THE CAPITAL MARKET

The capital market provides return to the savers in the

form of interest or divided and transfers funds to investors. Capital market diverts resources from wasteful and unproductive channels to productive investments. A well developed capital market helps to integrate the national economy with the global economy by allowing foreign investment in the national economy. The players in the capital market are broadly classified into three categories: (A) Companies Issuing Securities, (B) Financial Intermediaries and (C) Investors.[19]

1.6. A. Companies Issuing Securities

As per SEBI Guidelines, companies intending to issue securities are divided into three categories: (a) New Companies, (b) Existing Listed Companies and (c) Existing Unlisted Companies. If a company is said to be a new company it should be satisfy the three conditions: (i) It has not completed 12 months of commercial operations, (ii) Its audited operative results are not available and (iii) It is set up by entrepreneurs with or without track record. A company is called an existing listed company if its shares are listed in any one of the recognized stock exchanges. Existing closely held or private companies are called as existing unlisted companies.

1.6. B: Financial Intermediaries

Intermediaries are institutional or individual agencies who assist in the process of transforming savings into investment. The major intermediaries in the capital market are: (i) Merchant Bankers, (ii) Under-writers, (iii) Registrars, (iv) Brokers, (v) Depositories, (vi) Collection Agents, (vii) Advertising Agencies, (viii) Agents, (ix) Stock Brokers & Sub-Brokers and (x) Mutual Funds.

1.6. C. Investors

Investors comprising of financial and investment companies and the general public; these are employing funds with the hope of receiving future benefits. The institutions and companies raising capital from investors frame the schemes in such a way that these are suitable to all type of investors. The main objectives of investments are: (i) Safety, (ii) Profitability, (iii) Liquidity, (iv) Capital Appreciation and (v) Minimum Risk.

1.7: SEBI AND CAPITAL MARKET REFORMS

1.7. 1. Introduction

The functioning of the stock exchanges in India has shown many weaknesses, with long delays, lack of transparency in procedures and vulnerability to price rigging and insider trading. To counter these shortcomings, deficiencies and to regulate the capital market, the Government of India has set up the Securities Exchange Board of India (SEBI) in 1988. Initially, SEBI was set up as a non-statutory body, but in January 1992 it was as made a statutory body. SEBI was authorized to regulate all merchant banks on issue activity, lay guidelines and supervise and regulate the working of mutual funds and oversee the working of stock exchanges in India. SEBI, in consultation with the Government, has taken a number of steps to introduce improved practices and greater transparency in the capital markets in the interest of the investing public and the healthy development of the capital markets.[20]

The Capital Issues (Control) Act, 1947 governed capital issues in India so as ensure sound capital structure for corporate enterprises, to promote rational and healthy expansion of the joint stock companies in India and to protect the interests of the investing public from the fraudulent practices of operators. The capital issues control was administered by the Controller of Capital Issues (CCI) according to the principles and policies lay down by the Central Government. The Narasimham Committee on the Reform of the Financial System in India (1991) recommended the abolition of CCI and suggested that SEBI to protect the investors with autonomous powers and take over the regularity function of CCI. The Government of India accepted this recommendation, repealed the Capital Issues (Control) Act, 1947 and abolished the post of CCI. Companies were allowed to approach the capital markets without prior government permission subject to getting their offer documents cleared by SEBI. In other words, SEBI was given the autonomous powers to control and regulate the capital market.

1.7. 2. Capital Market Reforms

To reform means (improve) or become better by the removal

of faults or errors or abuses. A number of developments have taken place in the Indian capital market with the launching of financial reforms since July 1991. Some of the important developments that have taken place in the Indian capital market are given below:

1.7.2.1. From July 1991 to March 1996

* Setting up of Securities and Exchange Board of India (SEBI) with autonomous powers as a regulatory authority over various constituents of the capital market.
* Launching of Over the Counter Exchange of India a second tier bourse permitting smaller companies to raise funds.
* Controller of Capital Issues was abolished and free pricing introduced.
* Insider trading made an offence.
* New Industrial policy and a package of measures to boost industrial investment announced by the Government.
* Guidelines for disclosures and investor's protection issued.
* New guidelines were issued for preferential offers, issue of rights and bonus shares.
* Proportionate allotment of shares for all public issues cleared by SEBI after January 1, 1994 has been made mandatory.
* Capital adequacy norms for brokers announced: For brokers belonging to BSE and CSE minimum deposit required is Rs. 5 lakh each, for Delhi and Ahmedabad Rs. 3.5 lakh each etc; for remaining stock exchanges Rs. 2 lakh each.
* Rules relating to portfolio managers and mutual funds announced. A number of private sector mutual funds launched schemes to mobilize funds for investment.
* Relaxation in the provisions of Foreign Exchange Regulation Act, 1973 (FERA) and MRTP Act, 1969.

* Foreign Institutional Investors (FIIs) registered by SEBI and private placement of issues with FIIs.
* National Stock Exchange (NSE) began on line scrip less trading in India.
* Abolition of licensing system.
* Promoters required subscribing at least 25 per cent of the equity in each class of instrument when more than one instruments is offered to the public.
* Indian companies have been permitted to float Global Depository Receipts, Euro Equity Issues and Floating Rate of Interest Notes in various foreign countries.
* Clearance for financial institutions and banks for their capital issues has been made mandatory.
* Full convertibility of rupee on trade as well as on current account announced.
* Forward trading was banned and a new trading system called the 'twin-track' system was introduced.
* Foreign Equity Investments of Multi-National Corporations (MNC) have increased to 51 per cent of equity capital in their subsidiary companies in India.

1.7. 2.2. Capital Market Reform from April 1996 to March 2002

The process of capital market reforms was carried forward during 1996-2002. A number of reforms, both in the primary as well as secondary markets for equity, debt and foreign institutional investment were made. The following are some of the important reforms made during this period:

* The Depositories Act, 1996 was enacted in July 1996 and SEBI has notified (Depositories and Participants) Regulations in 1996.
* To provide greater flexibility, SEBI gave up vetting of public issue documents.
* To encourage the development of debt market, debt issues not accompanied by an equity component permitted

to be sold entirely by the book-building process subject to Section 19(2) (b) of the Securities Contracts (Regulation) Rules.

* Stock exchanges asked to modify the listing agreement to provide for payment of interest by companies to investors from the 30th day after the closure of a public issue.
* Uniform good-bad delivery norms and procedure for time bound resolution of bad deliveries, through Bad Delivery Cells, prescribed.
* Several restrictions including limits on the size of issues proposed to be listed on OTCEI removed, and listing criteria for OTCEI relaxed.
* The promoter's contribution for public issues has been made uniform at 20 per cent irrespective of the issue size.
* The SEBI Rules and Regulations, 1993 have been amended to provide for an arm's length relationship between the Issuer and the Registrar.
* Only body corporate is now allowed to act as merchant bankers.
* Companies are now required to make their partly paid up shares fully paid up or forfeit the same before making a public or rights issue.
* SEBI regulations enabling companies to buy-back their shares have been framed.
* Requirement to publish unaudited results by listed companies on quarterly basis.
* Introduction of rolling settlement in respect of demat securities.
* SEBI Regulations, 1997 issued and subsequently amended in 1998.
* Compulsory trading of shares in dematerialized form in specified scrips by institutional investors.

* Companies have been given freedom to determine the par value of shares issued by them.
* SEBI modified the framework for book-building.
* Securities Laws (Amendment) Bill, 1999 incorporating derivative instructions in the definition of securities.
* Introduction of rolling settlement for 10 select scrips from January 10, 2000.
* Insurance Regulatory and Development Authority (IRDA) Bill passed by Parliament in December, 1999.
* SEBI's Regulations for Collective Investment Schemes (CIS) were notified on October15, 1999.
* SEBI accepted a system envisaging the use of existing infrastructure of stock exchanges for marketing Initial Public Offers (IPOs).
* Investors can now place buy / sell orders through the internet.
* The SEBI Committee on Venture Capital, set up in July 1999, examined the impediments to the growth of Venture Capital Funds and suggested several measures to facilitate the growth of venture capital activity in India.
* Introduction of derivatives trading in June 2000.
* Introduction of compulsory rolling settlement.
* Compulsory trading of shares of all companies listed in stock exchanges in Demat form with effect from 2ndJanuary, 2002.
* Extension of derivatives trading in equity to index options, stock options and stock futures.
* Notification about the establishment of the Investor Education and Protection Fund with effect from October 1st, 2001.

1.7.2.3. Capital Market Reforms during 2002-03

* Implementation of T+3 rolling settlement for all listed securities across the exchanges from April 2nd, 2002 to

move on April 1st, 2003.

* Introduction of scientific model for risk management, based on Value at Risk.
* Introduction of Electronic Data Information Filing and Retrieval (EDIFAR) System to facilitate electronic filing of certain documents / statements by the listed companies and their immediate disclosure to the market participants.
* Launch of Securities Market Awareness Campaign.
* Introduction of rating corporate governance on the principles of wealth creation, wealth management and wealth sharing.
* Introduction of Straight Through Processing (STP) for the securities transaction.
* Implementation of a comprehensive risk management system for mutual funds.
* Introduction of the dual fungibility of ADRs and GDRs.
* Establishment of the Central Listing Authority (CLA).
* Issuance of necessary guidelines / circulars for Corporatization and Demutualization of stock exchanges.
* Introduction of the trading of government securities on the stock exchange.
* Posting all the orders passed by the Securities Appellate Tribunal (SAT) and the Board on the SEBI website, to bring in regulatory transparency.
* Introducing the consultative process on policy formulation by putting all reports of committees and draft regulations on the SEBI website for seeking comments, suggestions and opinions from public.
* Issuance of guidelines on delisting of securities from the stock exchanges.
* Establishment of inter-depository transfer through on-line connectivity between CDSL and NSDL.

* Review and amendment of the following regulations and guidelines- a measure of regulatory pro-activeness-
* SEBI (Insider Trading) Regulations, 1992
* SEBI (Underwriters) Regulations, 1993
* SEBI (Debenture Trustees) Regulation, 1993
* SEBI (Portfolio Managers) Regulations, 1993
* SEBI (Foreign Institutional Investors) Regulations, 1995
* SEBI (Substantial Acquisition of Shares and Takeovers) Regulations, 1997
* SEBI (Employee Stock Option Scheme and Employee Stock Purchase Scheme) Guidelines, 1999
* SEBI (Credit Rating Agencies) Regulations, 1999
* SEBI (Issue of Sweat Equity) Regulations, 2002
* SEBI (Procedure for Holding Enquiry by Enquiry Officer and Imposing Penalty) Regulations, 2002
* Announcement of Accounting Standards and disclosure practices of the Indian companies by ICAI in consultation with SEBI in accordance with International Accounting Standards.
* Expansion of the derivatives products market.
* Introduction of benchmarking of all the mutual fund schemes to facilitate the understanding of the investors about the performance of funds.
* Introduction of nomination facility for the unit holders of mutual funds.
* Simplification of documentation procedure for FII registration and reduction of registration fee for FIIs.
* Memoranda of Understanding (MoUs) for cooperation and information sharing were signed with international regulators like Securities and Finance Commission of Mauritius and Securities and Exchange Commission of Sri Lanka.

1.7.2.4. Capital Market Reforms during 2003-04

* In order to ensure the high quality of issuers accessing the primary securities market, SEBI has introduced an additional criteria of 'net tangible assets', 'minimum number of allottees in public issue' and 'profitability'.
* With a view to making Indian primary market more disclosure based and comparable with international standards, amendments have been made to the Guidelines to add additional disclosures in the offer documents. The offer documents should contain information relating to financial statements as per the Indian Accounting Standards.
* In order to make price discovery process more realistic, immune from artificial demand and more response to market expectations. The companies have been provided with some flexibility in the indication of price band either movable or fixed floor price in the Red Herring Prospectus. Qualified Institutional Buyers (QIBs) have been prohibited from withdrawing their bids after the closure of bidding.
* As a stabilization tool for listing price of newly issued shares, SEBI has introduced the green shoe option facility in IPOs.
* The Central Listing Authority (CLA) has been set up with Shri M.N. Venkatachalaiah, former Chief Justice of India as its President. The aim of CLA is to ensure uniform and standard practices for listing the securities on stock exchanges.
* With a view to provide greater liquidity in the secondary securities market, SEBI has allowed corporate brokers with a net worth of at least Rs. 3 crore to extend margin trading facility to their clients in the cash segment of stock exchanges.
* The brokers may use their own funds or borrow from scheduled commercial banks or NBFCs regulated by RBI but the total indebtedness for this purpose should not exceed five times the net worth.

* A clearing corporation / cleaning house, after registration with SEBI, under the SEBI scheme for Securities Lending and Borrowing, as an approved intermediary, may borrow securities for meeting shortfalls in settlement, on behalf of the members.
* With a view to providing greater transparency and protecting the interests of investors in debt securities, SEBI has prescribed new guidelines for regulating private placement of debt securities issued by the corporates.
* Full disclosure (initial and continuing) as per Companies Act 1956, SEBI (DIP) Guidelines 2000 and Listing Agreement are to be made by the companies.
* Credit rating of debt securities, appointment of debenture trustees, separate Listing Agreement, frequent furnishing of periodical reports to SEBI etc., have been made mandatory to enhance the protection of investors in debt instruments.
* With a view to promoting up-to-date information about all market participants, SEBI has made it mandatory for every intermediary, to make an application for allotment of unique identification numbers for itself and for its related persons, under the SEBI (Central Database of Market Participants) Regulations, 2003.
* With a view to provide further transparency and mitigating impacts of rumours and speculation, the brokers have been advised to disclose the details of bulk deals. Stock exchanges were advised to amend Clause 41 of the Listing Agreement to make it mandatory for the listed companies to publish the number of investor's complaints received, disposed of, unresolved along with their quarterly results.
* Clearing and settlement cycle time has been further contacted to T+2 with effect from April 1st, 2003 and this measure is expected to result in faster settlement, higher safety and lower settlement risk in the Indian capital market.
* With a view to strengthening the position, specifying

accountability and protecting the interest of investors, SEBI has defined the roles of Chief Executive Officer and Fund Manager of mutual funds.

* Regulatory practices should be fair to all concerned in the market place. In order to enhance fairness, a uniform cut-off time for calculating and applying NAVs, both for subscriptions and redemptions have been prescribed.
* Skewed holdings in mutual funds schemes may lead to distortion. To avoid any distortion in the unit holding pattern and its impact, minimum number of investors in a scheme has been prescribed. Further, it has been specified that no single investor should hold more than 25 percent of the corpus of any scheme / plan.
* Opportunities for investing have been widened for mutual funds by allowing them to invest in derivative securities. They have also been permitted to invest up to 10 per cent of the net assets as on January 31st of each year in the foreign securities with the limit of minimum U.S. $5 million and maximum of U.S. $50 million.
* To make Indian capital market more efficient and world class, new products have been permitted. Interest rate futures contracts were introduced in June 2003 and futures and options contacts on sectoral indices have been introduced in August 2003.
* FIIs and NRIs have been permitted to invest in all exchange traded derivative contracts.
* Exchange trade derivatives contracts on a notional 10 years Government bond have been allowed for trading.
* Stock brokers have been allowed to trade in commodity derivatives.
* To strengthen the "know your client" regime and in the interest of greater efficiency of the market, it has been made mandatory for the FIIs, to report issuance/renewal/ cancellations/redemption of off-shore derivatives instruments against underling Indian securities. Issuance of such derivatives has been limited only to regulated entities.

* FIIs have been allowed to participate in de-listing offers to afford an exit opportunity. They have also been allowed to participate in sponsored ADR / GDR programmes.
* FIIs have also been permitted to participate in divestment by the government in listed companies.
* With a view to making markets more competitive and complaint, SEBI has brought in the following new regulations.
* SEBI (Prohibition of Fraudulent and Unfair Trade Practices relating to Securities Market) Regulations, 2003
* SEBI (Ombudsman) Regulations, 2003
* SEBI (Central Listing Authority) Regulations, 2003
* SEBI (Central Database for Market Participants) Regulations, 2003
* SEBI. (Self Regulatory Organizations) Regulations, 2004
* SEBI (Criteria for Fit Proper Person) Regulations, 2004
* As a measure of regulatory pro-activeness, the existing regulations where reviewed and the following amendment to regulations where notified:
* SEBI (Foreign Institutional Investors) (Amendment) Regulations, 2003
* SEBI (Mutual Funds) (Amendment) Regulations, 2003
* SEBI (Depositories and Participants) (Amendment) Regulations, 2003
* SEBI (Debenture Trustees) (Amendment) Regulations, 2003
* SEBI (Prohibition of Insider Trading) (Amendment) Regulations, 2003
* SEBI (Issue of Sweat equity) (Amendment) Regulations, 2003
* SEBI (Stock Brokers and Sub-Brokers) (Amendment) Regulations, 2003
* SEBI (Procedure for Holding Enquiry and Imposing

Penalty) (Amendment) Regulations, 2003

* SEBI (Ombudsman) (Amendment) Regulations, 2003
* SEBI (Foreign Institutional Investors) (Amendment) Regulations, 2004

1.7.2.5. Capital Market Reforms during 2004-05

* Allocation of shares to retail individual investors has been increased from 25 percent to 35 percent of the total issue of securities in case of book-built issues.
* The retail investor has been redefined as one who applies or bids for securities of or a value not exceeding Rs. 1 lakh, as against the earlier limit of Rs. 50,000.
* The SEBI Disclosure and Investor Protection (DIP) Guidelines, 2000 were amended in order to ensure better readability of the issue advertisements appearing on television and to reduce the cost incurred in publishing pre-issue advertisements.
* The facility of shelf prospectus was introduced for public sector banks, scheduled banks and public financial institutions. They can file a draft shelf prospectus in the first instance disclosing the aggregating amount they intend to raise through various branches.
* All pre-IPO shareholders (including promoters) in case of IPOs and pre-issue shareholders holding more than 5 percent shares (including promoters) in case of follow-on offerings can lend their shares for the purpose of green shoe option.
* The SEBI (DIP) Guidelines 2000 on issue norms were amended to provide for a floor face value of Re.1 per share in order to restrict the pre-IPO splitting of shares. The face value has to be necessarily Rs. 10 per share for issue price below Rs. 500 and in case where the issue price is Rs. 500 or more, the issuer companies can fix the face value below Rs. 10 per share.
* The definition of the minimum application lot has been changed from Rs. 2,000 to a band of Rs. 5,000 - Rs. 7,000.

The applications can be made in multiples of such value.

* The DIP Guidelines for preferential allotment were amended to: (i) restrict sale of shares by shareholders who are allotted shares on preferential basis; (ii) impose lock-in period on pre-preferential shareholding from the relevant date till six months after the date of allotment; (iii) reduce the period for allotment from 30 to 15 days; and (iv) facilitate corporate debt restructuring.
* To improve the standards of corporate governance, SEBI amended Clause 49 of the Listing Agreement.
* In order to further develop the corporate debt market, SEBI prescribed a model debenture listing agreement for all debenture securities issued by an issuer irrespective of the model of issuance.
* The existing structure of dematerialization charges has been rationalized to provide benefits to investors. With effect from February 1st 2005, certain charges paid by investors were removed which include charges towards opening of a Beneficiary Owner (BO) account, credit of securities into BO account and custody charge for BO account opened on or after February 1st 2005.
* The first phase of BSE Indo Next trading platform was inaugurated by the Honorable Finance Minister on January 7th 2005 to provide for a nation-wide trading platform for the small and medium enterprises.
* Mandatory processing of all institutional trades executed on the stock exchanges through the Straight Through Processing (STP) was introduced with effect from July 1st, 2004.
* In order to encourage the trading and clearing members of stock exchanges to use infrastructure of special electronic fund transfer (SEFT) facility as laid down by RBI to the extent possible, the members are not given a choice to opt for payment of mark-to-mark margins, either before the start of trading next day i.e., on T day, or on the next day i.e., T+1.

* Units of money market mutual funds and units of gilt funds were permitted to be accepted towards cash equivalent as part of the liquid assets of a clearing member.
* The eligibility criteria for indices on which futures and options are permitted to be introduced was modified to encourage the introduction of derivatives contracts on sectoral indices.
* The Union Government announced, within an overall External Commercial Borrowing (ECB) ceiling of US $9 billion, a sub-ceiling of US $1.75 billion for FII investment in dated Government Securities and Treasury Bills, both under 100 percent debt route and normal 70:30 route.
* A cumulative sub-ceiling of US $500 million for FII investment in corporate debt was announced over and above the sub-ceiling of US $ 1.75 billion.
* FII position limit in all index options and futures contracts on a particular underlying index shall be Rs. 250 crore (separately for futures and options) or 15 percent of the total open interest of the market in index futures and index options, whichever is higher per exchange.
* The frequency of reporting of offshore derivative instruments by registered foreign institutional investors has been made monthly.
* The mutual funds and FIIs have been advised to enter the Unique Client Code (UCC) pertaining to the parent entity at the order entry level and enter the UCCs for their individual schemes/Sub-accounts on the post-closing session.
* A Securities Markets Infrastructure Leveraging Expert Task Force (SMILE Task Force) was constituted by SEBI to carry out a thorough 'health check' on the securities markets infrastructure encompassing all segments of the markets and covering all market participants and other intermediaries.
* SEBI signed a MoU with United States Commodity Futures Trading Commission (CFTC) at Washington on April

28th, 2004.

* As a measure of regulatory pro-activeness, the existing regulations where reviewed and the following amendment to regulations were notified:
* SEBI (Venture Capital Funds) Regulations, 2004.
* SEBI (Foreign Venture Capital Investors) (Amendment) Regulations, 2004.
* SEBI (Central Database of Market Participants) (Amendment) Regulations, 2004.
* SEBI (Portfolio Managers) (Amendment) Regulations, 2004.
* SEBI (Depositories and Participants) (Amendment) Regulations, 2004.
* SEBI (Buy-back of Securities) (Amendment) Regulations, 2004.
* SEBI (Procedure for Holding Enquiry by Enquiry Officer and Imposing Penalty) (Amendment) Regulations, 2004.
* SEBI (Substantial Acquisition of Shares and Takeovers) (Amendment) Regulations, 2004.
* SEBI (Procedure for Holding Enquiry by Enquiry Officer and Imposing Penalty) (Second Amendment) Regulations, 2004.
* SEBI (Substantial Acquisition of Shares and Takeovers) (Second Amendment) Regulations, 2004.
* SEBI (Procedure for Holding Enquiry by Enquiry Officer and Imposing Penalty) (Third Amendment) Regulations, 2004.

1.8: REVIEW OF LITERATURE

Liberalization, Privatization and Globalization (LPG) reform process in the economy have been influencing for increased role of the capital market in India. In the process of liberalization various amendments were made in the existing Acts of FERA, MRTP, abolition of Controller of Capital Issues and Licensing System and establishment of SEBI with autonomous powers.

All these measures have shown everlasting impact on capital market and its various parties such as Stock Exchanges, Investors, Financial Intermediaries, Brokers, Underwriters, and Mutual Funds etc. The literature on the changing pattern of capital markets are collected from various research studies and statistical information from the publications of RBI, SEBI, CMIE, Stock Holding Corporation of India Limited, NSE, BSE, the Institute of Cost & Works Accountants of India, the Institute of Chartered Accountants of India, the Hindu, the Economic Times, and Ministry of Finance etc.

The review of literature is presented as per the chapters covered in this study. Various institutions conducted several studies, seminars, symposia and conferences; and individual researchers also published their studies on the impact of economic reforms on the capital market performance. Distinguished Economists, Financial Advisors, Professionalists and Experts paid their attention to the problems and prospects of economic reforms in India like Chuppe & Atkin[21], Loklin[22], Miller-III (James. C)[23], R.K. Sinha[24], V.S. Mahajan[25], Dalip S.Swamy[26], Hari Shanker Singhania[27] N.K.P. Sinha & M.B. Singh[28], S.P. Gupta[29], A.N. Agarwal[30], Aggarwal & Chowdhary[31], and L.C. Gupta[32].

1.8.1. Studies on Capital Market Reforms

Prof. V. Gangadhar & Yadagiri (1993)[33]: In their research paper on "Capital Market Reforms in India", have stated that the financial market can be broadly grouped into the following two categories viz., (a) Capital Market, (b) Money Market, long term financial Instruments such as; shares-preference and equity, bonds and debentures; are traded in the capital market. For the balanced and sound economic development a sound and strong capital market is a must. Whereas money market consists of a group of markets in which low risk, high liquid large denomination debt instruments such as short-term bills, treasury bills, bankers' acceptance and commercial paper are traded. The Industrial Securities Market is further divided into two categories viz., (a) Primary Market and (b) Secondary Market. Primary Market refers to raising of capital in the form of fresh public issue of shares, debentures or bonds of private and public companies. The securities so issued in primary market i.e., existing financial instruments of existing companies are traded in secondary markets.

R. Nagaraj (1996)[34]: His study on "India's Capital Market Growth, Trends, Explanations and Evidence", has examined trends of the capital mobilization during the 1960-61 to 1992-93. The proportion of equity capital in capital mobilization accounted for 30 per cent in two decades.

L.M. Bhole & Shreeya Pattanaik (2002)[35]: They discussed the working of Indian Stock Market (ISM) from both quantitative and qualitative perspectives so as to find out how far the goal of liberalization policy has been achieved. In particular, they have stated whether and how far the ISM is characterized by volatility. Among other things, it finds that (a) the ISM is still speculative, volatile and riddled with certain drawbacks, (b) the share price behavior in India, particularly short-term one cannot be explained in terms of economic fundamentals, the state of ISM can hardly be said to be a barometer of the state of the Indian economy, (d) hyper liquidity on the secondary market does not necessarily ensure a vibrant new issue market and (e) a significant negative relationship between the rate of interest and stock market variables is absent.

R.N. Agrawal (2003)[36]: His study supports the Levine and Zervos argument that well developed stock markets may be able to offer different kinds of financial services. Also, the parameters of capital market development, the size and liquidity are found statistically significant to explain the economic activity. Correlation analysis reveals that the banking sector and capital market development indicators are complementary and not substitute for each other. The study has also inferred that the right variable to be a proxy for the expansion of economic activity is the totality of funds mobilized by the corporate sector from alternative sources and not merely the credit by the commercial banks.

M.T. Raju (2004)[37]: He pointed out that today's Indian capital market is one of the most modern, transparent, safe, efficient and highly investor centric in the world. Investors, issuers, stock exchanges, mutual funds, foreign institutional investors, intermediaries and other constituents of the market are all committed to promote and develop sustainable capital market. He presented the SEBI's role over the past one decade in the strengthening and active functioning of stock exchanges in the country for the protection of investors' interest. He also pointed out the number of reforms taken place in the capital market.

1.8.2. Studies on Primary Capital Market

Manoj Kumar et al., (2001)[38]: Their study assesses the impact of listing of ADRs / GDRs on the liquidity of the firm's underlying domestic shares by using a sample of 30 Indian Depository Receipt programmes that listed on the foreign markets between 1st January, 1996 and 30th June, 2001. Consistent with the theoretical assertions and results of Domowitz, Glen and Madhavan (1998), the authors record mixed results - while ADR listings in most cases reduce the liquidity of the domestic underlying shares, GDR listings in most cases increase the liquidity of the domestic underlying shares.

Dr. Madhu Kalimipalli & Dr. Latha Ramchand (2002)[39]: The Objective of the study is to document changes in returns, volatility and liquidity on the local market following foreign capital raising events by Indian firms. They examine a sample of 49 Indian firms that raised capital (via equity listing and/or ADR issue) abroad during 1999-00. They find that subsequent to gaining foreign exposure, firms experienced a decline in all the following: returns, volatility of returns, high / low price ranges and volatility of the daily price range on the local (Indian) market. These together imply lower bid-ask spreads and hence improved liquidity in the domestic market. Comparing these to firms that raise capital on the local (Indian) market only, they find that there are no significant differences in price ranges across the two groups. Firms gaining foreign exposure in fact experience a smaller decline in volatility of returns as well as volatility of the daily high / low price range compared to firms issuing equity only on the local market. The results suggest that foreign issue of equity does not improve liquidity on the local (Indian) market anymore than domestic issue.

Bharati Pathak (2003)[40]: He observed in his paper that the Government Securities Market in India was underdeveloped because of inefficient market prices, limited institutional infrastructure, absence of definite limits on the automatic monetization of the Central Government Budget deficits and little control of RBI on volume and maturity structure of securities. The government initiated reforms in the Government Securities Market in the early nineties. These reforms were undertaken as the vibrant Government Securities Market is significant for activating internal debt management policy and for effective conduct of monetary policy.

The objective of his paper is to study the impact of these reforms on the primary market segment and secondary market segment of the Government Securities Market for the period 1990-1991 to 1999-2000. The analysis reveals that the government securities market has attained width and depth but still some more policy measures are needed to make it more vibrant.

G.L. Malodia (2003)[41]: He has critically evaluated the legal provisions to curb the insider trading in India and some other countries. He made some suggestions for effective control of insider trading. They are (a) SEBI may organize seminars, symposiums and diploma programme to improve investment education, (b) companies must take necessary steps to provide all relevant information to their shareholders, (c) there should be a single regulatory body with the merger of SEBI and the Company Law Board and (d) to prevent misuse of material/ price sensitive information by company personnel, a full fledged internal corporate policy is required.

Sanjay K Hansda & Partha Ray (2003)[42]: Their study looks into the price interdependence of 10 India companies, which have floated ADRs. The strong correlation between the prices of the dually listed stocks is corroborated by the finding of bidirectional causality in a vector auto regression model. The competing domestic stock exchange, viz., NSE too is found to share the same bidirectional relation scrip-wise with the NASDAQ / New York Stock Exchange. Furthermore, the impulse responses pattern indicates that a positive shock in the domestic (international) price of scrip gets transmitted in terms of a strong positive movement in the international (domestic) price the very next day. Thus, the quotes of both the markets share not only stock-wise bidirectional causality, but markets also are efficient in processing and incorporating the pricing information.

Prof. V. Gangadhar & Arifa Begum (2004)[43]: They analyzed type-wise and industry-wise ownership pattern of capital issues in India and the role of public / private sector in mobilizing capital from the public. Some of the important conclusions drawn are: (i) The Average number of capital issues was at 978.8 and their amount stood at Rs. 43,040.7 crore. The year 2000-01 claimed with highest position with an amount of Rs.77,383 crore. (ii) The amount of capital issues steeply declined to -38.7 per cent in the year 2001-02 due to adverse capital market conditions, price volatility, attack on World Trade Center on September 11th 2001 etc. (iii) The ownership pattern of capital issues revealed that the private sector claimed 84.9 per cent of number of issues, whereas public sector has claimed 55.4 percent of the amount of capital issues. (iv) The amount of capital issues by the private sector was moving among 57.4 per cent to 74.9 per cent up to 1995-96 along with their number of issues accounting for 96 per cent. Alternatively the public sector has claimed 2.8 to 4 per cent of number of capital issues during that period.

Alan Blaylock & Edwin H. Duett (2004)[44]: Their study finds that the marginal listing firm experiences a significantly smaller change in the cost of capital during listing than that of previous listing firms from same market. A declining reaction found during the announcement period is not significant. The results are robust to changes in local and US market risks from period to period.

Manas Pandey (2004)[45]: He examines the contribution of domestic saving in the growth of new issue market. He concluded that the principle of economic growth focuses on generating saving and channelising them into productive investment. The behavior of the saving rate in India during the reform period proved to be an improvement in financial assets and emergence of marketable return. All these could be possible only when the government discourages the deposits specially bank deposit, limiting the saving in other sources and some extent the government taxation policy regarding taxes on income which may help in the investment in securities.

Prof. V. Gangadhar & Mr. G. Naresh Reddy (2005)[46]: They

have stated that the book-building system is a part of Initial Public Offer (IPO) of Indian companies. It was introduced by SEBI on the recommendations of Y.H. Malegam in October 1995. It is most practical, fast and efficient management of Mega Issues. Book-Building involves sale of securities to the public and the institutional bidders on the basis of predetermined price range. It is an innovative method of marketing securities involving price determination and quantum of securities on the basis of demand from the prospective shareholders. In this process the SEBI (Market Regulator) has issued various guidelines for control and regulation of book-building process. Since inception of book-building process in India, share of Mega Issues in total capital mobilized is increased from 60.1 percent in 1994-95 to 92.3 percent in 2003-04.

1.8.3. Studies on Secondary Capital Market

S. Amanulla & M Thiripalraju (2001)[47]: He tests whether the carry-forward transactions in different periods have any impact on week-end effect in the Indian stock market during the period January 1990- December 1999. He used the daily stock return of 82 companies traded in the BSE and three stock market price indices, Viz., BSE Sensitive Index, BSE National Index, and S&P CNX Nifty Index to investigate the week-end effect. The results from the sub-sample period strongly support the existence of week-end effect during the period of ban on carry-forward (Badla) transactions. This study also evidenced a reversal in week-end effect, i.e., positive Monday return and negative Friday return in modified carry-forward transactions and revised modified carry-forward transactions. This study further revealed that there was consistent positive return on Wednesday and negative return on Tuesday due to possible impact of NSE on the week-end effect.

Philip Maiyo & Subash Chander (2001)[48]: They examine the theory of random walks in stock prices with special reference to non-specified shares listed on the Bombay Stock Exchange. The analysis has been made using daily data of stock prices during the period 1-1-1996 to 30-11-2000. In addition, the market indices-BSE 100, BSE 200 and S&P CNX Nifty have also tested for the specified period, in order to examine the independence of these index series. The results show that the non-specified shares as well as marked indices duly follow the random walk hypothesis.

S. Amilan (2004)[49] : His paper is aimed at analyzing the influence of corporate fundamentals on the equity returns by testing the year wise consistency of equity returns with the corporate fundamentals in the selected industries. For this purpose he has considered four industries namely, textile, chemical, electrical equipment and computer and software. In each industry equity returns of the sample companies were regressed on the values of corporate fundamentals of the companies with one year lag. Based on the values of the regression coefficients of the independent variables the consistency of equity returns with the corporate fundamentals was tested. The regression result proved that in general the equity returns are not consistent with the corporate fundamental in the selected industries in India.

Prakash Nath Bhargva (2004)[50]: presented the application of Vector Auto Regressions (VARs) technique to assess share price movements. He has specified three variables VAR and applied it to cross-section stock market data from the Indian Stock Market on particular dates. The coefficients estimated are found to be very systematic and consistent and the equations show high statistical significance and determination. The estimated VARs and coefficients are demonstrated as useful in assessing whether the market is high or low, stable or unstable, volatile or non-volatile. The overall exercise gives encouraging results. The technique used here has wide scope of application, improvements and uses in the fields of equity and macroeconomic research.

R.L. Tamboli (2004)[51]: He analyzed the issues relating to accounting disclosure and investor protection. He analyzed impact of disclosure and regulatory authorities' efforts on investor protection. He discussed philosophy, concepts, accounting disclosure norms and actual practices. Based on the information collected from 100 respondents, his study concluded that the individual investors relied highly upon 'Materials on Financial Products' followed by 'Annual Reports' and 'Verbal Advice'. Investors preferred small saving schemes than corporate securities followed by consumer durables and real estates. Personal lending remained at last and least preference. The investors faced grievances on corporate investments remaining unknown about the right authorities to be approached.

S N Sarma (2004)[52]: His study aims at exploring the presence of seasonality in the Indian stock market returns during the post liberalization period. Using the log returns data on three popularly used BSE indices - SENSEX, NATEX, and BSE200- for the period January 1st 1996 to August 10th 2002, the study provides evidences as to the presence of seasonality across the days of the week. It confirms the conclusions of earlier studies as to the leptokurtic distribution of equity returns; presence of highest variance on Mondays; weekend effect, and regularity of returns across the indices. It also confirms the conclusions as to the futility of trading strategy based on the observed regularity of returns.

Suchismita Bose & Dipankor Coondoo (2004)[53]: They examined the impact of the FII policy reforms on FII portfolio flows to the Indian stock markets. They tried to assess the impact on FII flows of several policy revisions related to FII investment during the period January 1999 to January 2004, through a multivariate GARCH regression model. Their results suggest that liberalization policies have had the desired expansionary effect and have either increased the mean level of FII inflows and/or the sensitivity of these flows to a change in BSE return and/or the inertia of these flows. On the other hand, the restrictive measures aimed at achieving greater control over FII flows also do not show any significant negative impact on the net inflows; they find that these policies mostly render FII investments more sensitive to the domestic market returns and raise the inertia of the FII flows.

Joydeep Biswas (2005)[54]: He studied the role of foreign portfolio investments in the development of noise driven Indian stock market. The inflows of huge institutional investments in India increased the turnover and market liquidity. But excessive speculation indulged by institutional investors is the single most important reason for abnormal fluctuations of share price in Indian stock market in the post-liberalization period. The study concludes that foreign portfolio investments influence the share price movement in Indian stock market but their role in the development of stock market in India is still questionable.

1.8.4. Studies on Stock Market Volatility & Liquidity

1.8.4.1. Studies on Volatility

Edwards (1988)[55]: He studied whether stock Index futures trading destabilized the spot market in the long run. Using variance ratio of F tests for the period June 1973 to May 1987, he concluded that the introduction of futures trading did not induce a change in spot volatility in the long run.

Chan et.al, (1991)[56]: They estimated the intraday relationship between returns and returns volatility in the stock Index and Index Futures. Their study covered both S&P 500 and Major Market Index (MMI) futures. Bivariate GARCH models were used to estimate volatility. Their results indicate a strong inter market dependence in volatility of spot and futures returns.

Kamara (1992)[57]: He examined the influence of innovations in the rate of productive activity, unanticipated changes in the default risk premium, unanticipated changes in discount rate, unanticipated price level changes and changes in expected inflation on the volatility for the pre and post futures periods. The results indicate that the increase in volatility in the post futures period cannot be completely attributed to the introduction of futures trading.

Antoniou & Holmes (1995)[58]: They examined the relationship between information and volatility in FTSE 100 Index in the U.K using GARCH technique. They find that introduction of FTSE 100 Index Futures has changed volatility in the spot market and attributes this to better and faster dissemination of information flow due to trading in stock Index Future.

Gregory et.al, (1996)[59]: They examined how volatility of S&P 500 Index Futures affects the S&P 500 Index volatility. Their study also examined the effect of good and bad news on the spot market volatility. Volatility was estimated using EGARCH model. They find that bad news increased volatility more than good news and the degree of asymmetry was higher for futures market.

J.S. Pasricha & Umesh C. Singh (2001)[60]: Their study found that FIIs have remained net investors in the country except during 1998-99 and their investment has been steadily growing since their entry in the Indian markets. They are here to stay and have become the integral part of Indian capital market. Although their investment in relation to market capitalization is quite low, they have emerged as market movers. The market has been moving, in consonance with their investment behavior.

M.T. Raju & Kiran Karande (2003)[61]: They studied price discovery and volatility in the context of introduction of Nifty futures at the NSE in June 2000. Co integration and Generalized Auto- Regressive Conditional Heteroscedasticity (GARCH) techniques are used to study price discovery and volatility respectively. The major findings are that the futures market (and not the spot market) responds to deviations from equilibrium; price discovery occurs in both the futures and the spot market, especially in the later half of the study period. The results also show that volatility in the spot market has come down after the introduction of stock index futures.

Kalyan Mukherjee (2003)[62]: He finds that the time of buying of scrip, 'Monday' would be the most appropriate day and 'Wednesday' would be the most appropriate day for selling of scrip. Monthly analysis shows that month of December would be the most appropriate month for buying of scrip and the month of May would be the most appropriate month for selling.

Harvinder Kaur (2004)[63]: His study described the extent and pattern of stock return volatility of the Indian stock market during the last decade of the previous millennium, i.e. from 1990 to 2000. He covers the two most prominent spot price indices viz. BSE Sensex and S&P CNX Nifty. It is found that the stock market volatility was the highest during 1992 followed by 1990 and 2000, in that order. It fell sharply after 1992 until 1995, after which it started increasing again. This result is confirmed by findings, based on daily as well as monthly returns.

M.T. Raju & Anirban Ghosh (2004)[64]: Their study concludes that mature markets continue to provide over long period of time high return with low volatility. Amongst emerging markets except India and China, all other countries exhibited low returns. India with long history and China with short history, both provide as high a return as the US and UK market could provide but the volatility in both the countries is higher. The third and fourth order moments exhibit large asymmetry in some of the developed markets. Comparatively, Indian market shows less of Skewness and Kurtosis. Indian markets have started becoming informationally more efficient. Contrary to the popular perception in the recent past, volatility has not gone up.

A. K. Seth & Saloni Gupta (2005)[65]: They used the quality control approach to study the volatility of common stock in India at the market level and devised a trading behavior at BSE. They examined how the returns in the Indian stock market behaved in the financial liberalization. Volatility is an important indicator of stock market efficiency and development. He measured the average level of volatility from the year 1980 to 2003. This period covers a wide range of political and economic events that may have influenced the economy and the stock market. Estimates of the standard deviation of monthly return in a year, daily return in a year and daily return in a month are made to have a complete idea of the level (size) and nature of volatility. Further, he established the acceptable limits of volatility that may be embedded in the decision making of investors, depending on the type of investors.

Parthapratim Pal (2005)[66]: He has studied the volatility in Stock Market in India and Foreign Institutional Investors - Post-election Crash. The influence of FIIs on the movement of the Sensex became apparent after the 2004 general elections in India when the sudden reversal of FII flows triggered a panic reaction which resulted in very high volatility in the India stock market. During this period, the Sensex experienced the worst single-day decline in its history. In the three months between April and June 2004, the index declined by about 17 percent. And it all started because of the selling pressure exerted by the FIIs after the elections when they became less confident about the continuation of the reform process in India. FII control in the companies that constitute the Sensex is very high. Data on the shareholding pattern show that the FIIs are currently the most dominant non-promoter shareholder in most of the Sensex companies and they also control more tradable shares of these companies than any other investor group.

1.8.4.2. Studies on Liquidity

A study conducted by the World Bank (1997)[67] reported that stock market liquidity improved in those emerging economies that received higher portfolio investments.

Levine & Zervos (1998)[68] *Kim & Singhal* (2000)[69] have opined that the evidence for the liquidity enhancing effects of capital inflows.

Chandra (2002)[70] concluded that the stock market liberalization improves liquidity of stock markets.

Patro & Wald (2003)[71]: They examined the company level analysis on the impact of capital market liberalization in 18 emerging economies they found that the cost of raising equity capital for firms reduced considerably after stock market liberalization. Lowered cost of raising capital is one of the important indicators of stock market liquidity and therefore, it leads credence to the prediction of theory that stock market liberalization improves stock market liquidity.

Gurcharan Singh (2004)[72]: His Study highlighted that the securities market in India has come a long way in terms of infrastructure, adoption of best international practices and introduction of competition. Today, there is a need to review stock exchanges and improve the liquidity position of various scrips listed on them.

1.8.5. Studies on Financial Derivatives & Commodity Futures

B. K. Vashist & Ashutosh Vashist (2002)[73]: He has made an attempt to conceptualize the determination of equilibrium price, of an agricultural futures contract and its relationship with the expected spot price at maturity of the contract. There are two distinctive features of this theoretical study: (i) The spot market demand and supply conditions expected (by the hedgers) to prevail at the maturity of the futures contract, the risk aversion of hedgers, and finally, the expectations of speculators regarding current spot market and their responsiveness to the same, are the three important determinants of equilibrium contract price. (ii) The equilibrium relationship between the contract price and the expected spot price over the different seasonal phases of the crop-year is due basically to shifts in the net position (in futures) of hedgers & speculators as a whole rather than simply to shifts in the net hedging interest.

Dr. Premalata Shenbagaraman (2004)[74]: Author explored the impact of the introduction of derivative trading on cash market volatility using data on stock index futures and options contracts traded on the S&P CNX Nifty. The results suggested that futures and options trading have not led to a change in the volatility of the underlying stock index, but the nature of volatility seems to have changed post-futures. This study also examined whether greater futures trading activity (volume and open interest) is associated with greater spot market volatility. It finds no evidence of any link between trading activity variables in the futures market and spot market volatility. The results of this study are especially important to stock exchange officials and regulators in designing trading mechanisms and contract specifications for derivative contracts, thereby enhancing their value as risk management tools.

Sunil Kumar (2004)[75]: He has investigated into the futures markets in agriculture commodities in India. The results obtained from regressions for a sample of five commodities traded in six exchanges reveal that these futures exchanges fail to discover prices and provide efficient hedge against the risk emerging from price volatility. The futures markets in these commodities are not efficient and futures prices are not unbiased predictors of the future ready rates. The analysis also reveals that futures markets are unable to effectively incorporate information. The time series data in respect of spot prices and futures prices exhibit presence of unit roots implying weak-form of market efficiency. The cointegration tests reveal that the futures and ready markets do not have long-term equilibrium relationship.

Basab Dasgupta (2004)[76]: His study suggested that the allegation against futures market in India 'that it distorts the spot market price and creates artificial scarcity by allowing unnecessary hoarding', is a misconception. This study finds out that there is a co-movement among futures price, production decision and the inventory decision. With the assumption that future market is monopolistically competitive, the study finds that future price elasticity of production always being greater than or equal to one, an increase in profit by increasing price is not possible. Therefore, the doubt about its distorting effect on spot price can be ruled out. The suspicion about the increasing hoarding resulting from futures market can also be proved unjustified from results. His results show that futures price elasticity on inventory is inversely related with the carrying cost. Therefore, an unnecessary hoarding will increase the carrying cost leading to a lower responsiveness of inventory to futures prices. This study also finds out the effect of expected production shocks on futures price elasticity of supply.

1.9. STATEMENT OF PROBLEM

In a broad context, the research problem is to identify major issues encountered in the capital markets in India and its impact on the individual and institutional investors. The study will make an attempt to critically evaluate the growth, pattern and trends in capital markets and to seek solutions for various problems. The research will address the following:

* What changes have occurred and what will be their impact on investors of both Primary and Secondary Markets in India?
* What will be the performance of stock exchanges in India?
* What will be the role played by SEBI in the protection of interests of investors?
* What will be the relationship and impact between volatility and liquidity in the Indian stock market?
* How the Derivatives Markets will be functioning and how these will be minimizing the risk and price volatility?
* What will be the growth and development of commodity futures market in India?

1.10: OBJECTIVES OF THE STUDY

The following are the objectives of the study:

* To examine the patterns of the capital market in the post reforms period.

* To analyze the impact of various guidelines and regulations framed by the SEBI for the protection of investors as well as the capital markets.
* To study the capital issues in the primary market according to sector-wise, industry-wise, size-wise and region-wise in order to bring out the diversities if any in them as well as to present the possible reasons for such position.
* To evaluate the performance of both primary and secondary capital markets in India.
* To examine the strengths and weaknesses of derivatives market in India with regard to minimization of risk and price volatility.
* To discuss the pattern and development of commodity futures market in India.

1.11: HYPOTHESES OF THE STUDY

An industrializing economy like India can greatly benefit in different ways by introducing changing policies and procedures in the capital market from time to time. The research study purposes to test and prove the following hypotheses:

* Whether the performance of primary market is fairly satisfactory for mobilizing savings from various sections of investors?
* The sector-wise, region-wise, industry-wise, size-wise public issues do not have major diversities.
* Whether the pre-pricing of public issues has created confidence in the investing public and helped for mobilization of the capital?
* The performance of secondary market both to investors as well as players do not differ significantly.
* The SEBI through its regulatory measures has not controlled the price rigging and price volatility and ensured safety to the investors.
* Whether the financial derivatives in the secondary markets enabled to minimize speculative tendencies, price volatility?

* Whether the introduction of commodity futures exchanges in India has minimized the commodity price fluctuations in the economy.

1.12: SIGNIFICANCE OF THE STUDY

Major reforms in the capital markets have been carried out during decade of the 1990's. Reforms in India were initiated after the market has experienced unprecedented decline in security prices. Ironically, securities scams have kept pace with reforms. From Harshad Mehta through Ketan Parekh, price manipulation has plagued the capital market with regularity. While the capital market reforms have grown scams and skepticism has also grown during the 1990's. Therefore, in the light of the above, the present study makes an attempt to critically evaluate the capital markets in India.

1.13: SCOPE OF THE STUDY

The present study of "Changing Pattern of Capital Markets in India - An Analytical Study" covers the following:

* The analysis and critical evaluation of primary and secondary markets in India.
* The role and importance of SEBI in regulation and monitoring of capital markets.
* Maintaining price stability and minimization of price volatility in the secondary market.
* Management of financial derivatives and their role in risk minimization.
* The trends and patterns of commodity futures market in India.

1.14: RELEVANCE OF THE STUDY

The present study of "Changing Pattern of Capital Markets in India- An Analytical Study" is relevant, in view of the following:

* There are no studies conducted to examine the changing pattern of capital markets in India with a comprehensive

coverage in post reforms era.

* The study analyses trends in the capital market with reference to post-liberalization and globalization.
* The study attempts to analyze the primary and secondary market performance.
* The study examines the role of derivatives in the process of minimization of price volatility and risk in the capital market.

1.15: METHODOLOGY

In order to conduct the research study of the "Changing Pattern of Capital Markets in India-An Analytical Study", the following methodology is adopted:

1.15.1. Sources of Data

The study will be based on both primary and secondary sources of data.

1.15.1.1. Primary Data

The primary source of data is to be collected by administering well designed questionnaires to various people involved in policy making, industry and other agencies including the investors.

1.15.1.2. Secondary Data

The secondary source of data relevant to the study will be collected from various libraries, stock exchanges, SEBI publications, CMIE reports etc. In this context, I will also be making use of the data available from RBI Bulletins and Web Sites, etc.

1.15. 2. Research Techniques

In order to analyze and present the data collected both from primary and secondary sources, the research analysis techniques such as Ratios, Percentages, Trend Analysis, Averages, Techniques of Regression, Correlation, Multiple Regression and Scaling Techniques etc., will be used.

1.16: PERIOD OF THE STUDY

The study covers period starting from first year of economic reforms i.e., 1991 up to 2005. It is also proposed to cover data relating to pre-reforms and post-reforms periods.

1.17: LIMITATIONS OF THE STUDY

The study may have the following limitations:

* The primary data relevant for the study may be much depending upon the co-operation of the officials of the various investors, players in the capital markets, regulatory authorities etc.
* The secondary data collected through various journals and bulletins may have impact of price level changes on rupee indicated values.
* The various statistical, mathematical techniques used for analyzing both primary and secondary data may have their inherent limitations.
* The study based on long-term data relating to pre and post liberalization periods may possible to avoid seasonal or short-term trends in the capital markets.
* The study includes various aspects of primary and secondary markets, covering long period of time therefore it may not be possible to include all the other aspects relating to the capital markets.

1.18: ORGANISATION OF THE STUDY

The study of "Changing Pattern of Capital Markets in India-An Analytical Study" will be divided into the following chapters:

Chapter-I: *Introduction to Capital Market*: This chapter is devoted to cover- Meaning of Capital Market, Capital Market Reforms, Review of Literature, Statement of Problem, Objectives of the Study, Hypothesis of the Study, Significance of the Study, Scope of the Study, Methodology, Period of the Study and Limitations of the Study.

Chapter-II: *Primary Market*: Introduction, Meaning, Functions of New Issue Market, Types of New Issues, Factors to be considered for Investment in New Issue Market, Responsibilities of Intermediaries in the New Issue Market, Review of Policies,

Programmes, Trends and role of Domestic Savings in the Growth of New Issue Market.

Chapter-III: *Changing Pattern of Capital Issues*:. Sector-wise, Industry-wise, Size-wise, Region-wise Capital Issues and their Diversities in India, Foreign Investment Flows through Euro Issues and Book-building Mechanism in India.

Chapter-IV: *Secondary Market*: Introduction, Meaning, Changing Regulations of Secondary Market, Secondary Market Selective Indicators, Trading Intensity, Regional Stock Exchanges Threats and Opportunities and Investors Protection in India.

Chapter-V: *Volatility and Liquidity*: Introduction, Meaning, Definitions, Stock Market Volatility A Comparative Analysis of NSE and BSE, Relationship between Volatility and Liquidity in the Indian Stock Market and the Impact of Foreign Institutional Investment on Stock Market Liquidity and Volatility.

Chapter-VI: *Financial Derivatives*: Meaning, Features of Financial Derivatives, Historical Development of Financial Derivatives, Players in Financial Derivatives Trading, Components of Financial Derivatives, Development of Derivatives Market in India, Trading Mechanism, Clearing and Settlement Mechanism, Trends and Pattern of Derivatives Market in India.

Chapter-VII: *Emerging Pattern of Commodity Futures Market*: Nature of Commodity Price problems, Traditional Methods for Managing Commodity Price-risk, Managing Price Risk by Commodity Derivatives, Evolution of Commodity Futures Markets in India, Present Status of Commodity Futures Market and Commodity Futures Trading in India.

Chapter-VIII: *Summary of Findings, Conclusions and Suggestions*: This Chapter covers summary of findings and suggestions for deficiencies identified in various chapters.

REFERENCES

1 Kamlesh Vikamsey: "Capital Market-Future in India, Monthly Public Opinion Surveys, September, 2002, P.14.

2 Gokarm.S: "Indian Capital Market Reforms, 1992-96", *Economic and Political Weekly*, April13, 1996, p.956.

3 *Ibid.* p. 956.

4 Majumdar.N.A: "Financial Sector Reform an Exercise in Introspection", *Economic and Political Weekly,* March 23, 1996, p. 727.

5 Mukherjee D N & George P: "Corporate India in the Age of Reform", *Business World,* 6-19 September, 1995, p. 34.

6 Mukherjee. D.N. and George. p. *Ibid.* p. 34.

7 Singh.K.K: The Times of India, Bombay, November11, 1995.

8 *Ibid.*

9 *Ibid*

10 James C. Van Horne: Fundamentals of Financial Management, Prentice Hall of India, p. 526, 1997.

11 Arun K. Datta: Government, Finance and Capital Market, P.G. Book Market, Calcutta, p.17.

12 S.K. Gupta and Others: "Financial Institutions and Markets", Kalyani Publishers, New Delhi, 2004, p. 3.1.

13 Ruddar Datt and K.P.M. Sundharam: "Indian Economy", S. Chand and Company, 2004, p. 868.

14 F. Livingston: The English Capital Market, Methuen, London, 1929.

15 *Ibid.* Ruddar Datt and K.P.M. Sundaram, P.868.

16 S.K. Misra and V.K.Puri: "Indian Economy", Himalaya Publishing House, Mumbai, 2004, P.714.

17 M.Y. Khan: "Indian Financial Systems", Tata McGraw-Hill Publishing Company Limited, New Delhi, 2004, P.17.3.

18 Ravi M. Kishore: "Financial Management", Taxmann's, New Delhi, August, 2003, p. 1067.

19 Prof. V. Gnagadhar and G. Ramesh Babu: "Investment Management", Anmol Publications Pvt. Ltd., New Delhi, 2003, p. 129.

20 Ruddar Datt and K.P.M. Sundharam: "Indian Economy", S. Chand and Company Ltd., New Delhi, 2004, p. 880.

21 Chuppe & Atkin: "Regulation of Securities Markets; Some Recent Trends for Emerging Markets", Washington, D.C., World Bank, 1992.

22 Loklin: "Regulation of Security Issues by the Interest Rate Commerce Commission", David, Philip.

23 Miller III (James.C) "Regularity Return; Some Problems and Approaches.

24 R.K. Sinha: "Indian Economy in Transition", Deep & Deep Publications, New Delhi, 1994.

25 V.S. Mahajan: "Manmohan's India", Deep & Deep Publications, New Delhi, 1994.

26 Dalop S. Swamy: "The Political Economy of Industrialization", Sage Publication, New Delhi, 1994.

27 Hari Shanker Singhania: "Economic Issues Global & National", Vikas Publishing House Pvt. Ltd., New Delhi, 1995.

28 N.K.P. Sinha & M.B. Singh: "Industrial Development in India", Rawat Publications, New Delhi, 1993.

29 S.P. Gupta: "Liberalization: It's Impact on the Indian Economy", Macmillion India, New Delhi, 1993.

30 A.N. Aggarwal: "Indian Economy, Current Development", Willey Eastern Limited, New Delhi, 1992.

31 A.N. Aggarwal & Chowdhary: "Indian Economy, Crisis and Reforms", Shirpa Publications, 1991.

32 L.C. Gupta: "Indian Share Owners, A Survey Society for Capital Market Research and Development, New Delhi, 1991.

33 Prof. V. Gangadhar & Yadagiri: "Capital Market Reforms in India", The Indian Journal of Commerce, December, 1993.

34 R. Nagaraj: "India's Capital Market Growth: Trends, Explanations and Evidence", Economic and Political Weekly, September, 1996.

35 L.M. Bhole and Shreeya Pattanaik: "The State of Indian Stock Market Under Liberalization", Finance India, Vol.XVI No.1, March 2002, p. 159.

36 R.N. Agarwal: "Capital Market Development, Corporate Financing Pattern and Economic Growth in India", The Asian Economic Review, April, 2003, Vol.45, No.1, p. 23.

37 M.T. Raju: "Capital Market Reforms in India An Evaluation", The Indian Journal of Commerce, Vol. 57, No.4, Oct-Dec. 2004, p.1.

38 Manoj Kumar et al: "The Impact of International Listings on Liquidity: Evidence from the Indian Stock Market", Vikalpa, Vol. 26, No.4, October - December 2001, pp. 35 to 50.

39 Dr. Madhu Kalimipalli and Dr. Latha Ramchand: "Changes in Liquidity Following Exposure to Foreign Shareholders: The

Effect of Foreign Listing and Issues of American Depository Receipts by Indian Firms", NSE Working Paper No. 7, 2002.

40 Bharati Pathak: "The Government Securities Market-Post Reforms Scenario &Policy Issues", Finance India, Vol. XVII No.2, June2003, p. 535.

41 G.L. Malodia: "Rules and Regulations to Curb Insider Trading in Indian Stock Market", The Indian Journal of Commerce, October-December 2001, Vol.54, No. 4, p. 48.

42 Sanjay K. Hansda & Partha Ray: "Stock Market Integration and Dually Listed Stocks Indian ADR and Domestic Stock Prices", Economic and Political Weekly, February 22nd 2003, Vol. XXXVIII, No.8, pp. 741 to 754.

43 Prof.V. Gangadhar & Arifa Begum: "Critical Analysis of Pattern of Capital Issues in India", The Management Accountant, April, 2004, p. 324.

44 Alan Blaylock and Edwin H. Duett: "The Declining Market Reaction to ADR Issuers in Emerging Markets", Global Business and Finance Review Fall 2004, pp. 1 to 12.

45 Manas Pandey: "Contribution of Domestic Saving in the Growth of New Issue Market", The Indian Journal of Commerce, Vol.57, No.4, Oct-Dec.2004, pp. 93.

46 Prof. V. Gangadhar & Mr. G. Naresh Reddy: "Book-Building Process: An Efficient Mechanism for Management of Mega Public Issues in India", Research Bulletin of the Institute of Cost and Works Accountants of India, Vol. XXVII, July, 2005, p.31 to 45.

47 S. Amanulla & M. Thiripalraju: "Week-end Effect: New Evidence from the Indian Stock Market", Vikalpa, Vol. 26, No. 2, April - June 2001, pp. 33 to 50.

48 Philip Maiyo & Subash Chander: "Testing Stock Market Efficiency: A Study of Non-Specified Shares", The Indian Journal of Commerce, October-December 2001, Vol.54, No.4, P.14.

49 S.Amilan: "Consistency of Equity Returns with Corporate Fundamentals in India", Indian Journal of Commerce, Vol.57, No.4, Oct-Dec.2004, p. 31.

50 Prakash Nath Bhargava: "Using VARs to Assess Share Price Movements Some Hypotheses and Tests", The Indian Journal of Commerce, Vol.57, No.4, Oct-Dec.2004, p.41.

51 R.L. Tamboli: "Analysis of Accounting Disclosure and Investor

Protection", The Indian Journal of Commerce, Vol.57, No.4, Oct-Dec.2004, p. 108.

52 S N Sarma: "Stock Market Seasonality in an Emerging Market", Viklpa, Volume-29, July-September 2004, No.3, pp. 35 to 41.

53 Suchismita Bose and Dipankor Coondoo: "The Impact of FII Regulations in India: A Time Series Intervention Analysis of Equity Flows:, ICRA Bulletin, Money & Finance Vol.2 Nos. 18-19, July-December 2004, pp. 54 to 83.

54 Joydeep Biswas: "Foreign Portfolios Investments and Stock Market Behavior in a Liberalized Economy: An Indian Experience, Asian Economic Review, August Issue 2005, Volume 47, No. 2, pp. 221 to 232.

55 Edwards F R: "Does futures trading increase stock market volatility"? , Financial Analysis Journal, Jan/Feb 1988, pp. 63-69.

56 Chan K, K C Chan and G A Karolyi: "Intra day volatility in the stock Index and stock Index futures markets", Review of Financial Studies, Vol. 4, 1991, pp. 657-683.

57 Kamara A, T Miller and A Siegel: "The effects of futures trading on the stability of the S&P 500 returns", The Journal of Futures Markets, Vol.12, 1992, pp. 645-658.

58 Antoniou A and P Holmes: "Futures trading, information and spot price volatility: evidence for the FTSE 100 stock Index and futures contract using GARCH", Journal of Banking and Finance, Vol. 19, 1995, pp. 117-129.

59 Gregory K and T Michael: "Temporal relationships and dynamic interactions between spot and futures markets", The Journal of Futures Markets, Vol.16, No.1, 1996, pp. 55-69.

60 Pasricha J.S and Umesh C. Singh: "Foreign Institutional Investors and Stock Market Volatility", The Indian Journal of Commerce, Vol. 54, No. 3, July-September, 2001.

61 M.T. Raju and Kiran Karande: "Price Discovery and Volatility on NSE Futures Market", SEBI Working Paper Series No.7, March 2003, p. 7.

62 Kalyan Mukherjee: "Seasonality Pattern of Stock Indices Volatility: A Study of Selected Indices", Vitta Shodh, The Journal of Finance, Vol.1, No.2, July-December, 2003, pp. 7-15.

63 Harvinder Kaur: "Stock Market Volatility in India", The Indian Journal of Commerce, Vol.57, No.4, Oct-Dec.2004, P.55.

64 M.T. Raju, Anirban Ghosh: "Stock Market Volatility - An International Comparison", SEBI Working Paper Series No.8, April 2004, p. 8.

65 A. K. Seth & Saloni Gupta: "Understanding Volatility at BSE: A Quality Control Approach Implications for Investors", Decision, Vol.32, No.1, January - June, 2005, pp. 1 to 37.

66 Parthapratim Pal: "Volatility in the Stock Market in India and Foreign Institutional Investors -A Study of the Post-election Crash", Economic and Political Weekly, February 19th 2005, p. 765 to 772.

67 World Bank: "Private Capital Flows to Developing Countries: The Road to Financial Integration", World Bank Policy Research Report, Oxford University Press, New York, 1997.

68 Levine and Zervos: "Capital Control Liberalization and Stock Market Development", World Development, Vol. 26, 1998, p. 1169-1183.

69 Kim and Singal: "Stock Market Openings: Experience of Emerging Issues", Journal of Business, Vol. 73, #1, 2000.

70 Chandra: "The Impact of Stock Market Liberalization on Liquidity and Efficiency in Emerging Equity Markets", Paper presented at the Annual Conference of the Columbia Business School, September 2002.

71 Patro and Wald: "Firm Characteristics and the Impact of Emerging Market Liberalizations", Rutgers University Working Paper, 2003.

72 Gurucharan Singh: "Illiquidity in Stock Exchanges: Some Issues", The Indian Journal of Commerce, Vol.57, No.4, Oct-Dec.2004, p. 71.

73 B. K. Vashist & Ashutosh Vashist: "Agricultural Futures Markets: Analysis of Equilibrium conditions and Inter-Market Relations", Finance India, Vol. XVI, No. 1, March 2002, pp. 121 to 146.

74 Dr. Premalata Shenbagaraman: "Do Futures and Options Trading Increase Stock Market Volatility?" NSE Working Paper, 2004.

75 Sunil Kumar: "Price Discovery and Market Efficiency: Evidence from Agricultural Commodities Futures Markets", South Asian Journal of Management, Vol. 11, Issue No. 2, April -June 2004, p. 12 to 47.

76 Basab Dasgupta: "Role of Commodity Futures Markets in Spot Price Stabilization, Production and Inventory Decisions with Reference to India", Indian Economic Review, Vol. XXXIX, No. 2, 2004, p. 315 to 325.

CHAPTER-II

PRIMARY MARKET

2.1: INTRODUCTION

To keep pace with the globalization and liberalization process, the government of India was very keen to bring the capital market in tune with the international practices through gradual deregulation of the economy. It led to liberalization of capital market in the country with more expectations from primary market to meet the growing needs for funds for investment in trade and industry.[1]

The industrial enterprises for financing their projects resort to equity and preference share capital, reserves and surplus, subsidies from the government, debentures and bonds, deferred payments and loans from the developmental financial institutions, banks, and others wherein the contributions of equity and preference share capital and debentures/bonds constitute the contribution of the new issue market through individuals/households, financial institutions, government and semi-government bodies, joint stock companies, investment trusts and charitable institutions and others.[2] Therefore, there was a vital need to strengthen the capital market which, it left, could only be achieved through structural modifications, introducing new mechanism and instruments, and by taking steps for safeguarding the interest of the investors through more disclosures and transparency.

2.2: MEANING

The Primary Market is a mechanism through which resources of the community are mobilized and invested in the various types of industrial securities. New Issues are made in the primary market. The secondary market is also known as stock exchange taken together, is a mechanism which provides easy liquidity, transferability and continuous price formation of securities to enable investors to buy and sell them with ease.[3] The New Issue Market is also known as Primary Capital Market is a permanent source of industrial securities of the secondary market. The secondary market activates the primary market when it is buoyant and vice-versa.[4] The mobilization of funds through the new issue market is adopted by the state government and the corporate sector. The investor in these securities is banks, insurance companies, investment trust companies and individuals.[5] The organic development of the security as well as the scope for higher productive capacity and social welfare depend upon the efficiency of the new issue market.[6]

2.3: OBJECTIVES

The important objectives of this chapter are presented below:

- To present the meaning, functions, types and methods of the NIM.
- To analyze the factors influenced for investment in the NIM.
- To understand the responsibilities of intermediaries in the NIM.
- To know the reviewed policies and programmes of the NIM.
- To examine the share of Gross Domestic Savings (GDS) in the Gross Domestic Product (GDP).
- To study the contribution of House-hold Sector, Private Corporate Sector and Public Sector for the Gross Domestic Savings.
- To bring out the savings of House-hold Sector in Financial Assets.

2.4: FUNCTIONS OF NEW ISSUE MARKET

The general function of the New Issues Market (NIM) mainly, channeling of investible funds into industrial enterprise, can be split from the operational stand point into three distinct services;[7] (i) Origination, that is investigation and processing of proposals for new issues; (ii) Underwriting of new issues; and (iii) Distribution of new securities to ultimate investors. A developed new issue market is characterized by the presence of specialized agencies to perform each of these three sources.[8]

2.5: TYPES OF NEW ISSUES

The new issues can be divided into various ways. It may be classified on the basis of issues by the new companies and old companies.[9] The securities which the companies issue for the first time either after incorporation or on conversion from private into public company limited is called 'initial issues'. The securities which have already been issued at the time of incorporation of the company, if issued further to procure funds for modernization/diversification / expansion etc., such issues are called 'Further Issues' or 'Rights Issues'.

The new issues may also be classified on the basis of flow of funds into the market as well as flow of new money.[10] The new money issues provide additional funds to the company. New money refers to the sum of money mobilized which is equivalent to the number of newly created shares multiplied by the price per share/minus all administrative costs associated with the issue.

2.6: METHODS OF ISSUE

Methods of Issue of Securities is a process of approaching a large number of investors, both individual and institutional, to invest their savings and surpluses in the shares or debentures of a company. A company may adopt any one or more than one of these methods. The various methods adopted by corporate entities for marketing of securities in the new issues market[11] are:

(1) Pure Prospectus Method,

(2) Offer for Sale Method,

(3) Private Placement Method,

(4) Rights Issue Method,

(5) Bonus Issue Method,

(6) Initial Public Offers (IPOs) Method,

(7) Book-Building Method,

(8) e-IPO Method,

(9) Employee Stock Option Method,

(10) Bought-Out Deal Method, and

(11) Euro Issues Method.

2.6.1. Pure Prospectus Method

According to this method, a corporate enterprise mops up capital funds from the general public by issue of a prospectus and also called 'Pure Prospectus Method'. Section 2(36) of the Companies Act, 1956 defines prospectus as 'any document described or issued as a prospectus and includes any notice, advertisement or other document inviting deposits from the public or inviting offers from the public for the subscription or purchase of any shares in, or debentures of a body corporate'. The main futures of this method includes: (i) A minimum of 49 percent of the total issue at a time is to be offered to public, (ii) The securities may be issued either at par, at a discount, or at a premium, (iii) This issue is usually underwritten.

2.6.2. Offer for Sale Method

Under this method, marketing of securities takes place through intermediaries, such as issue houses, stockbrokers and others. The sale of securities takes place in two stages. In the first stage, the issuer company makes an en-block sale of securities to intermediaries such as houses and share brokers at an agreed price. Under the second stage, the securities are re-sold to ultimate investors at a market-related price. The biggest advantage of this method is that it saves the issuing company the hassles involved in selling the shares to the public directly through prospectus.

2.6.3. Private placement

It is defined as an issuance of securities to fewer than 50 persons, without issuing prospectus/letter of offer and without seeking permission for listing on the stock exchanges for the debt securities issued. This definition is derived on the basis of non-compliance of Rule 19 (2) (b) of SC (R) Act, 1957 a pre-condition for listing of the securities to be issued. The specified investors of private placement include institutional buyers, high net worth individuals and corporates. Usually, the companies reserve certain number of securities for private placement. The SEBI has laid down certain restrictions on the reservation of securities in any public issues. The maximum permissible allotment through reservation is restricted to 10 percent for permanent employees, 10 percent for shareholders of promoting companies, 20 percent for Indian mutual funds, 24 percent for foreign institutional investors and 20 percent for Indian and multilateral development-financial institutions.

2.6.4. Rights Issue Method

Rights issue is an invitation to the existing shareholders to subscribe for further shares to be issued by a company. The relevant guidelines issued by the SEBI in this regard are: (i) Only the listed companies shall be issued, (ii) Announcement regarding rights issue once made, shall not be withdrawn and where withdrawn, no seçurity shall be eligible for listing up to 12 months, (iii) Underwriting as to rights issue is optional and appointment of Registrar is compulsory, (iv) Appointment of category-I Merchant Bankers holding a certificate of registration issued by SEBI shall be compulsory, (v) Rights shall be issued only in respect of fully paid shares, (vi) Letter of Offer shall contain disclosures as per SEBI requirements, (vii) Agreement shall be entered into with the depository for materialization of securities to be issued, (viii) Issue shall be kept open for a minimum period of 30 days and for maximum period of 60 days, and (ix) A minimum subscription of 90 percent of the issue shall be received.

2.6.5. Bonus Issue Method

Where the accumulated reserves and surplus of profits of a company are converted into paid up capital, it takes the form of issue of 'bonus shares'. It merely implies capitalization of existing reserves and surplus of a company. Bonus shares issued under Section 205(3) of the Companies Act, 1956 such shares are governed by the guidelines issued by the SEBI (applicable to listed companies only) as: (i) In respect of FCDs and PCDs, bonus shares must be reserved in proportion to such convertible part of FCDs and PCDs, (ii) The bonus issue shall be made out of free reserves built of the genuine profits or share premium collected in cash only, (iii) The declaration of bonus issue, in lieu of dividend, is not made, (iv) The bonus issue is not made unless the partly paid shares, if any are made fully paid-up, (v) A company that announces its bonus issue after the approval of the Board of Directors, and (vi) The Articles of Association of the company shall contain a provision for capitalization of reserves.

2.6.6. IPO Method

The public issue made by a corporate entity for the first time in its life is called 'Initial Public Offer' (IPO). Under this method of marketing, securities are issued to successful applicants on the basis of the orders placed by them, through their brokers. Full disclosure of all material information in connection with the offering of new securities must be made as part of the new offerings. A statement and preliminary prospectus (also known as red herring) is to be filed with the Registrar of Companies containing: (i) A description of the issuer's business, (ii) The names and addresses of the key company officers, (iii) The amount of ownership of the key officers, (iv) The company's capitalization and description of how the proceeds from the offering will be used, and (v) Any legal proceedings that the company is involved in.

2.6.7. Book-Building Method

Book Building Mechanism of IPOs was recognized by SEBI in India after having the recommendations of the committee under the chairmanship of Y.H. Malegam in October, 1995. It is a most practical mechanism for the quick and efficient management of mega issues (including offers of sale). SEBI guidelines, 1995 defines book building as "a process undertaken by which a demand for the securities proposed to be issued by a body corporate is elicited and built up and the price for such securities is assessed for the determination of the quantum of such securities to be issued by means of a notice, circular, advertisement, document or information memoranda or offer document". In general the word Book Building is a method of marketing the shares of a company whereby the quantum and the price of the securities to be issued will be decided on the basis of the 'bids' received from the prospective shareholders by the lead merchant bankers. According to this method, share prices are determined on the basis of real demand for the shares at various price levels in the market.

2.6.8. e-IPO Method

SEBI has come up with guidelines for e-IPO (i.e. online initial public offer). The concept of e-IPO has not picked up, since the primary market for initial public offer itself was dull. The e-IPO is applicable to the fixed price issue as well as for the fixed price portion of book-built issues. The issuing companies would have the option to issue securities to the public either through the online system of the stock exchange or through the existing banking channel. Under this concept, the applications for securities are made through the terminals allotted by the exchange to its members. These members of the exchange act as a collection centre. They process the applications of their clients through their allotted terminals. All the applications are then received by the exchange and are sent through the Registrar for further processing. The applicant will issue; the cheque in favors of the broker who shall then deposit the said amount to the exchange in its pay in obligation. The whole process will reduce the time for processing the application and allotment. It is expected that this route of making IPO would catch up because of its obvious advantages.

2.6.9. Employee Stock Option Method (ESOP)

Under section 2(15A) of the Companies Act, 1956 "Employees Stock Option means the option given to the whole-time directors, officers or employees of a company, which gives such directors, officers or employees the benefit or right to purchase or subscribe at a future date, the securities offered by the company at a pre-determined price". It is a voluntary scheme on the part of the company to encourage employees' participation in the company. The scheme also offers an incentive to the employees to stay in the company. The scheme is particularly useful in the case of companies whose business activity is dominantly based on the talent of the employees, as in the case of software industry.

2.6.10. Bought Out Deal Method (BOD)

BOD is a process of investment by a sponsor or a syndicate of investors/sponsors directly in a company. Such direct investment is being made with an understanding between the company and the sponsor to go for public offering in a mutually agreed time. A company allots shares in full or in lots to a sponsors at a price negotiated between the company and the sponsor(s). After a particular period of agreed upon between the sponsorer and the company the shares are issued to the public by the sponsorer with a premium. The holding costs of such shares by the sponsor may either be reimbursed by the company or the sponsor may absorb the profit in part or full as per the agreement, arising out of the public offering at a premium. After the public offering the shares are listed in one or more stock exchanges.

2.6.11. Euro Issues Method

The term 'Euro issue' means an issue made abroad through instruments denominated in foreign currency and listed on a European stock exchange, the subscriptions for which may come from any part of the world.[12] Most of the Indian companies get their issues listed on the Luxembourg Stock Exchange and New York Stock Exchange. The Indian corporates have been allowed to tap the global market with (i) Global Depository Receipts (GDRs), (ii) American Depository Receipts (ADRs)/American Depository Shares (ADS) and (iii) Foreign Currency Convertible Bonds (FCCBs) since 1993.[13]

2.7: FACTORS TO BE CONSIDERED FOR INVESTMENT IN NEW ISSSUE MARKET

Investors are aware that under the present free pricing environment, issuers are free to decide the issue price subject to SEBI guidelines for disclosure and investor protection. The set of guidelines is intended to educate the investors about certain aspects which they normally should look for in the memorandum containing salient features of prospectus accompanying all application forms before making investment in any issue. Merchant bankers should look into the proper disclosures on all the following counts:[14]

2.7.1. Promoters' Track Record

It includes (i) adequacy of knowledge and experience in the field relating to the project, (ii) past performance particularly with reference to the companies earlier promoted by them and their track record and (iii) to ascertain the reputation and integrity of the promoters with regard to their involvement in the affairs of other companies through independent inquiries with reference to financial newspapers, magazines, journals, etc.

2.7.2. Professional Management

Verify the managing director's backgrounds and experience in the field and also check the composition of the board of directors.

2.7.3. Objects of the Issue

Check whether the purpose of the issue is likely to result in enhancement of the profitability and growth of the company.

2.7.4. Project Details

It covers (i) to appreciate and understand the location of the project, availability of tax concessions, etc., (ii) whether the issuing company obtained appraisal of the project by financial institutions, banks and if so whether the appraising agency has any financial stake in the project and (iii) provision for monitoring the implementation of the project by financial institutions and banks or any other agency.

2.7.5. Product/Technology/Market

It consists of (i) whether disclosure of demand-supply projection for the product has been made, (ii) the product is susceptible to fair competition, (iii) the chances of the product becoming obsolete in view of the technological developments, (iv) the availability of substitutes having a bearing on the demand for the product and (v) the export potential for the product in case of an export oriented project.

2.7.6. Financial Data

The Financial Data relating to capital, reserves, turnover, profits, dividend record, profitability ratios, book value, earning per share, relative percentage of profit from the operations of the company and other sources.

2.7.7. Profitability Projections

The profitability projections as indicated by the company or by the appraising institution and likelihood of achieving the same in the light of its past performance or that of the industry.

2.7.8. Pricing

Justification for pricing with reference to the past performance and future projections; whether future projections are based on company's own estimates or independent appraisal by financial institutions, banks, etc. In case of issues of existing companies' movement of prices immediately before the issue to ascertain whether prices are fair market prices or there has been rigging of the market prices.

2.7.9. Report of the Auditor

Auditor's report forming part of the offer document, especially with reference to significant notes to accounts, qualifying remarks and changes in accounting policies, in order to know the reliability of the figures reflected in the balance sheet.

2.7.10. Statutory Clearances

Whether various statutory clearances are required for the implementation of the project have been obtained. If not, the current status of such clearances.

2.8: RESPONSIBILITIES OF INTERMEDIARIES IN THE NEW ISSUE MARKET

In a market economy, primary securities market of capital market plays a significant role in helping mobilization of capital and investment formation. Many types of intermediaries carry out this role very effectively. Some of the major intermediaries in this segment are:[15] (1) Merchant Bankers/Lead Managers, (2) Underwriters, (3) Bankers to an Issue, (4) Brokers to an Issue,

(5) Registrars to an Issue and Share Transfer Agents, (6) Debenture Trustees and (7) Portfolio Managers.

2.8.1. Merchant Bankers/Lead Managers

Merchant bank is an institution or an organization which provides a number of services including management of securities issues, portfolio management services, underwriting of capital issues, insurance, credit syndication, financial advices and project counseling etc. They mainly offer financial services for a fee. SEBI has laid down various responsibilities for a merchant banker. They are: (i) he shall enter into a contract with the issuing company, (ii) a registration certificate has to be obtained by him from the SEBI, (iii) he is duty-bound to accept on his own or through its associate, a minimum underwriting obligation of 5 percent of total underwriting commitment or Rs. 25 lakh, whichever is less, (iv) he has to submit 'Due Diligence Certificate' to SEBI at least two weeks before the opening of the issue for subscription, (v) he shall submit to SEBI various documents containing details such as issue, draft prospectus/letter of offer and other literature to be circulated to the investors/shareholders, etc at least two weeks before the date of filing them with the Registrar of Companies and Regional Stock Exchanges, (vi) he shall make a disclosure of responsibilities regarding the management of the issue to the SEBI, and (vii) he shall also fulfill the obligations like continuing to remain fully associated with the issue till the subscribers have received share/debenture certificates or the refund of excess application money; not to acquire securities of any company on the basis of unpublished price sensitive information; and submission of complete particulars with SEBI within 15 days of the acquisition of securities of the company.

2.8.2. Underwriters

According to SEBI Rules 1993, underwriting means an agreement with or without conditions to subscribe to the securities of a body corporate when the existing shareholders of such body corporate or the public do not subscribe to the securities offered to them. 'Underwriter' means a person who engages in the business of underwriting of an issue of securities of a body corporate. Role of underwriters in the corporate financing are: (i) assurance of adequate finance in the event of non-subscription by the public, (ii) supplying valuable information to companies in regard to capital market conditions, general response of the investors, etc., (iii) after purchasing securities they distribute the same to the real investors, (iv) the underwriting of capital issues by prestigious institutions generates confidence among investors and improve their response to the issues, (v) they encourage people to save more and direct their savings in corporate securities and (vi) they play a very important role in setting up of new projects, increasing employment, production and per capita income.

2.8.3. Bankers to an Issue

Bankers who are engaged in the function of acceptance of applications for shares and debentures along with application money from investors in respect of issue of securities and also refund of application money to the applicants to whom securities could not be allotted, are called 'bankers to an issue'. The intermediary to act as a banker has the various responsibilities as ordained by the SEBI. They are: (i) Bankers who are desirous of acting as bankers to an issue are required to obtain the necessary certificate of registration from the SEBI, (ii) Annual registration fee of Rs. 2.5 lakh for the first two years is payable to the SEBI by the intending banker and Rs. 1 lakh is to be paid for the third year, (iii) The issuer company has to enter into a contract with the banker to an issue shall include detailed information, (iv) A daily statement giving the details regarding the number of applications and the amount of money received from the investors shall be submitted by the banker to the issuing company/registrar to an issue and (v) Books of accounts, records and documents pertaining to all matters regarding which the banker may be required to submit details to SEBI shall be maintained by the banker.

2.8.4. Brokers to an Issue

Intermediaries that are responsible for procuring the subscription to the issue from the prospective investors are called 'brokers to the issue'. Responsibilities of brokers to an issue are: (i) Registration with SEBI is mandatory for both stock brokers and sub-brokers and (ii) Stock brokers are required to maintain books of account and documents as stipulated by SEBI.

2.8.5. Registrars to an Issue and Share Transfer Agents

Registrars and share transfer agents are of two categories such as category-I which carry on activities of both registrars to an issue and also of share transfer agents and category-II which carry on activities either of a registrar to an issue or as a share transfer agent. The role and responsibilities of registrars and share transfer agents are:

(i) A certificate of registration is to obtain from the SEBI and

(ii) They shall show such details as applications received from investors relating to the issue, rejected applications together with the reasons for rejection, basis of allotment of securities in consultation with the stock exchange, terms and conditions of purchase of securities, allotment of securities, list of allotters and non-allotters, refund orders, names of transferors and transferees and the date of transfer of securities.

2.8.6. Debenture Trustees

The Regulations define a debenture trustee as a trustee of a trust deed for securing any issue of debentures of a body corporate. Trust deed means a deed executed by the company in favor of trustees named therein for the benefit of the debenture holders. Role and responsibilities of debenture trustees are:

(i) An institution shall be registered with the SEBI to be in a position to function as a debenture trustee,

(ii) Consent in writing must be given to the body corporate to act as debenture trustee before the debenture issue,

(iii) They shall carry out the inspection of books of accounts, records, registers of the body corporate, (iv) They shall take possession of trust property in accordance with the provisions of the trust deed,

(v) They shall carry out any act as would be necessary for the protection of the interest of and the resolution of grievances of the debenture holders,

(vi) They should exercise due diligence to ascertain whether or not the assets of the body corporate which are available by way of security or otherwise,

(vii) They shall call or cause to be called by the body corporate, a meeting of the entire debenture holders where a requisition for the meeting has been made at least one-tenth of the debenture holders,

(viii) They shall maintain books of accounts, records and documents relating to the trusteeship functions for a period of not less than 5 financial years preceding the current financial year and

(ix) They shall abide by the prescribed code of conduct.

2.8.7. Portfolio Managers

The SEBI Regulations define portfolio manager as any person who pursuant to a contract or arrangement with a client, advises or directs or undertakes on behalf of the client, the management or administration of a portfolio of securities or the funds of the client. General responsibilities of a portfolio manager is:

(i) He shall individually and independently manage the funds of each client,

(ii) He shall not accept from the client, funds or securities worth less than 5 lakh rupees,

(iii) He shall act in a fiduciary capacity with regard to the client's funds,

(iv) He shall keep the funds of all clients in a separate account to be maintained by it in a scheduled commercial bank,

(v) He shall transact in securities within the limitation placed by client himself with regard to dealing in securities under the provisions of the RBI Act, 1934,

(vi) He shall not derive any direct or indirect benefit out of the client's funds or securities,

(vii) He shall not borrow funds or securities on behalf of the client,

(viii) He shall not pledge or give on loan securities held on behalf of clients to third person without obtaining a written permission from the client and

(ix) He shall ensure proper and timely handling of complaints from his clients and take appropriate action immediately.

Table 2.1 provides details of various classes of intermediaries from the year 1992-93 to 2003-04. A close examination of the total number brings out two important revelations. Traditionally, the number of intermediaries has gone down substantially. This is led by registrars to an issue and share transfer agents category. Their number fell by 65 from 143 to 78 and in terms of percentage, it declined by about 45 percent. The next category in this class includes bankers to an issue, whose number has come down to 55 from 67, a decline of 12. The other two categories-merchant bankers and debenture trustees also registered a decline of one percent to stand at 123 and 34 respectively. Only two categories of intermediaries; portfolio managers and underwriters showed positive growth of six and four at 60 and 47 respectively. The overall decline can be attributed to the excessive supply, i.e., the large number of intermediaries who have entered the market. Compared to many of the international markets, the number of intermediaries registered in India, in certain categories, still continues to be on the high side.

2.9: REVIEW OF POLICES AND PROGRAMMES

The reforms process continues unabated with significant changes in the capital market. For the first time, in the history of Indian capital market, a public offer of more than 10,000 crore was made by a listed Government of India company. The primary market has witnessed a highly encouraging response from foreign institutional investors (FIIs). These have become possible because of many proactive issuer as well as investor friendly regulatory reforms initiated by SEBI. The reviewed policies and programmes are: (1) information and investor protection and (2) other policy initiatives.

2.9.1. Information and Investor Protection

SEBI has been pro-active and dynamic in responding to national and international challenges in the primary securities market and to make the Indian market more scientific, transparent

Table 2.1: No. of Intermediaries Registered in New Issue Market

Year	Merchant Bankers		Under-writers		Bankers to an Issue		Bankers to an Issue		Registrars to an Issue & Share Transfer Agents		Debenture Trustee		Portfolio Managers		Total	
1992-93	74	(00.0)	NA	(00.0)	NA	(00.0)	5290	(00.0)	NA	(00.0)	NA	(00.0)	28	(00.0)	5392	(00.0)
1993-94	422	(470.2)	NA	(00.0)	NA	(00.0)	6413	(21.2)	100	(00.0)	NA	(00.0)	40	(42.8)	6975	(29.4)
1994-95	790	(87.2)	36	(00.)	70	(00.0)	6711	(04.6)	264	(164.0)	20	(00.0)	61	(34.4)	7952	(14.0)
1995-96	1012	(28.1)	40	(11.1)	77	(10.0)	8476	(26.3)	334	(26.5)	23	(15.0)	13	(–78.7)	9975	(25.4)
1996-97	1163	(14.9)	38	(–5.0)	80	(03.9)	8867	(04.6)	386	(15.6)	27	(17.4)	16	(23.1)	10577	(06.0)
1997-98	802	(–31.0)	43	(13.2)	72	(–10.0)	9005	(01.5)	334	(–13.5)	32	(18.5)	16	(00.0)	10304	(–2.6)
1998-99	415	(–48.3)	17	(–60.5)	66	(–8.3)	9069	(00.7)	251	(–24.8)	34	(06.3)	18	(12.5)	9870	(–4.2)
1999-00	186	(–55.2)	42	(147.1)	68	(03.0)	9192	(01.4)	242	(–3.6)	38	(11.7)	23	(27.87)	9791	(–0.8)
2000-01	233	(25.3)	57	(35.7)	69	(01.5)	9782	(06.4)	186	(–23.1)	37	(–2.6)	39	(69.6)	10403	(06.3)
2001-02	145	(–37.7)	54	(–5.3)	68	(–1.4)	9687	(–0.9)	161	(–13.4)	40	(08.1)	47	(20.5)	10202	(–1.9)
2002-03	124	(–14.5)	43	(–20.4)	67	(–1.5)	9519	(–1.7)	143	(–11.2)	35	(–12.5)	54	(14.9)	9985	(–2.1)
2003-04	123	(–0.8)	47	(09.3)	55	(–17.9)	9368	(–1.6)	78	(14.5)	34	(–2.8)	60	(11.1)	9765	(–2.2)

NA = Not Available: Figures in Brackets indicate the Annual Growth Rate of respective Intermediaries.

Source: Hand Book of Statistics on the Indian Securities Market SEBI 2004, p. 5.

and investor-centric; SEBI has taken several new policy initiatives. A few of them are: (i) revision of issue standards (ii) enhanced disclosure requirements and (iii) enhanced corporate governance standards.

2.9.2. Other Policy Initiatives

These include (i) definition of small investor, (ii) book building guidelines, (iii) green shoe option, (iv) role of debenture trustees, (v) withdrawal of the concept of regional stock exchange, (vi) modified guidelines for employee stock option schemes and (vii) standardization of listing requirements and their implementation in all the exchanges.

2.10: TRENDS OF DOMESTIC SAVINGS IN THE GROWTH OF NEW ISSUE MARKET

During the late 1980s, the developing countries started liberalizing their financial sectors. Increased emphasis was put on the development of equity markets. India also followed this path. Stock markets grew rapidly in India during the late 1980s and early 1990s. Capital markets have taken a prominent place in the developing countries' financial system during the last decade. In the fast growing financial system, new issue market occupy a very crucial position by enabling the corporate sector to mobilize capital from household savings and canalize such savings into productive area of investment.

A substantial portion of the security issues are offered to the public for whose subscription the domestic saving particularly the household saving serve as the primary source of the capital resources. In other words, a major portion of total domestic saving comprises of public and private corporate sector saving are accruing to the household sector which is the main source from which new issue market financial resources for the corporate enterprises.[16]

2.10.1. Savings-Meaning

The Central Statistical Organization (CSO) defines Saving as "the excess of current income over current expenditure and is the balancing item on the income and outlay accounts of producing enterprises, and households, government administration and other final consumers." For the purpose of estimating the domestic saving, the economy has been divided into three broad institutional sectors: (a) household; (b) private corporate; and (c) public.

(a) Saving of the household sector is measured as (i) the total of financial saving, and (ii) saving in the form of the physical assets. The financial saving involves possession of currency, net deposits, investment in shares and debentures, net claims on government in the form of Central and State Government Securities and small savings, net increase in the claims in life insurance and provident funds. Physical assets include construction, machinery, equipment and stocks held by individuals, firms and other institutions constituting the household sector.

(b) Private corporate sector comprises non-government non-financial companies, private financial institutions and cooperative institutions. The basic data for the non-government non-financial corporate enterprises are obtained from the analysis of balance sheets and profit and loss accounts of these companies.

(c) Public sector comprises government administrative departments and enterprises, both departmental and non-departmental. The saving of the government administration is defined as the excess of current receipts over current expenditure. The net savings of the government companies and statutory corporations are estimated from the results of the analysis of their Annual Accounts.

2.10.2. Share of GDS in GDP

National income is one of the major factors influencing for the savings in the economy. However, the rate of savings can be improved through certain incentives. Such incentives need not be in financial terms. Creation and offer of a variety of financial assets and ensuring liquidity could also improve the propensity to save. Within a two-way broad classification of equity and debt on the one hand and long term and short term on the other, the primary market offers a whole array of financial assets. These assets vary in terms of liquidity, return and stability thereof over a period of time. By offering such asset differentiation, the capital market is expected to attract savings from different sources. The share of GDS in GDP was presented in Table-2.2 and Fig.2.1.

Table-2.2: GDP and GDS

(Rs. In Crore)

Year	*GDP*	*GDS*	*GDS as % of GDP*
1990-91	5,68,674 (——)	1,31,340 (——)	23.10
1991-92	6,53,117 (14.8)	1,43,908 (09.6)	22.03
1992-93	7,48,367 (14.6)	1,62,906 (13.2)	21.77
1993-94	8,59,220 (14.8)	1,93,621 (18.8)	22.53
1994-95	10,12,770 (17.9)	2,51,463 (29.9)	24.83
1995-96	11,88,012 (17.3)	2,98,747 (18.8)	25.15
1996-97	13,68,208 (15.2)	3,17,261 (06.2)	23.19
1997-98	15,22,547 (11.3)	3,52,178 (11.0)	23.13
1998-99	17,40,985 (14.3)	3,74,659 (06.4)	21.52
1999-00	19,36,831 (11.2)	4,68,680 (25.1)	24.20
2000-01	20,89,499 (07.9)	4,95,986 (05.8)	23.74
2001-02	22,82,143 (09.2)	5,35,185 (07.9)	23.45
2002-03	24,69,564 (08.2)	5,97,696 (11.7)	24.20
2003-04	27,60,025 (11.8)	7,76,420 (29.9)	28.13
Total	2,11,99,962	51,00,050	330.97
Average	15,14,283	3,64,289	23.64

Note: (1) GDP and GDS represent Gross Domestic Product and Gross Domestic Savings respectively.

(2) Both GDP and GDS are at current prices.

(3) Figures in (——) indicates Annual Growth Rate.

Source: National Income Statistics, October 2004, CMIE.

Between 1990-91 and 2003-04, the primary market has witnessed introduction of variety of financial instruments with a varying maturity, return and other features in tune with that of new liberalized economic policies. Not only had there been a flush of financial instruments, but also a variety of tax incentives were extended to promote savings and investments. From the

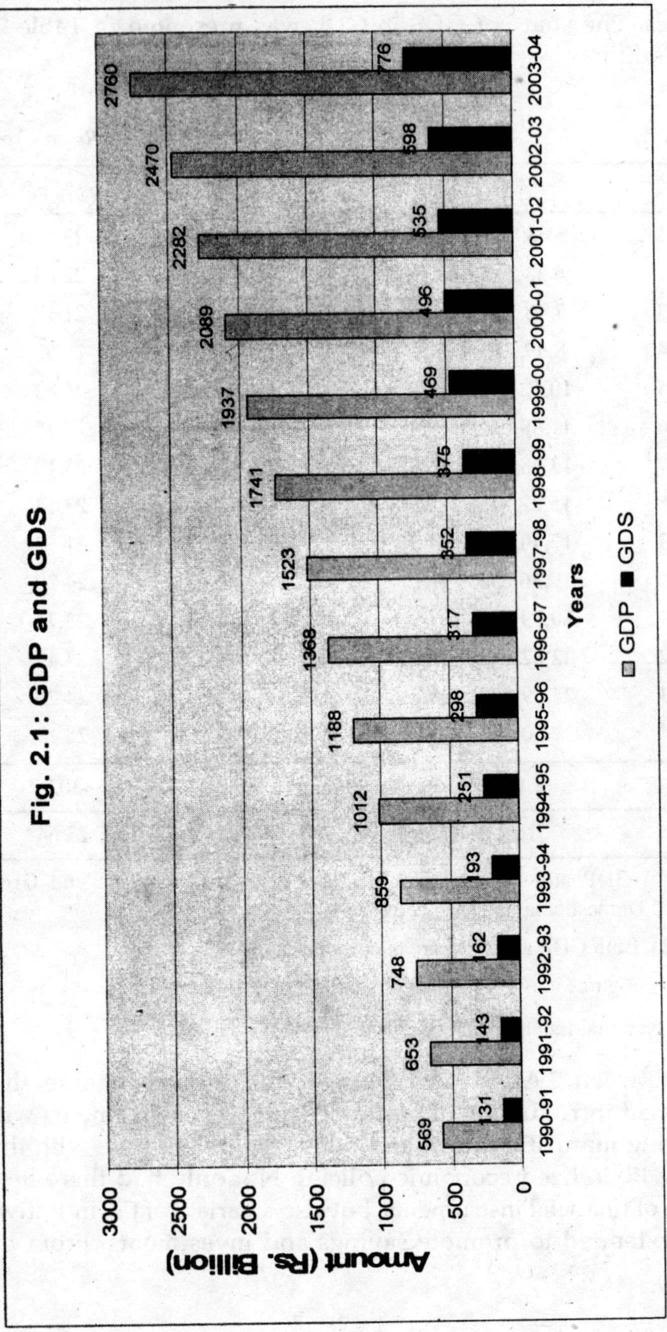

Fig. 2.1: GDP and GDS

Table-2.2, we observe that GDP had gone up from Rs.5,68,674 crore (1990-91) to Rs.27,60,025 crore (2003-04) - a 385 percent increase. During the same period, the GDS recorded a 491 percent increase, i.e., from Rs.1,31,340 crore to Rs.7,76,420 crore. Annual growth rate of GDP and GDS ranges in between 7.9 percent to 17.9 percent and 5.8 percent to 29.9 percent respectively. The average annual growth rate of GDP and GDS are recorded at 13 percent and 15 percent respectively. According to this trend we can say that the growth rate in GDS is higher than that of GDP. The ratio of GDS to GDP is increased from 23.10 percent (1990-91) to 28.13 percent (2003-04) with a net increase of 5.03 percent barring ups and downs in a couple of years. In the above background, it can be concluded that the array of financial instruments and incentives had improved the savings rate. Further, they have also helped to prevent decline in savings rate.

2.10.3. Sector-wise Analysis of Savings

It is proposed to examine the sector-wise contribution of savings to the total savings along with analyzing their trend during the period under review. Table-2.3 and Fig.2.2 presents the relevant data.

From the Table-2.3, we can find out that the gross domestic savings during 2003-04 amounted to Rs. 7,76,420 crore. A bulk of the savings amounting to Rs. 7,31,387 crore (94.20%) was contributed by the household sector. Private corporate sector accounted for Rs.1,10,484 crore, while the public sector's share has negative at Rs. -65,451 crore. What is relevant to note is that over the years, the proportion of savings by household sector has been going up with a slight variations. While the household sector accounted for about 83.67 percent of the savings in 1990-91, it went up to 94 percent of the savings in 2003-04. Therefore, it is the savings of the household sector have fuelled for encouraging trend in the primary market.

Household sector keeps its savings in financial or physical assets. Savings in financial assets can be in the form of currency, deposits, shares and debentures, net claims on Government, life insurance, provident and pension funds. The proportion of savings in financial vs. physical assets, has been varying over the years. From the Table-2.4, we observed that the savings in the form

Table 2.3: Sector Wise Gross Domestic Savings (At Current Prices)

(Rs. Crore)

Year	Household Sector						Private Corporate Sector		Public Sector		Gross Domestic Savings	
	Financial Savigs		Physical Savings		Total							
	Value	%	Value	%	Value	%	Value	%	Value	%	Value	%
1990-91	49,640	45.17	60,257	54.17	109,897	83.67	15,164	11.55	6,279	4.78	131,340	100.00
1991-92	61,101	56.08	48,635	43.92	110,736	76.95	20,304	14.11	12,868	8.94	143,908	100.00
1992-93	65,267	49.87	65,706	50.13	131,073	80.46	19,968	12.26	11,865	7.28	162,906	100.00
1993-94	94,738	59.84	63,572	40.16	158,310	81.77	29,866	15.42	5,445	2.81	193,621	100.00
1994-95	120,95	60.56	78,625	39.44	199,358	79.28	35,260	14.02	16,845	6.70	251,463	100.00
1995-96	105,719	48.91	110,421	51.09	216,140	72.35	58,542	19.60	24,065	8.05	298,747	100.00
1996-97	141,661	60.73	91,591	39.27	233,252	73.52	61,092	19.26	22,917	7.22	317,261	100.00
1997-98	146,777	54.68	121,660	45.32	268,437	76.22	63,486	18.03	20,255	5.75	352,178	100.00
1998-99	180,346	55.19	146,456	44.81	326,802	67.23	65,026	17.36	–17,169	–4.59	374,659	100.00
1999-00	205,743	50.88	198,658	49.12	404,401	86.29	84,329	17.99	–20,049	–4.28	468,680	100.00
2000-01	222,721	48.61	235,494	51.39	458,215	92.38	86,142	17.37	–48,371	–9.75	495,986	100.00
2001-02P	254,304	49.00	264,736	51.00	519,040	96.98	78,849	14.73	–62,704	–11.72	535,185	100.00
2002-03Q	254,407	45.49	304,851	54.51	559,258	93.57	84,169	14.08	45,730	–7.65	597,696	100.00
2003-04Q	348,799	47.69	382,588	52.31	731,387	94.20	110,484	14.23	–65,451	–8.43	776,420	100.00
Total	2,253,056	732.68	2,173,250	666.64	4,426,306	1,174.86	812,681	219.99	–138,935	5.11	5,100,050	1,400.00
Mean	160,933	52.33	155,232	47.62	316,165	83.92	58,049	15.71	–9,908	0.37	364,289	100.00

Source: National Icome statistics, October 2004 CMIE, P = Provisional, Q = Qick Estimates.

Fig. 2.2: Sector-wise Domestic Savings

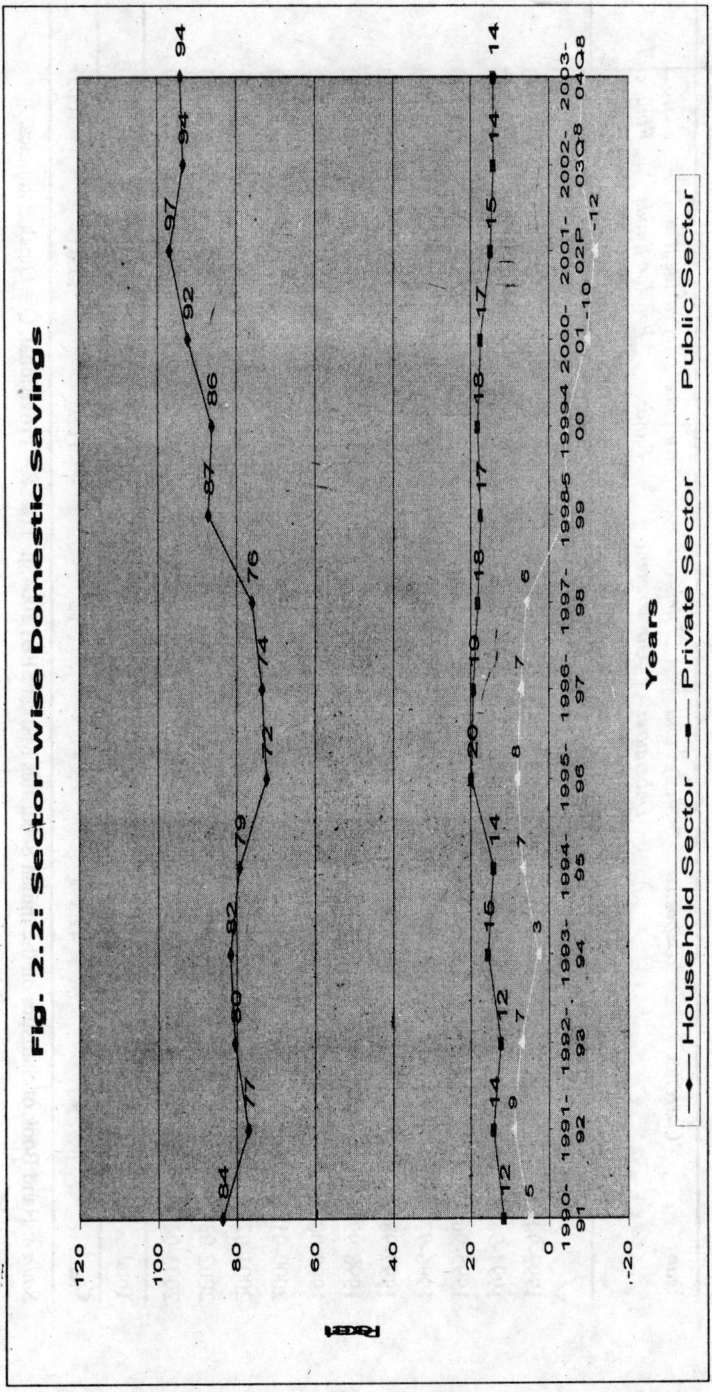

Table 2.4: Financial Savings of Household Sector (At Current Prices)

(Percent)

Year	*Currency*	*Deposits*	*Shares and Debentures*	*Claims on Government*	*Insurance Funds*	*Provident and Pension Funds*	*Gross Financial Savings*
			New Series (Base: 1993-94)				
1993-94	12.2	42.6	13.5	6.3	8.7	16.7	100.0
1994-95	10.9	45.5	11.9	9.1	7.8	14.7	100.0
1995-96	13.3	42.5	7.3	7.7	11.2	18.0	100.0
1996-97	8.6	48.1	6.6	7.4	10.2	19.2	100.0
1997-98	7.4	46.6	2.9	12.9	11.3	18.8	100.0
1998-99	10.5	38.8	3.4	13.6	11.3	22.4	100.0
1999-00	8.8	36.3	7.7	12.3	12.1	22.8	100.0
2000-01	6.3	41.0	4.1	15.7	13.6	19.3	100.0
2001-02P	9.7	39.4	2.7	17.9	14.2	16.1	100.0
2002-03Q	8.5	41.5	1.6	18.6	15.5	14.3	100.0
2003-04Q	10.1	42.9	1.4	17.7	14.5	13.0	100.0
Total	106.3	465.2	63.1	139.2	130.4	195.3	1,100.0
Mean	9.7	42.3	5.7	12.7	11.9	17.8	100.0

Source: Hand Book of Statistics on the Indian Securities Market SEBI 2004, p. 118. P = Provisional, Q = Quick Estimates.

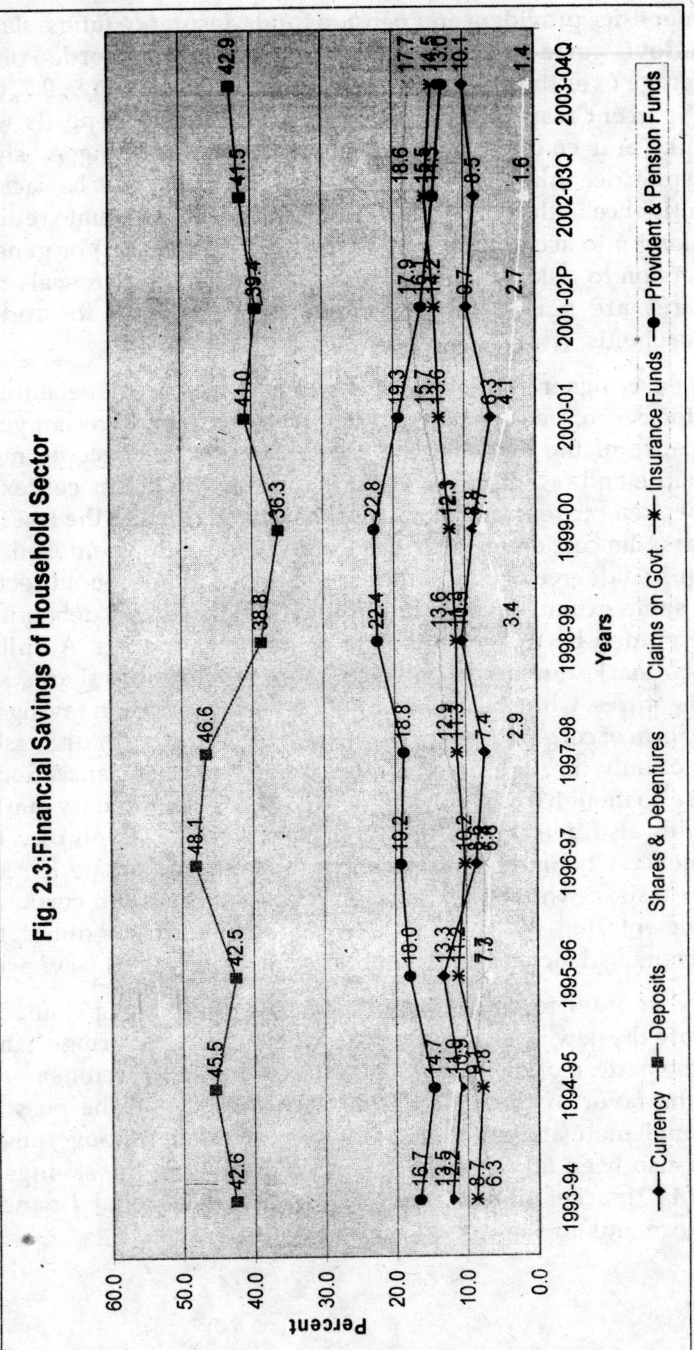

Fig. 2.3: Financial Savings of Household Sector

of deposits, provident and pension funds, insurance funds, claims on Govt., currency and shares and debentures rerecorded on an average over the study period are 42.3, 17.8, 12.7, 11.9, 9.7, and 5.7 percent respectively. Savings in the form of deposits with banks and contractual savings accounted for a bigger share despite declining interest rates. The reason could be lack of confidence in the corporate sector securities, inadequate returns (taking into account the risk associated with shares) or general aversion to risk. Whatever be the reason, the data reveals that shares are not preferred vehicle of investment for Indian households.

Savings in the form of investments in shares/ debentures of the corporate sector enterprises have declined in recent years because of the fact that the capital market has become more volatile and faced scams. What is noteworthy in this context is that even far-reaching stock market reforms during the last few years, the corporate securities do not seem to have infused the required degree of confidence in the minds of household sector. To some extent, savings in the form of shares and debentures are guided by the general state of the stock market. A bullish stock market invariably attracts more savings into shares and debentures, while bearish market tends to dissuasion savings in the form of corporate sector securities. The attraction or dissuasion is not only through diversion (secondary market transactions), but also though fresh infusion (new issues). The secondary market health also determines the flow of securities (supply) by the issuers. A booming market encourages the corporate to float new issues, while a bearish market discourages the corporate from entering the market. It is against this background the phenomenal increase in the public issues during 2003-04 viewed.

In order to develop capital market there is big challenge before the new issue market and stock exchange to bring change in the pattern of the investment of the household sector savings in the favor of those industrial securities. It will be possible through motivating the masses for such investments. Government has also been taken certain steps in promoting the savings in capital market divert saving from the traditional financial instruments to the capital market instrument.

The principle of economic growth focuses on generating saving and canalizing them into productive investment. The behavior of the saving rate in India during the reform period proved to be an improvement in financial saving, which provide an opportunity for diversification across financial assets and emergence of marketable return. All these could be possible only when the government discourage the deposits specially bank deposit, limiting the saving in other sources and some extent the government taxation policy regarding taxes on income which may help in the investment in securities.

REFERENCES

1 Siddhartha Sankar Sharma: "The Book Building Mechanism of IPOs", The Chartered Account, August 2004, Vol. 53, No. 2, p. 198

2 Manas Pandey: "Contribution of Domestic Saving in the Growth of New Issue Market", The Indian Journal of Commerce, Vol. 57, No. 4, October-December 2004, p. 93.

3 Fortune India, Bombay, Monthly Journal, November 1, 1990, p.21.

4 Krishan, Bal: "Industrial Securities Market in India", Common Wealth Publishers, New Delhi, 1989, p.53.

5 Bhatia. B.: "New Issue Market in India", Vora Publications, Bombay, 1976, p. 9.

6 Kulkarni. P.V.: "Corporation Finance", Himalaya Publishing House, New Delhi, 1987, p. 317.

7 Briston. R.J. and Liversidge. J.: "Practical Approach to Business Investment Decision", London, Mac million, 1979, p.75.

8 Gupta. L.C.: "The Changing Structure of Industrial Finance in India", Clarendon Press, Oxford, 1969, p. 200.

9 Henderson. R.F.: "New Issues Market and Finance for Industry", Bower and Cambridge, New York, 1951, p.24.

10 Merrent. Howe and New Bould: "Equity Issue and London Capital Market", 1967, p.4.

11 Guruswamy. S.: "Financial Markets and Institutions", Vijay

Nicole Imprints Private Limited, Chennai, 2004, p.146.

12 Gupta S.K. and Others: "Financial Institutions and Markets", Kalyani Publishers, New Delhi, 2004, p.21.19.

13 Alexander, G, J, Eun, C S, and Janakiramanan, S: 'International Listings and Stock Returns: Some Empirical Evidence', Journal of Financial and Quantitative Analysis, 23 (2) 839-55.

14 Avadhani. V.A.: "Capital Market Management", Himalaya Publishing House, Mumbai, 2001, p. 128.

15 http://www.sebi.gov.in/annualreport/2003-04/pt1b4.html

16 Manas Pandey: "Contribution of Domestic Saving in the Growth of New Issue Market", Indian Journal of Commerce, Vol. 57, No. 4, October-December 2004, p. 93.

CHAPTER-III

CHANGING PATTERN OF CAPITAL ISSUES

The decade of eighties witnessed emergence of stock markets as a major source of finance for industry and trade. Average annual capital mobilization from the primary market, which used to be about Rs. 700 million in 1960 and about Rs. 900 million in 1970, increased manifold during the eighties, with the amount raised in 1990-91 being Rs. 43,120 million. The Indian economy has been experiencing a dynamic change since 1991 due to introduction of Liberalization, Privatization and Globalization policies. The major capital market reforms with relating to IPOs are: (i) Government of India permitted since 1993, the good track record Indian companies to raise funds from the international market through Euro Issue and (ii) Book-Building mechanism was recognized by SEBI in India on the basis of the recommendations of the committee constituted under the chairmanship of Y.H. Malegam in October, 1995. This chapter is divided into three sections. They are: (I) Aggregate Analysis of Primary Issues, (II) Foreign Investment Flows through Euro Issues and (III) Capital Issues through Book-Building System.

SECTION-I:

AGGREGATE ANALYSIS OF PRIMARY ISSUES:

3. 1: INTRODUCTION:

Strong fundamentals of the economy, encouraging corporate results, buoyant secondary market, and revival of structural reforms by the government and an investor friendly regulatory framework provided by SEBI attracted the investors to the primary market. Several mega issues apart, a number of small issues entered the market. There has been overwhelming response to most of the public issues from FIIs, other institutional investors and the retail investors. Large number of the issues was over-subscribed indicating the quality of issues and the appetite for public issues by the investors. The post-listing performance of most of the IPOs was encouraging and these are presented in the form of aggregate analysis of primary issues in the following pages.

3.2: OBJECTIVES

The Aggregate Analysis of Primary Issues is aimed at analyzing the following:

* To examine the aggregate pattern of capital issues with a view to identify the changing pattern in number and amount of issues and identify major diversities along with the contributing factors therein.
* To study ownership pattern of capital issues in order to bring out the role of public sector or private sector undertakings to mobilize capital from the public.
* To discuss industry wise pattern of capital issues to pin point the predominance of a specific industrial sector in the capital issues.
* To bring out the size wise analysis of capital issues in order to know whether the mega issues or small issues have claimed major/minor number and amount of capital issues.
* To analyze the region-wise pattern of capital issues to point out the predominance of a specific region in the capital issues.

3.3: AGGREGATE PATTERN OF CAPITAL ISSUES

It is proposed to analyze the changing pattern of new capital issues in India during the period of 1991-92 to 2004-05 for a period of 14 years with a view to bring out the diversities in the Capital Issues as well as to point out the various attributing factors for such diversities. This analysis is made with the help of data relating to number and amount of public issues and their related indices.

Table-3.1 presents the data of number and amount of public issues. The total number of public issues over a period of 14 years was stood at 12,650 with an average of 904 issues. Whereas the amount of public issues was at Rs.6,95,846 crore with an average of Rs. 49,703 crore per annum it reflects that the companies have raised every year Rs. 49,703 crore of rupees from the public. The number of issues were highest in 1994-95 at 2,122 indicating 311.2 percent over 1991-92. The year 2001-02 has accounted for lowest number at 405 issues. Alternatively 2000-01 has accounted for Rs. 77,383 crores from the public claiming highest amount of capital raised during the study period. 1991-92 the first year of reforms process has helped to mobilize Rs. 14,042 crores from the public. This was the year of high expectation for the investors who were trying to invest the money in changed economic and liberalized period that has ignited the attitude of investors to invest their savings in the various public issues in the later years. The number of issues was constantly increased from 516 in 1991-92 to 2,122 in 1994-95 then onwards continuously declined year after year due to volatility in the prices of shares in secondary market, coupled with scams due to price manipulation of Harshad Mehta 1992 to Kethan Parekh 2001. Thereafter, the number of issues was increased from 501 to 816.

However, this trend is reversed in the amount of capital issues whereas, it has increased from Rs.14,042 crore in 1991-92 to Rs.77,383 crore in 2000-01 indicating a growth of 451.1 percent. The decline in the number of public issues did not bring down the amount of public issues due to the fact that the numbers of companies with heavy amount of public issues have increased. For instance in October 2002 Rs.2490 crore has been raised through the primary capital market. This includes Rs.100 crore of IPO from Allahabad Bank and its issue was over subscribed many times. Further, the number of investors increased during the early 90's was persistently continued in the rest of the period. The survey conducted by the Society for Capital Market Research and Development indicates that there were 9 to 10 million shareholder in 1990 and they grew 14 to 15 million by 1993 and 20 million by 1997. A SEBI-NCAER study showed that of 12.8

million investors, house holds, and 37 percent entered the capital market prior to 1991, 47 percent among 1991-95 and 17 percent after 1995.

The annual growth rate of number of issues has gone unto 106.8 percent in 1992-93, after Harshad Mehta's scam in 1992 the issues have gone down abnormally even indicating negative growth by 30.9 percent in the year 1998-99. Further, there was an improvement in the number of issues in 1999-00 and after Kethan Parekh scam in March 2001, these further declined to -29.4 percent.

Table 3.1: Aggregate Pattern of Capital Issues in India

Years	*No. of Issues*	*Rate of Change (%)*	*Amount (Rs. Crores)*	*Rate of Change (%)*
1991-92	516	100.0	14,042	100.0
1992-93	1,067	106.8	18,375	101.1
1993-94	1,307	22.5	47,297	66.7
1994-95	2,122	62.4	55.920	18.2
1995-96	1,928	-9.1	33,515	-40.1
1996-97	1.128	-14/5	34.685	3.5
1997-98	653	-42.1	50,470	45.5
1998-99	451	-30.9	61,774	22.4
1999-00	616	36.6	69.974	13.3
2000-01	574	-6.8	77,383	10.6
2001-02	405	-29.4	47,419	-38.7
2002-03	501	23.7	42,786	-9.8
2003-04	566	12.9	57,220	33.7
2004-05	816	44.2	74,986	31.0
Total	12,650		695,846	
Average	904		49,703	

Source: CMIE Capital Markets Special Issues 2002, 2003, 2004 and 2005.

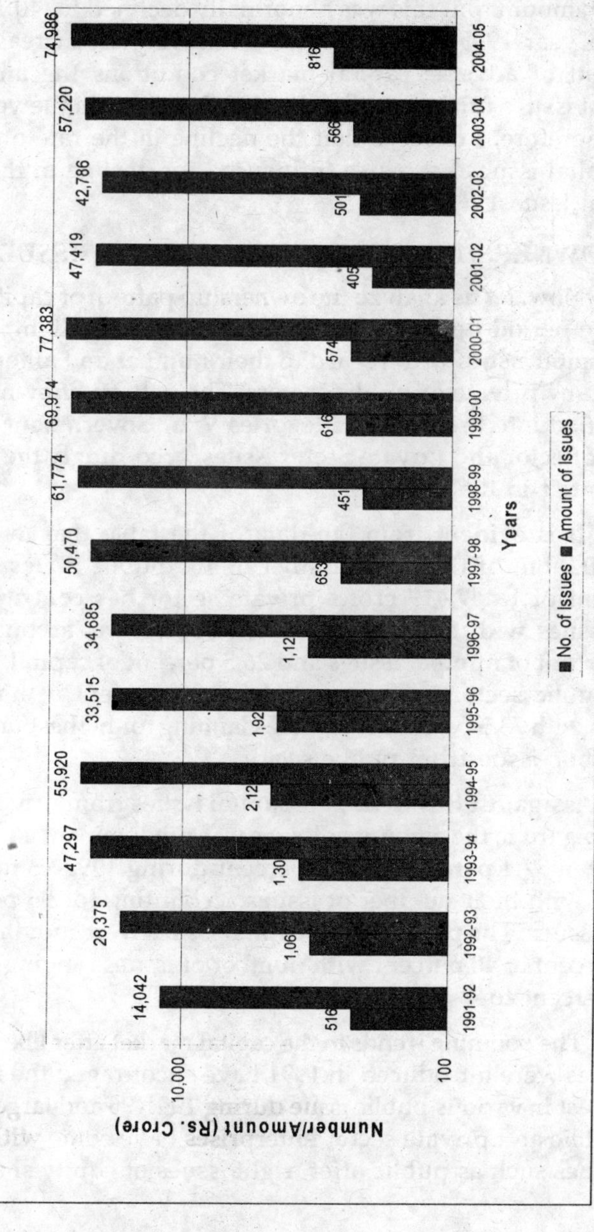

Fig. 3.1: Aggregate Pattern of Capital Issues in India

The similar trend was also evident in the case of amount of capital issues. However, there was no significant steep decline in the amount. But this was abnormally declined to -40.1 percent in the year 1995-96. Then after witnessing an increase under account of adverse capital market conditions the amount of capital issues further declined to -38.7 percent in the year 2001-02. Therefore, I observe that the decline in the rate of number of capital issues have also influenced for decline in the rate of capital issues.

3.4: OWNERSHIP PATTERN OF CAPITAL ISSUES

Now, let us analyze the ownership pattern of capital issues for the period under review with a view to highlight, whether the capital issues with regard to their number and amount were issued by private or public sectors. The pattern of ownership is classified into broad two categories Viz., Government Sector / Public Sector and Private Sector issues, accordingly the data has presented in the Table-3.2.

It is evident from the data of the table that in the year 2001-02, out of the total number of 405 public issues with the amount of Rs.47,419 crore, private sector has contributed for 247 issues with the amount of Rs.12,585 crore, accounting for 61 percent of number issues and 26.5 percent of capital, whereas the public sector has accounted for 39 percent of number of issues with 73.5 percent of capital, claiming for highest proportion of public issue from public sector.

As against this trend, the capital issues from private sector with regard to the amount of issues was predominant and moving between 57.4 percent to 74.9 percent during 1992-93 to 1995-96 along with their number of issues accounting for 96 percent of total issues. The public sector capital issues were moving among 29 percent to 40 percent with number of issues ranging between 2.8 percent to 4 percent.

The booming trends in the capital market after liberalization policies were introduced in 1991 have encouraged the investors to invest in various public issue during 1991-96 and large number of public and private sector enterprises have come with variety of issues such as public offer, right issues of equity shares with premium and convertible bonds and debentures. This has ignited many traditional investors to enter into the capital market by applying to various public issues. During this period the major issues such as Reliance, L&T, S R Gujarat, ONGC, GAIL (India) Ltd., IPCL, Maruti Udyog Ltd., IDBI Patni Computer Systems, ICICI Bank Ltd., IBP Company Ltd., etc have come with mega issues.

After witnessing the Harshad Mehta's capital market scam, there was partial change in the attitude of investors with regard to premium public issues and also the several cases of defaulting and misusing of capital raised through public issues by the companies such as M S Shoes, C R B Capital Markets and Usha Rectifier Corporation etc., have cautioned the investors to be away from the unreasonable public issues.

On account of such developments, the Government has taken up various measures, prominent among them setting up of SEBI with autonomous powers to monitor and regulate capital markets and public issues, and various reforms were also introduced at different time periods. These measures did not repose confidence of investors and public issues were not attractive to them.

From 1999-00 onwards the total number of public issues is not only declined but also their amount has substantially gone down during this period. Many public issues were under-subscribed.

If we observe the rate of change with regard to number of public sector enterprises we find that it was increased to 78 percent in 1993-94 and 93 percent in 1997-98. But, in the rest of the years it has moved between -4.1 to -14.6 percent reflecting that the number of issues has significantly declined in view of the various adverse conditions prevailing in the capital market as well as the portion of Disinvestment and privatization programmes. As against to this, the amount of capital issue of the public sector enterprises significantly increased to 52.7 percent in 1998-99 and 126.2 percent in 1993-94. But in the rest of the years these were moved between -24.1 percent to +48.5 percent. It is also evident that the increased growth rate in number of issues have also influenced for increased growth in the amount of capital issues on account of mega and multiple capital issues of public sector enterprises.

Alternatively, the position of private sector is quite different in those years of highest number and amount of capital issues of public sector have shown a negative impact on private sector capital issues, because these were abnormally low in all such years not only in number of issues but also the amount. The year 1992-93 has witnessed with an unprecedented rate of growth at 119.2 percent along with the amount of 258.2 percent. This was the second year of post liberalization and economic reforms have ignited with much confidence among the house hold sector investors to canalize their savings towards capital market. However after the Harshad Mehata's scam in 1992, the number of issues and the amount has continuously declined and reached to -8.9 percent and -54:1 percent in the year 1995-96 respectively. Then onwards the numbers of issues have shown a negative growth rate touching a maximum of -49.6 percent with regard to their number and -35.8 percent with regard to amount.

On the basis of observations made in the preceding paragraphs, we can conclude the following:

* The years of highest rate of growth in number and amount of capital issues of public sector have accompanied a negative growth in the private sector capital issue indicating a negative relationship. This may be due to the fact that if both the sectors are tapping the capital market with mega issues the market may not absorb such huge amount and issues may be under subscribed. Hence, the issues were planned in such a way that in the years of mega issues of public sector were associated with lower number of private sector capital issues.

* The second year of the post Economic Reforms period has shown greater impact on the private sector to come out with mega issues offering huge amount for the public. This trend was caught by the public sector capital issues in the 1993-94. This indicates that there is a lag and lead relationship between public and private sector capital issues.

* The growth rate of capital issues in both the sectors has

Table 3.2: Capital Issues Distribution Based on Ownership Pattern

Year	Public Sector				Private Sector				Grand Total	
	No. of Issues	*% to Total*	*Amount (Crore)*	*% to Total*	*No. of Issues*	*% to Total*	*Amount (Crore)*	*% to Total*	*No. of Issues*	*Amount (Crore)*
1991-92	48 (100.0)	9.3	8406 (100.0)	59.9	468 (100.0)	90.7	5636 (100.0)	40.1	516	14,042
1992-93	41 (–14.6)	3.8	8185 (–2.6)	28.6	1026 (119.2)	96.2	20190 (258.2)	71.4	1,067	28,375
1993-94	73 (78.0)	5.6	18517 (126.2)	39.2	234 (20.3)	94.4	28780 (42.5)	60.8	1,307	47,297
1994-95	70 (–4.1)	3.3	14051 (–24.1)	25.1	2052 (66.3)	96.7	41869 (45.5)	74.9	2,122	55,920
1995-96	59 (–15.7)	3.1	14051 (1.6)	42.6	1869 (–8.9)	96.9	19235 (–54.1)	57.4	1,928	33,515
1996-97	59 (0.0)	5.2	14280 (48.5)	61.2	1069 (–42.8)	94.8	13475 (–29.9)	38.8	1,128	34,685
1997-98	114 (93.2)	17.5	21210 (50.3)	63.2	539 (–49.6)	82.5	18587 (37.9)	36.8	653	50,470
1998-99	124 (12.3)	28.4	31883 (52.7)	78.8	323 (–40.1)	71.6	13097 (–29.5)	21.2	451	61,774
1999-00	158 (23.4)	25.7	48677 (–9.6)	62.9	458 (41.8)	74.4	25937 (98.0)	37.1	616	69,937
2000-01	144 (–8.9)	25.1	44000 (31.3)	74.4	430 (–6.1)	74.9	19613 –24.4)	25.3	574	77,383
2001-02	158 (9.7)	39.0	57770 (–39.7)	73.5	247 (–42.6)	61.0	12585 (–35.8)	26.5	405	47,419
2002-03	130 (–17.7)	25.9	29223 (49.4)	68.3)	371 (50.2)	74.1	13563 (7.8)	31.7	501	42,786
2003-04	107 –17.7)	18.9	39581 (35.4)	69.1	459 (23.7)	81.1	17640 (30.1)	30.9	566	57,220
2004-05	81 (–24.3)	9.9	31397 (–20.7)	41.8	735 (60.1)	90.1	43589 (147.1)	58.2	816	74,986
Total	1366 (213.6)	220.7	381231 (398.7)	788.6	10280 (291.5)	1179.4	293796 (593.4)	611.1	12,650	695,809
Average	98 (15.3)	15.8	27231 (28.5)	56.3	734 (20.8)	84.2	20985 (42.4)	43.7	904	49,701

Note: Figures in Brackets indicates the Annual Index of Capital Issues Distribution Based on Ownership Pattern
Source: CMIE Capital Markets Special Issues 2002, 2003, 2004 and 2005.

Fig. 3.2: Capital Issues Distribution Based on Ownership Pattern

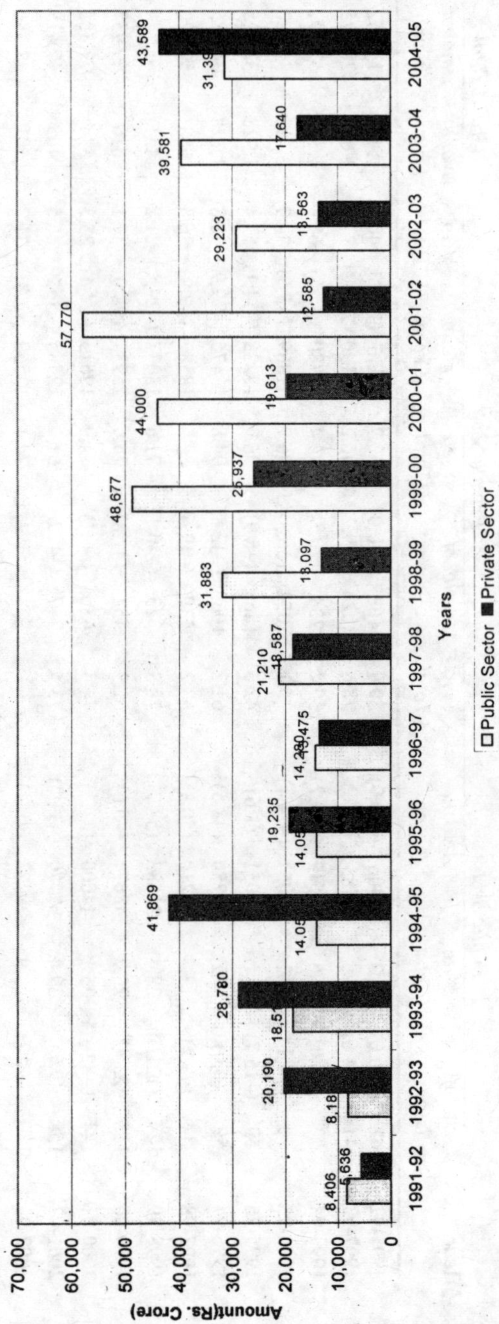

declined significantly from 1993-94 on wards in view of depressed market conditions, different scams and political instability along with September 11, 2001 event.

* The average growth rate of amount of capital issues of the public sector was at 30.4 percent and that of the private sector was at 37.1 percent.

3.5: INDUSTRY-WISE ANALYSIS OF CAPITAL ISSUES:

The total number and the amount of capital issues are classified into the following industry groups:

A. Manufacturing.

B. Mining and Electricity.

C. Services and others.

The basic purpose of this analysis is to identify the industry group, which has come out with the maximum number and amount of capital issues with response to liberalization, privatization and globalization policies of the government. Further, it is also proposed to point out industry-wise diversities and the growth rate in the capital issues as well as to point out possible reasons for such diversities. The data relating to industry-wise distribution of capital issues presented in the Table-3.3 and it also presented in the Fig. 3.3.

The manufacturing sector has accounted for 73 to 82.3 percent, numbers of capital issues from 1991-92 to 1994-95, claiming significantly highest number of capital issues from that sector.

Alternatively, the number of issues in service sector have accounted for highest position ranging between 61.7 percent to 74.5 percent from the year 1996-97 to 2002-03. This reflects that in the first four years of post liberalization the manufacturing sector has come out with large number of public issues, whereas in the rest of the period due to encourage given to the service sector more specifically telecommunications, transportation, treasury sector, growth of mutual funds have contributed for maximum number of capital issues. The mining industry's number of issues moved among 1.3 percent to 5.0 percent reflecting very insignificant role in the total capital issues.

Table 3.3: Capital Issues Distribution by Industry

Year	Manufacturing Sector				Mining & Electricity Sector				Services & Others				Grand Total	
	No. of Issues	% to Total	Amount (Crore)	% to Total	No. of Issues	% to Total	Amount (Crore)	% to Total	No. of Issues	% to Total	Amount (Crore)	% to Total	No. of Issues	Amount (Crore)
1991-92	403	78.1	5,198	37.0	19	3.7	1,436	10.2	94	18.2	7,408	52.8	516	14,042
1992-93	878	82.3	18,224	64.2	18	1.7	539	1.9	171	16.0	9,612	33.9	1,067	28,375
1993-94	1,040	79.6	26,650	56.3	52	4.0	3,617	7.6	215	16.4	17,030	36.0	1,307	47,297
1994-95	1,50	73.0	34,802	62.2	32	1.5	1,218	2.2	540	25.4	19,990	35.6	2,122	55,920
1995-96	1,127	58.5	13,788	41.2	25	1.3	1,300	3.9	776	40.2	18,427	55.0	1,928	33,515
1996-97	634	56.2	11,809	34.0	21	1.9	1,483	4.3	473	41.9	21,393	61.7	1,128	34,685
1997-98	401	61.4	12,740	25.2	27	4.1	4,093	8.1	225	34.5	33,637	66.6	653	50,470
1998-99	237	52.5	10,564	17.1	24	5.3	3,721	6.0	190	42.1	47,489	76.9	451	61,774
1999-00	320	51.9	16,294	23.3	26	4.2	5,698	8.1	270	43.8	47,945	68.9	616	69,937
2000-01	307	53.5	14,188	18.3	29	5.1	5,490	8.4	238	41.5	56,705	73.3	574	77,383
2001-02	153	37.8	8,542	18.0	20	4.9	4,965	10.5	232	57.3	33,912	71.5	405	47,419
2002-03	171	34.1	7,140	16.7	25	5.0	3,768	8.8	305	60.9	31,878	74.5	501	42,786
2003-04	178	31.4	7,236	12.6	23	4.1	19,585	34.2	365	64.5	30,399	53.2	566	57,220
2004-05	264	32.4	16,434	21.9	20	2.5	9,557	12.7	532	65.1	48,989	65.4	816	74,980
Total	7,663	782.7	203,609	448.0	361	49.3	67,470	126.9	4,626	567.8	424,724	825.3	12,650	695,803
Average	547	55.9	14544	32.0	26	3.5	4,819	9.1	330	40.6	30,337	59.0	904	49,700

Source: CMIE Capital Markets Special Issues 2002, 2003, 2004 and 2005.

Fig. 3.3: Capital Issue Distribution by Industry

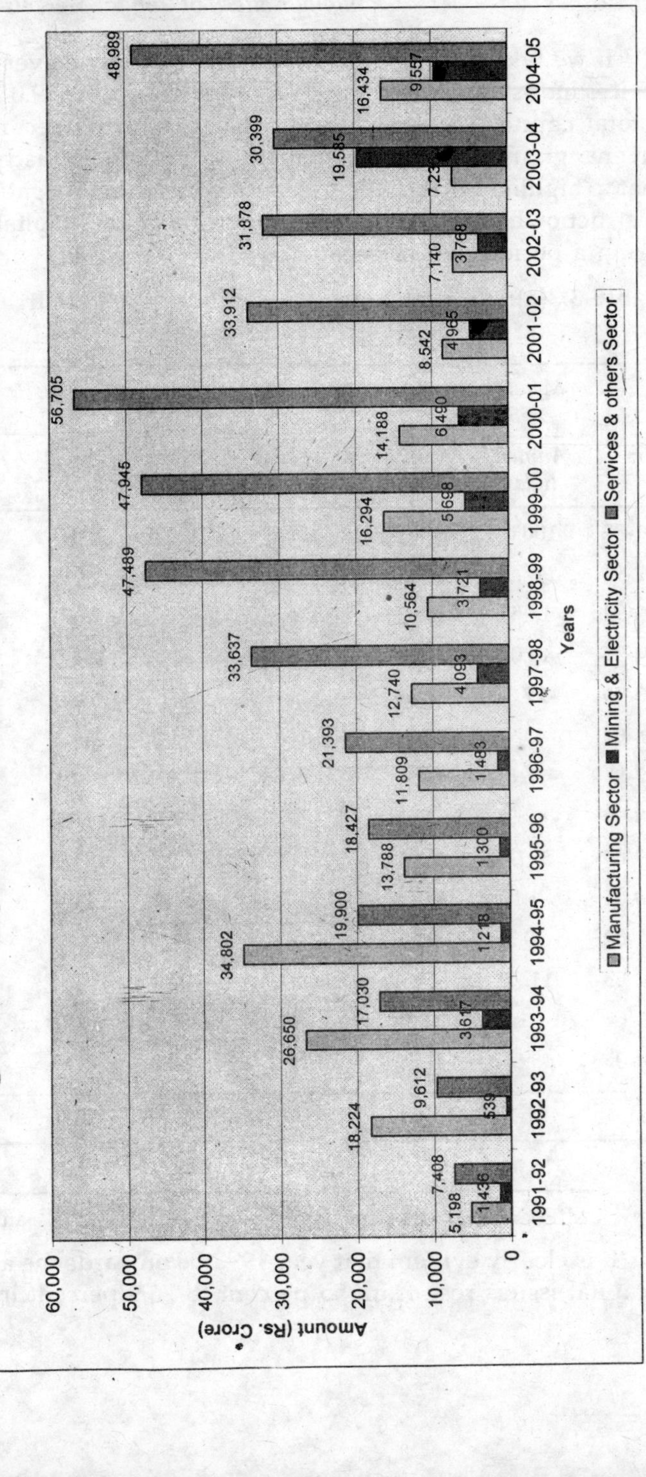

If we take the amount of capital issues, on an average the services industry has accounted for major share with 59.0 percent of total capital issues, while the manufacturing sectors 32.0 percent, giving very meager share to mining industry. This went to highlight that the service sector including irrigation and construction has gained highest proportion of total capital issues during a period over a decade of study.

Table 3.3(a): Annual Index of Capital Issues Distribution Based on Industry

	Manufacturing Sector		*Mining & Electricity Sector*		*Services & others*	
Years	*Annual Index*	*Annual Index*	*Annual Index*	*Annual Index*	*Annual Index*	*Annual Index*
1991-92	100.0	100.0	100.0	100.0	100.0	100.0
1992-93	117.9	250.6	-5.3	-62.5	81.9	29.8
1993-94	18.5	46.2	188.9	571.1	25.7	77.2
1994-95	49.0	30.6	-38.5	66.3	151.2	16.9
1995-96	-27.3	-60.4	-21.9	6.7	43.7	-7.4
1996-97	-43.7	-14.4	-16.0	14.1	-39.0	16.1
1997-98	-36.8	7.9	28.6	176.0	-52.4	57.2
1998-99	-40.9	-17.1	-11.1	-9.1	-15.6	41.2
1999-00	35.0	54.2	8.3	53.1	42.1	1.0
2000-01	-4.1	-12.9	11.5	13.9	-11.9	18.3
2001-02	-50.2	-39.8	-207.0	23.5	-2.5	-40.1
2002-03	11.7	-16.4	25.0	-24.1	31.5	-6.0
2003-04	4.1	1.3	-8.1	419,7	19.7	-4.6
2004-05	48.5	127.1	-13.0	-52.2	45.8	61.1
Total	181.5	456.9	41.5	1,249.5	420.2	360.7
Average	13.0	32.6	3.0	89.3	30.0	25.8

Source: CMIE Capital markets Special Issues 2002, 2003, 2004 and 2005.

It is clearly evident that year 1995-96 onwards the amount of capital issues rose from 55 percent to 76.9 percent in 1998-

99 and 71.5 percent in 2001-02. As against a significant decline in the manufacturing sector from 41.1 percent to 18 percent during the similar period. Therefore, we can conclude that the second half of the post economic reforms period was dominated by service sector with the highest amount of capital issues and mobilized significantly greater proportion of funds of the total capital issues. The growth rate in the amount of capital issues suggest that there was significantly greater rate of decline in the manufacturing sector than compared to service sector over a period of the study. The rate of growth in amount of capital issues on year wise basis has declined in both the sectors; however, more than proportionate decline was in the case of manufacturing sector.

Thus we conclude that the second half of the post liberalization period was dominated by the service sector companies to mobilize highest amount of capital from the public issues. This may be on account of the fact that on the basis of Narsimham Committee Recommendations, the banking sector reforms were introduced and many banks have come out with the mega public issues, on the other hand have launched variety of innovative schemes by public sector and private sector mutual funds in order to mobilize resources from the primary capital market.

3.6: DISTRIBUTION OF CAPITAL ISSUES BY TYPES OF ISSUES

This analysis is aimed at examining the dominance of types of issues during the period under review. For this purpose total capital issues are classified into the following:

(a) Public Issues

(b) Rights Issues

(c) Private Placements

(d) Euro Issues.

The data relating to the types of issues with regard to their number and amount along with percent to total are presented in the Table-3.4 and 3.4(a) and it also shown in the Fig. 3.4.

In the first six years of post liberalization period number

Table 3.4: Capital Issues Distribution by based on Type of Issues

Year	Public Issues				Rights Issue				Private Placements				Euro Issues				Grand Total	
	No. of Issues	% to Total	Amount (Crore)	% to Total	No. of Issues	% to Total	Amount (Crore)	% to Total	No. of Issues	% to Total	Amount (Crore)	% to Total	No. of Issues	% to Total	Amount (Crore)	% to Total	No. of Issues	Amount (Crore)
1991-92	219	42.4	5,976	42.6	236	45.7	3,466	24.7	6	1.2	4,600	32.8	0	0.0	0	0.0	516	14,042
1992-93	537	50.3	13,593	47.9	458	42.9	12,166	42.9	70	6.6	1,862	6.6	2	0.2	754	2.7	1,067	28,375
1993-94	786	60.1	18,759	39.7	359	27.5	12,935	27.3	133	10.2	7,618	16.1	29	2.2	7,986	16.9	1,307	47,297
1994-95	1,344	64.4	24,906	44.5	343	16.4	11,577	20.7	401	19.2	11,536	20.6	34	1.6	7,901	14.1	2,088	55,920
1995-96	1,429	74.1	18,258	54.5	256	13.3	6,124	18.3	235	19.2	6,560	19.6	8	0.4	2,573	7.7	1,98	33,515
1996-97	768	68.1	15,815	45.6	119	10.5	2,663	7.7	229	12.2	10,5528	30.4	12	1.1	5,679	16.4	1,128	34,685
1997-98	1,105	16.1	12,448	24.7	49	7.5	3,004	4.0	496	20.3	34,914	69.3	3	0.5	1,103	2.2	653	50,407
1998-99	76	16.9	14,123	22.9	27	6.0	3,610	5.8	346	76.0	25,944	42.0	2	0.4	18,097	9.3	451	61,774
1999-00	124	20.1	18,711	26.8	33	5.4	1,505	2.2	453	76.7	45,732	65.4	6	1.0	3,989	5.7	616	69,937
2000-01	151	26.3	11,285	14.6	24	4.2	581	0.8	390	73.5	37,162	48.0	9	1.6	28,354	36.6	574	77,383
2001-02	78	19.3	8,982	18.9	14	3.5	1,077	2.3	310	67.9	35,167	74.2	3	0.7	2,193	4.6	405	47,419
2002-03	66	13.2	6,275	14.7	11	2.2	811	1.9	417	83.2	34,791	81.3	7	1.4	910	2.1	501	42,786
2003-04	39	6.9	20,888	36.5	19	3.4	783	1.4	494	87.3	30,988	54.2	14	2.4	4,561	7.9	566	57,220
2004-05	41	5.0	25,340	33.8	31	3.8	3,822	5.1	711	87.1	30,717	41.0	33	4.1	15,107	20.1	816	74,986
Total	6,763	483.2	215,359	467.7	1,979	192.3	63,124	165.1	4,691	640.6	318,119	601.5	162	17.6	99,207	166.3	12,616	695,746
Average	483	34.5	15383	33.4	141	13.7	4,509	11.8	335	45.8	22,723	43.0	12	1.3	7,086	11.9	901	49,696

Source: CMIE Capital Markets Special Issues 2002, 2003, 2004 and 2005.

Fig.3.4: Capital Issues Distribution Based on Type of Issues

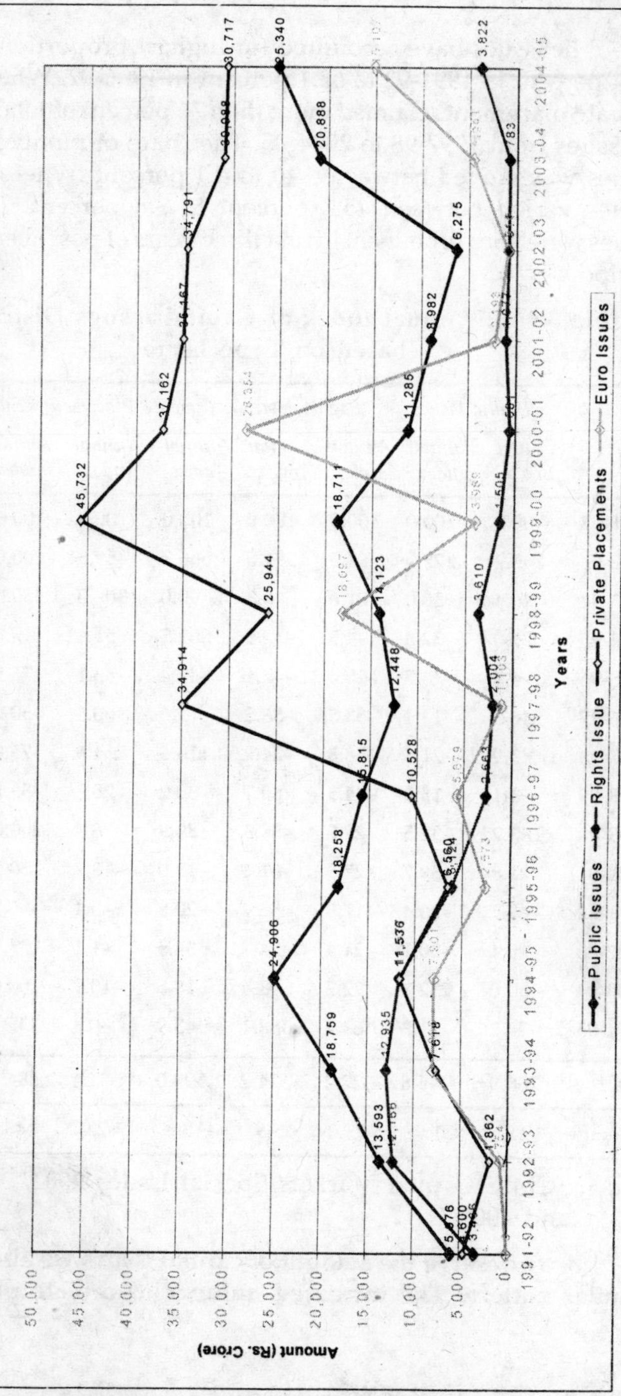

of public issues have accounted for highest proportion ranging 42.4 percent in 1991-92 to 68.1 percent in 1996-97. Whereas, the private placements claimed more than 76 percent of total number of issues from 1997-98 to 2004-05. The share of number of Euro issues was moved between 0.40 to 4.1 percent. Whereas rights issues varied between 45.7 percent to 3.8 percent. The right issues were very prominent in first three years of post liberalization period.

Table 3.4(a): Annual Index of Capital Issues Distribution based on Type Issue

	Public Issues		*Rights Issues*		*Private Placement*		*Euro Issues*	
Years	*Annual Index*	*Annual Index*	*Annual Index*	*Annual Index*	*Annual Index*	*Annual Index*	*Annual Index*	*Annual Index*
1991-92	100.0	100.0	100.0	100.0	100.0	100.0	100.0	100.0
1992-93	145.2	127.5	94.1	251.0	1,066.7	-59.5	200.0	75,400.0
1993-94	46.4	38.0	-21.6	6.3	90.0	309.0	1,350.0	959.2
1994-95	71.0	32.8	-4.5	-10.5	201.5	51.4	17.2	-1.1
1995-96	6.3	-26.7	-25.4	-47.1	-41.4	-43.1	-76.5	-67.4
1996-97	-46.3	-13.4	-53.5	-56.5	2.6	60.5	50.0	120.7
1997-98	43.9	-21.3	-58.8	-24.7	116.6	231.6	-75.0	-80.6
1998-99	-93.1	13.5	-44.5	80.1	-30.2	-25.7	-33.3	1,540.7
1999-00	63.2	32.5	22.2	-58.3	30.9	76.3	200.0	-78.0
2000-01	21.8	-39.7	-27.3	-61.4	-13.9	-18.7	50.0	610.8
2001-02	-48.3	-20.4	-417.0	85.4	-20.5	-5.4	-66.7	-92.3
2002-03	-15.4	-30.1	-21.4	-24.7	34.5	-1.1	133.3	-58.5
2003-04	-50.0	232.8	72.7	-3.5	18.5	-10.9	100.0	401.2
2004-05	24.2	21.3	63.2	388.1	43.9	-0.8	135.7	231.2
Total	268.9	446.8	-322.2	624.2	1,594.0	587.4	2,084.7	78,985.9
Average	19.2	31.9	-23.0	45.9	113.8	42.0	148.9	5,641.8

Source: CMIE Capital Markets Special Issues 2002, 2003, 2004 and 2005

If we observe the amount of capital issues we also confirm similar pattern. The increased number of private placements from 1997-98 on wards have also attributed for highest proportion of amount of capital issues over public, right and Euro issues. This may be on account of fact that companies have gone for private placements in order to mobilize required funds (i) when there was no favorable conditions in the capital market due to scams, instability, price volatility and lukewarm response to the public issues; (ii) the exemption of private placements from the public disclosure regulation and registration requirements of the regulatory body; (iii) possibilities of completing the resource raising exercise in a much shorter time span and hence utilization of the same in a more efficient manner; and (iv) the reduction in cost (as the issuer through private placement need not issue advertisement and incur only a limited expense on printing) and feasibility of innovating products catering to the specific needs of the investor and preferences of issuer could also play their role. However, the capital mobilized through private placements will have a lacking period of three years for listing in stock exchanges to create a marketability and liquidity to the security holders.

A cursory glance at the public issues will reveal that the banking, TMT and chemical industries dominated the scenario. UCO Bank, Vijaya Bank, Indian Overseas Bank and Bank of Maharashtra between themselves mobilsed Rs. 9.5 billion. The TMT sector accounted for another Rs. 6 billion. Chemical and Pharmaceutical industry, needless to state, accounted for a lion's share.

A noteworthy feature of the public issues made during the year 2003-04 is the growing popularity of book building route. The public offers can be made through fixed price route or book building route. Under the book building route, the price of the offer is determined through a process of transparent bidding using the network of the NSE/BSE/Lead Managers. The floor price is fixed as a starting point for the bidding process. SEBI has stipulated suitable rules for making public offer through book building route. The book building route has gained importance over the years. During the year 2003-04, 14 out of 39 issues were made through book building route as against 2 out of 66 issues made during 2002-03. ONGC topped the list, whose shares were offered at Rs. 750 to institutional investors and at Rs.712.50 to retail investors followed by IBP Co. Ltd., with Rs. 620 for institutional and Rs.589 for retail investors.

The share of Euro issues in the total amount of capital issue was ranged between 2.7 percent to 36.6 percent, whereas the right issues moved between 42.9 percent to 0.8 percent indicating no encouragement for such issues and now a days no company is coming out with right issues at all, but the first four years of the study up to 1995-96, the right issues were significant.

On the basis of this analysis we conclude that the public issues were dominant in number and amount of capital issues from 1991-92 to 1996-97 i.e. first half period of the post liberalization and claimed dominant share in both number as well as amount.

3.7: ANALYSIS OF CAPITAL ISSUES BASED ON SIZE

Next it is proposed to examine the pattern of capital issues based on size of the issue. The objective of this analysis is to find out which size group has accounted for major/minor number and amount of capital issues. For this purpose the total capital issues are grouped into the following sizes:

(A) Below Rs. 10 crores.

(B) Rs. 10 crores to Rs. 50 crores.

(C) Rs. 50 crores to Rs. 100 crores

(D) Rs. 100 crores and above (Mega Issues).

The relevant data of the size-wise capital issues with the number, amount, percent to total and their annual growth rate is presented in the Table-3.5, 3.5 (a) and in Fig. 3.5.

The average number of capital issues was 63.4 percent in the size group of below Rs.10 crores, 18.0 percent in the size group of Rs.10 to Rs.50 crores, 6.1 percent in the size group of Rs. 50 crores to Rs. 100 crores and 12.6 percent in the size group of Rs. 100 crores and above. The capital issues were highest and moved among 70.3 percent to 82.3 percent from 1991-92 to 1996-97 in the capital issue size group of below Rs. 10 crores. Whereas in the mega issues of above Rs. 100 crores these were moved between 27.7 percent to 41.5 percent from 1998-99 to 2001-02. However the capital issue size group of below Rs. 10 crores has

Table 3.5: Capital Issues Distributionbased on Size

Year	Below 10 Crrores				Between Rs. 10 - 50 Crores				Between Rs. 50 - 100 Crores				Rs. 100 Crores and Above				Grand Total	
	No. of Issues	% to Total	Amount (Crore)	% to Total	No. of Issues	% to Total	Amount (Crore)	% to Total	No. of Issues	% to Total	Amount (Crore)	% to Total	No. of Issues	% to Total	Amount (Crore)	% to Total	No. of Issues	Amount (Crore)
1991-92	363	70.3	1,255	8.9	10.5	20.4	2,253	16.0	18	3.5	1,245	8.9	30	5.8	9,289	66.2	516	14,042
1992-93	734	68.8	3,188	11.2	243	22.8	5,220	18.4	39	3.7	2,701	9.5	51	4.8	17,266	60.8	1,067	28,375
1993-94	877	67.1	3,760	7.9	278	21.3	6,143	13.0	61	4.7	4,462	9.4	91	7.0	32,932	89.6	1,307	47,297
1994-95	1,457	68.7	6,184	11.1	450	21.2	9,368	16.8	95	4.5	6,765	12.1	120	5.7	33,603	60.1	2,122	55,920
1995-96	1,587	82.3	6,350	18.9	228	11.8	4,488	13.4	55	2.9	3,731	11.1	58	3.0	18,946	56.5	1,928	33,515
1996-97	872	77.3	3,547	10.2	162	14.4	3,351	9.7	36	3.2	2,296	6.6	58	5.1	25,491	73.5	1,128	34,685
1997-98	337	51.6	1,092	2.2	130	19.9	3,011	6.0	54	8.3	3,499	6.9	132	20.2	42,868	84.9	653	50,470
1998-99	154	34.1	542	0.9	99	22.0	2,198	3.6	73	16.2	4,589	7.4	125	27.7	54,445	88.1	451	61,774
1999-00	198	32.1	724	1.0	143	23.2	3,333	4.8	78	12.7	4,987	7.1	197	32.0	60,893	87.1	616	69,937
2000-01	224	39.0	747	1.0	115	20.0	2,572	3.3	71	12.4	4,341	5.6	164	28.6	69,723	90.1	574	77,383
2001-02	97	24.0	285	0.6	83	20.5	2,258	4.8	57	14.1	3,669	7.7	168	41.5	41,207	86.9	405	47,419
2002-03	238	47.5	343	0.8	75	15.0	2,022	4.7	46	9.2	2,736	6.4	142	28.3	37,685	88.1	501	42,786
2003-04	342	60.4	375	0.7	65	11.5	1,407	2.5	45	8.0	3,008	5.3	114	20.1	52,430	91.6	566	57,220
2004-05	536	65.7	242	0.3	90	7.4	2,319	3.1	41	5.0	2,756	3.7	149	18.3	69,669	92.9	816	74,986
Total	8,016	788.9	28,634	75.7	2,266	251.2	49,943	120.1	769	108.3	50,785	107.6	1,599	248.1	566,447	1096.4	12,650	695,809
Average	573	56.4	2045	5.4	162	17.9	3,567	8.6	55	7.7	3,628	7.7	114	17.7	40,461	78.3	904	49,701

Source: CMIE Capital Markets Special Issues 2002, 2003, 2004 and 2005.

Fig. 3.5: Capital Issues Distribution Based on Size

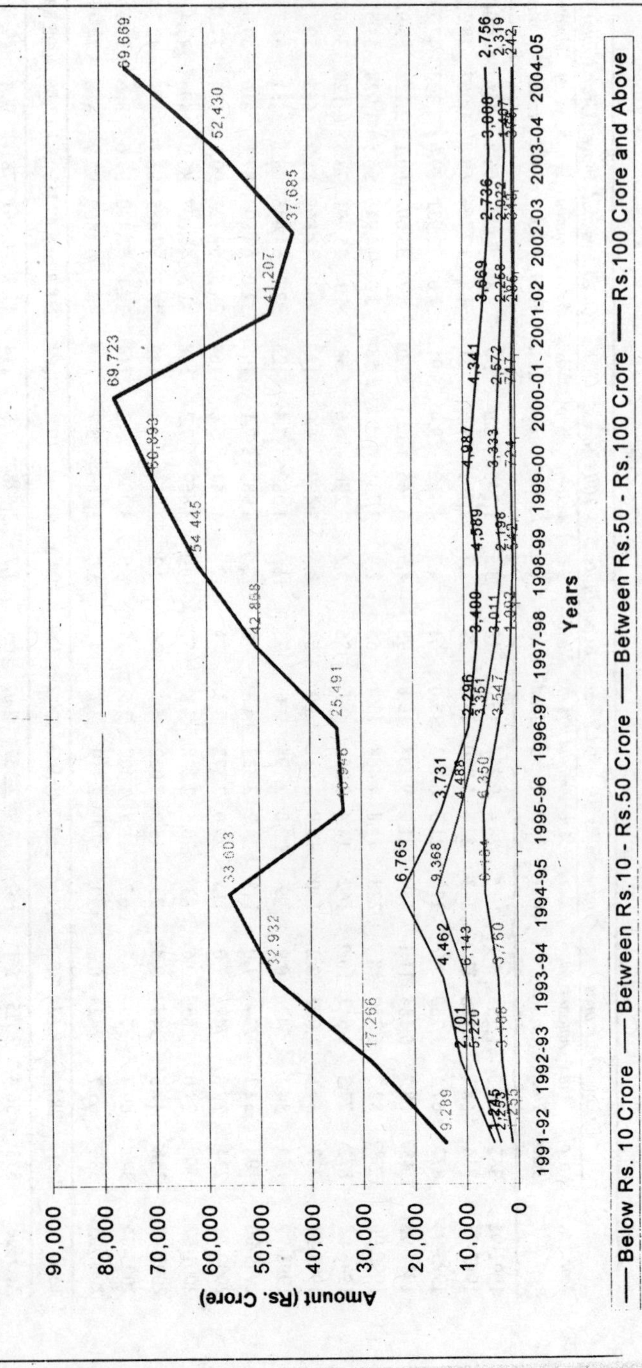

attributed for maximum number, over the period under review.

Table 3.5(a): Annual Index of Capital Issues Distribution based on Size

	Below 10 Crores		*10-50 Crores*		*50-100 Crores*		*100 Crores*	
Years	*Annual Index*	*Annual Index*	*Annual Index*	*Annual Index*	*Annual Index*	*Annual Index*	*Annual Index*	*Annual Index*
1991-92	100.0	100.0	100.0	100.0	100.0	100.0	100.0	100.0
1992-93	102.2	154.0	131.4	131.7	116.7	116.9	70.0	85.9
1993-94	19.5	17.9	14.4	17.7	56.4	65.2	78.4	90.7
1994-95	66.1	65.5	61.9	52.5	55.7	51.6	31.9	2.0
1995-96	8.9	2.7	-49.3	-52.1	-42.1	-44.8	-51.7	-43.6
1996-97	-45.4	-44.1	-28.9	-25.3	-34.5	-38.5	0.0	34.5
1997-98	-61.4	-69.2	-19.8	-10.1	50.0	52.4	127.6	68.0
1998-99	-54.3	-50.4	-23.8	-27.0	31.2	31.2	-5.3	27.0
1999-00	28.6	33.6	44.4	51.6	6.8	8.7	57.6	11.8
2000-01	13.1	3.2	-19.6	-22.8	-9.0	-13.0	-16.8	14.5
2001-02	-56.7	61.8	-27.8	-12.2	-19.7	-15.5	2.4	-40.9
2002-03	145.4	20.4	-9.6	-10.5	-19.3	-18.8	-15.5	-8.5
2003-04	43.7	9.3	-13.3	-30.4	-2.2	9.9	-19.7	39.1
2004-05	56.7	-35.5	38.5	64.8	-8.9	-8.4	30.7	32.9
Total	366.7	269.2	198.4	228.0	285.1	297.0	289.6	413.5
Average	26.2	19.2	14.2	16.3	20.4	21.2	27.8	29.5

Source: CMIE Capital Market Special Issues 2002, 2003, 2004 and 2005

If we observe the amount of capital issues we find interesting and distinctive features as compared to number of capital issues. The mega issues which were accounting for on an average 12.6 percent of total number of issues have claimed 81.4 percent of total amount of capital issues, and it was 90.1 percent in the year 2000-01. The striking change in the capital market is the arrival of mega issues and exit of small companies, as reflected in the increase of the average size of issues, which worked out to Rs. 470 crore per issue in 2004-05 compared to Rs. 11.7 crore in 1995-96. This is also supported by the large number of issues (1,725) in 1995-96 for only Rs. 28,800 crore compared to only 60 issues for Rs. 20,800 crore in 2004-05. Twenty-six mega issues were made for Rs. 27,000 crore and each of these on an average amounted to Rs. 1,081 crore. It is apparent from the data that small companies raised relatively small amounts from the market probably due to high transaction cost, high listing fees and stringent disclosure norms set by the SEBI to protect investors. Over the previous five years period (2000-01 to 2004-05), IPOs have begun playing a major role in resource mobilization, especially with the entry of government companies with mega offers.

The capital issues size group of below Rs.10 crores has claimed highest number, however its share in total amount of capital issues was very insignificant and moved between 0.3 percent to 18.9 percent during the period under review. The size group of Rs. 10 crores to Rs. 50 crores has mobilized 8.6 percent of total amount of capital issues. Whereas the size group of Rs. 50 to 100 crore has claimed 7.7 percent.

Thus we conclude that with regard to number of capital issues the size group below Rs.10 crores with 63.4 percent claimed major share, whereas in respect of amount of capital issues the mega size group of Rs. 100 crores and above has mobilized 81.4 percent of total capital issues.

3.8: DISTRIBUTION OF CAPITAL ISSUES BY REGION-WISE

This analysis is aimed at examining the major contribution of a region in the primary capital issues during the period under consideration. For this purpose the issues within the country was taken into consideration and it is also divided into the following:

(A) Northern Region.

(B) Eastern Region.

(C) Western Region.

(D) Southern Region.

The data relating to the region-wise issues with regard to their number and amount, percent to total along with annual

Table 3.6: Region-wise Distribution of Capital Raised

Year	Northern Region				Eastern Region				Western Region				Southern Region				Grand Total	
	No. of Issues	% to Total	Amount (Crore)	% to Total	No. of Issues	% to Total	Amount (Crore)	% to Total	No. of Issues	% to Total	Amount (Crore)	% to Total	No. of Issues	% to Total	Amount (Crore)	% to Total	No. of Issues	Amount (Crore)
1993-94	314	27.5	5,828	23.9	94	8.2	1,352	5.5	503	44.0	14,559	59.7	232	20.3	2,633	10.8	1,143	24,372
1994-95	399	23.6	6,554	23.7	178	10.5	2,216	8.0	740	43.7	10,824	39.2	375	22.2	8,039	29.1	1,692	27,633
1995-96	467	27.1	5,109	24.6	168	9.7	1,416	6.8	680	39.4	10,811	52.0	410	23.8	3,467	16.7	1,725	20,804
1996-97	221	25.1	3,381	23.7	114	12.9	767	5.4	360	40.8	9,041	63.3	187	21.2	1,087	7.6	882	14,276
1997-98	18	16.2	302	6.6	26	23.4	1,164	25.5	46	41.4	2,391	52.3	21	18.9	713	15.6	111	4,570
1998-99	10	17.2	171	3.1	10	17.2	266	4.8	29	50.0	4,856	86.9	9	15.5	293	5.2	58	5,587
1999-00	13	14.0	1,900	24.3	7	7.5	106	1.4	46	49.5	5,235	67.0	27	29.0	577	7.4	93	7,817
2000-01	10	6.6	207	3.4	9	6.0	240	3.9	43	28.5	4,105	67.2	89	58.9	1,555	25.5	151	6,108
2001-02	3	8.6	1,002	13.3	2	5.7	180	2.4	23	65.7	5,942	58.8	7	20.0	419	5.6	35	7,543
2002-03	1	3.8	78	1.9	3	11.5	117	2.9	13	50.0	3,358	82.5	9	34.6	588	14.4	26	4,070
2003-04	15	26.3	14,576	62.6	7	12.3	636	2.7	21	36.8	6,782	29.1	14	24.6	1,234	5.3	57	23,272
Total	1,471	196.0	39,108	211.1	618	125.1	8,460	69.3	2,504	489.9	77,904	678.0	1,380	289.0	20,605	143.2	5,973	146,052
Average	134	17.8	3555	19.2	56	11.4	769	6.3	228	44.5	7,082	61.6	125	26.3	1,873	13.0	543	13.277

Source: Hand Book of Statistics on the Indian Securities Market SEBI 2004, p. 23..

Fig. 3.6: Region-wise Distribution of Capital Rasied

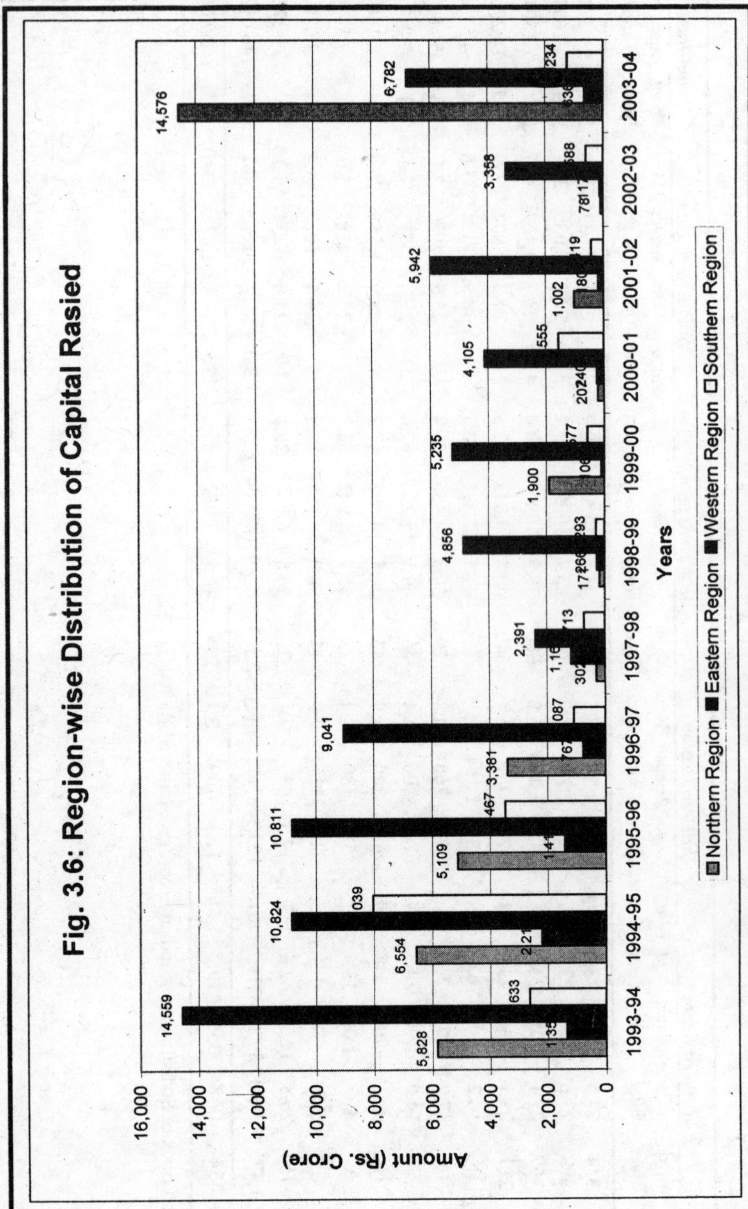

index of capital issues are presented in the table-3.6 and 3.6(a). This information is also presented in the Fig. 3.6.

We observe from the table that the first four years recorded a three digit number of issues and in the remaining period of the study it was recorded only a two and one digit number of issues in all the four regions. The amount of issues was also recorded the similar trend in all the four regions. From this observation we can say that the region-wise capital raised is also influenced by liberalization, privatization and globalization policies of the country.

Table 3.6 (a): Annual Index of Capital Issues Distribution based on Region

	Northern Region		*Eastern Region*		*Western Region*		*Southern Region*	
Years	*Annual Index*	*Annual Index*	*Annual Index*	*Annual Index*	*Annual Index*	*Annual Index*	*Annual Index*	*Annual Index*
1993-94	100.0	100.0	100.0	100.0	100.0	100.0	100.0	100.0
1994-95	27.1	12.5	89.4	63.9	47.1	-25.6	61.6	205.3
1995-96	17.0	-22.0	-5.6	-36.1	-8.1	-0.1	9.3	-56.8
1996-97	-52.7	-33.8	-32.1	-45.8	-47.1	-16.4	-54.4	-68.6
1997-98	-91.8	-91.1	-77.2	51.7	-87.2	-73.6	-88.8	-34.4
1998-99	-44.4	-43.4	-61.5	-77.1	-36.9	103.1	-57.1	-58.9
1999-00	30.0	1,011.1	-30.0	-60.2	58.6	7.8	200.0	96.9
2000-01	-23.1	-89.1	28.6	126.4	-6.5	-21.6	229.6	169.5
2001-02	-70.0	384.1	-77.7	-25.0	-46.5	44.8	-92.1	-73.1
2002-03	-66.7	92.2	50.0	-35.0	-43.5	-43.5	28.6	40.3
2003-04	1,400.0	18,587.2	57.1	443.6	61.5	102.0	55.5	109.8
Total	1,225.4	19,907.7	41.0	506.4	-8.6	176.9	392.2	430.0
Average	111.4	1,809.8	3.7	46.0	-0.8	16.1	35.7	39.1

Source: Hand Book of Statistics on the Indian Securities Market SEBI 2004, p. 23.

The average number of capital issues was 42.0 percent in the Western Region, 24.7 percent in the Northern Region, 23.0 percent in the Southern Region and only 10.3 percent in the

Eastern Region. The average amount of capital issues was 53.3 percent in the Western Region, 26.7 percent in the Northern Region, 14.2 percent in the Southern Region and only 5.8 percent in the Eastern Region. From the above, we can say that the average number and amount of capital issues were shows the varying proportion of contribution from the four regions. Hence, we conclude that the Western Region contributes above 50 percent of the total capital issues and the remaining was contributed by the other three regions.

SECTION-II

IPOs THROUGH EURO ISSUES

3.9: INTRODUCTION

Globalization is the process of denationalization of markets, politics and legal systems ultimately leading to a global economy. It is the integration of economies around the world, particularly through trade and financial flows. Globalization has been a major driving force motivating industries to become globally competitive in new economic environment. It provides competitive firms tremendous opportunities for growth and profitability at the same time. Many countries have restructured to better integration with the interconnected global economy. The globalization process has created waves of changes, leading higher adoptiveness and responsiveness on the part of industry. The corporate global competitiveness has emerged as a useful indicator of the long term health, prosperity of the corporate entity. The corporate sector in India found its way to global capital markets for meeting their resource requirements.

With the opening-up of Indian economy and as a part of the reforms process undertaken since July, 1991, there has been an inflow of foreign investment through direct and portfolio routes. Foreign portfolio investments in India have taken place through Euro Issue and also by direct purchase of securities by FIIs in domestic capital market. Government of India permitted since 1993, the good track record Indian companies to raise funds from the international market through Euro Issue. Today, a large number of Indian companies are tapping global financial funds from the foreign market through Euro Issue viz. Global

Depository Receipts (GDRs), American Depository Receipts (ADRs), American Depository Shares (ADS) and Foreign Currency Convertible Bonds (FCCBs).[1]

3.10: MEANING

3.10.1. Euro Issue

The term 'Euro issue' means an issue made abroad through instruments denominated in foreign currency and listed on a European stock exchange, the subscriptions for which may come from any part of the world.[2] Most of the Indian companies get their issues listed on the Luxembourg Stock Exchange.

3.10.2. Global Depository Receipts (GDRs)

A GDR is an instrument which allows Indian Corporates, Banks, Non-Banking Financial Companies etc., to raise funds through equity issues abroad to augment their resources for domestic operations. As per the recent guidelines on issue of GDRs, a corporate entity can issue any number of GDRs in a year and the Corporate involved in infrastructure projects need not have a past track record of financial performance.[3]

3.10.3. American Depository Receipts (ADRs)

ADRs are the US version of GDRs. ADRs are negotiable receipts issued to investors by an authorized depository, normally a US bank or depository, in lieu of shares of the foreign company, which are actually held by the depository. It is a negotiable instrument, denominated in US dollars representing a non-US company's local currency equity shares. ADRs are listed on an American stock exchange. The issue process is governed by American laws and Securities and Exchange Commission (SEC), US, the market regulator, monitors the issue.

3.10.4. Foreign Currency Convertible Bonds (FCCBs)

FCCBs are bonds issued to and subscribed by a non-resident in foreign currency which are convertible into certain number of ordinary shares at a pre-fixed price. Euro convertible bonds are listed on a European Stock Exchange. The issuer company has to pay interest on FCCBs in foreign currency till the conversion takes place and if the conversion option is not exercised by the investor; the redemption of bond is also to be made in foreign currency.

3.11: OBJECTIVES

The Initial Public Offers through Euro Issues is aimed at covering the following objectives:

* To discuss the concept of Euro Issues and its constituents.
* To present critical stages in the process of ADRs and GDRs issue.
* To analyze the trends and pattern of Euro Issues.

3.12: THE PROCEDURE

3.12.1. The following are some of the critical stages in the process of ADRs issue

(a) The company shall present its accounts in conformity with US GAAP. US GAAP requires presentation of consolidated financial statements.

(b) Appointment of legal experts, lead experts, leads managers, investment bankers and their due diligence.

(c) Preparation of the offer document and its vetting by legal counsels.

(d) Filing of the offer document and its review by Securities and Exchange Commission (SEC).

(e) Replying to the comments of SEC and obtaining its clearance.

(f) Road shows and book running.

(g) Appointment of domestic and international depositary. Domestic depositary will act as a custodian of the underlying shares.

(h) Selection of an American Stock Exchange.

(i) Allotment of underlying shares and creation of ADRs.

(j) Listing of ADRs on American Stock Exchange.

(k) Listing of underlying shares with domestic Stock Exchanges.

3.12.2. The broad steps leading to the GDR issue are as follows:

a) Approval of the Board of the Company for GDRs issue.

b) Appointment of Various Agencies like: Book Runners, Global Coordinators and Underwriters, International Lawyers, Local/Company's Lawyers, Auditors and International Depository.

c) Organizing meetings, management presentations with regard to features and prospects of GDRs.

d) Commence Financial, Business & Legal attentiveness.

e) Finalize Offer Memorandum (OM).

f) Obtain preliminary listing approval.

g) Print and file Red Herring Offer Memorandum. Submit Red Herring Offer Memorandum to Indian stock exchanges (BSE, NSE) SEBI and Registrar of Companies for record purpose.

h) Arranging road shows for book building.

i) Complete road show, signing / pricing meeting and finalization of allocation to investors.

j) Allotment of underlying shares and GDRs

k) Closing of all the activities.

l) File the final offering document with SEBI and Indian Stock Exchanges.

m) Listing of Shares at the local stock exchanges.

3.13: TRENDS AND PATTERN OF EURO ISSUES:

Starting with the maiden issue of the Reliance Industries in May 1992, around 100-odd Indian companies have so far tapped the global market with a cumulative mobilization of Rs. 99,207 crore by the end of 2004-05 through 162 issues (Table-3.7 and Fig. 3.7). Indeed, India has the distinction of issuing the maximum number of Depository Receipts (DRs) among the emerging economies. The genesis of Indian multinational corporations (MNCs) with not only international operations, but also a global ownership is logical fallout of this process.

While bunching of Depository Receipt issues took place in

the early 1990s possibly in view of the pent-up overseas demand for Indian scrips, it seemed to have been primarily motivated by the existing costly procedure of floatation in the Domestic market96 . Initially GDRs were the preferred mode with the majority of listings in the Luxembourg or the London Stock Exchange in view of their less stringent disclosure requirements vis-_-vis the requirements under the US GAAP (Generally Accepted Accounting Principles). Besides, a majority of the Indian GDRs were issued pursuant to the US Rule 144A and/or Regulations of the US Securities Exchange Commission, which enabled their trading in the US market too mainly through the PORTAL system. Nevertheless, ADRs have since emerged as the star attraction through its higher global visibility, particularly

Table 3.7: Euro Issue by Indian Companies

(Rs. Crore)

Year	*No. of Issues*	*Annual Growth Rate*	*Amount Raise*	*Annual Growth Rate*
1992-93	2	–	754	–
1993-94	29	1,350.0	7,986	959.2
1994-95	34	17.2	7,901	-1.1
1995-96	8	-76.5	2,573	-67.4
1996-97	12	50.0	5,679	120.7
1997-98	3	--75.0	1,103	-80.6
1998-99	2	-33.3	18,097	1,540.7
1999.00	6	200.0	3,989	-78.0
2000-01	9	50.0	28,354	610.8
2001-02	3	-66.7	2,193	-92.3
2002-03	7	133.3	910	-58.5
2003-04	14	100.0	4,561	401.2
2004-05	33	135.7	15,107	231.2
Total	162	1,784.7	99,207	3,486.0
Average	12	137.3	7,631	268.2

Source: CMIE Capital Markets Special Issues 2002, 2003, 2004 and 2005

Fig. 3.7: Euro Issue by Indian Companies

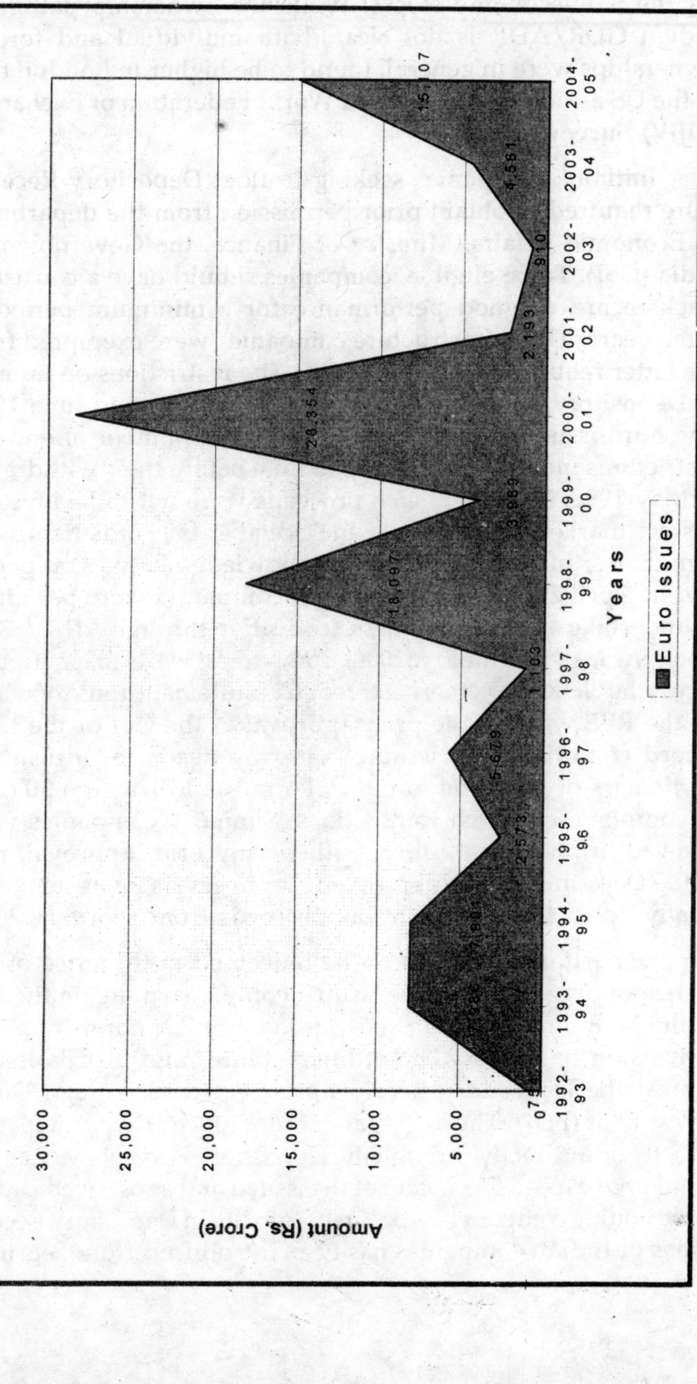

for the new-economy stocks. While the ownership pattern of Indian GDR/ADR is not clear, both individual and foreign ownerships were in general, found to be higher in London than in the US as per the Paris-based World Federation of Exchanges (FIBV) Survey (1999).

Initially, companies seeking to float Depository Receipts were required to obtain prior permission from the department of Economic Affairs, Ministry of Finance, the Government of India (GoI). To be eligible, companies should have a consistent track record of good performance for a minimum period of three years. The infrastructure companies were exempted from the latter requirement in June 1996. The restrictions on number of Depository Receipt issues were also removed in June 1996. The Euro issue proceeds were subject to a number of end-use restrictions modified from time to time before their withdrawal in May 1998. However, such proceeds were not to be invested in stock market and real estate. In December 1999 Indian software companies, in March 2000 other knowledge-based companies and in April 2001 different types of companies were permitted to undertake overseas business acquisition through ADR / GDR stock swaps. In January 2000, companies were made free to access the GDR/ ADR market through an automatic route operated by the RBI, without the prior approval of the GoI or the track record condition. The issuing company needs to furnish full particulars of the issue to the GoI and the RBI within 30 days of completion of such transactions. Similarly companies were allowed in phases to utilize, without any prior approval, part of the Depository Receipt proceeds for overseas investment and finally up to 100 percent of the proceeds from February 2001.

Depository Receipts can be redeemed at the price of the corresponding shares of the issuing company ruling on the BSE or the NSE on the date of redemption. Similar norms apply to conversion of FCCBs. The ordinary shares and FCCBs issued against the Depository Receipts are treated as Foreign Direct Investment (FDI). The aggregate of foreign equity participation directly or indirectly through the Depository Receipt mechanism should not exceed 51 percent of the issued and subscribed capital of the issuing company. Two-way fungibility in Depository Receipt issues of Indian companies has been introduced from February

13, 2002 whereby converted local shares could be reconverted into Depository Receipts subject to sectoral caps on FDI.

Interest payment and dividend on these instruments are subject to tax deduction at source at the rate of 10 percent. Capital gains on account of transactions among non-resident investors outside India are free from any income tax liability in India. However, transfer of the aforesaid shares in India to the non-resident investor is liable to income tax at the rate of 10 percent. Holding of Depository Receipts by non-resident investors, holding of underlying shares by ODB in a fiduciary capacity and transfer of Depository Receipts between non-resident investors and ODB are exempted from wealth tax and gift tax. Provisions of avoidance of double taxation agreement (entered into by the GoI with the country of residence of the ODB) are applicable to the Depository Receipts.

There are two alternatives, albeit not mutually exclusive, ways of investment in Indian shares by a foreign concern. As an FII registered with the SEBI, it can directly participate in trading and investment in the Indian stock market. Alongside or alternatively, it can buy Depository Receipts of the Indian companies in the overseas markets. Given the legal and institutional requirements as also the tax implications for an FII, small and medium sized investors' and particularly foreign individuals might find it convenient to invest in the Indian GDR / ADR rather than in the Indian market parse. While virtual capital account convertibility for the non-residents has provided such alternative avenues of investment, its absence for the resident citizens of India has confined them to the domestic market. Indian fund managers including mutual funds are, however, now permitted to invest in ADR / GDR of Indian companies, and foreign debt securities up to 4 percent of their net assets subject to a maximum of $ 50 million per mutual fund and $ 500 million for the overall industry.

Euro Issues by the Indian Companies are presented in Table-3.7; the following important observations are presented below:

* The lowest and highest numbers of Euro Issues are recorded in the year 1992-93 and 1994-95 respectively.

* The lowest and highest amounts of Euro Issues are witnessed in the year 1992-93 and 2000-01 respectively.
* The highest number and amount of Euro Issues are recorded in different years. From this observation we can say that the highest numbers of Euro Issues are not necessarily to contribute the highest amount and this is depending on the size of capital offered by the companies at that time.
* The annual growth rate in number and amount of Euro Issues were witnessed greater fluctuations. These fluctuations are highlighted because of various reasons like, steps taken by the Government from the time to time, rate of growth / expansion of individual companies and their ambition to raise funds from overseas, etc.
* The last two years of the study witnessed the positive growth rate in number as well as amount of Euro Issues. This is because of the companies permitted to make Euro Issues are broaden by the Government of India.

Portfolio investment flows to India was presented in the Table-3.8. We observed that the Portfolio investment inflows have since then substantial, with the lone exception of 1998-99. On an annual average basis, India received cross-border portfolio investment to the tune of US $ 3,426 million per year among 1992-93 to 2004-05; the contribution of FIIs was close to US $ 2,520 million, on an average. The cumulative FII investment in India is close to US $ 32,755 million. ADR / GDR issues by Indian companies are another important source of cross-border portfolio investment in India. On an average basis, ADR / GDR accounted for over one-third of the total cross-border portfolio investment to India. The overall contribution of ADR/GDR, FII and Offshore Funds to total portfolio flows to India are recorded at 23.7 percent, 73.5 percent and 2.8 percent respectively. The first highest contribution is came from FIIs and the next highest is from ADRs/GDRs. Offshore Funds contribution is very less and in the last three years of the study its evidence is nil. The average annual growth rate (from the year 1994-95 to 2004-05) of ADRs/GDRs, and FIIs are 13.1 percent and 285.7 percent respectively. The growth rate of FIIs is 22 times higher than that of ADRs/GDRs.

Table-3.8: Portfolio Investment Flows to India

(US $ Million)

Year	*ADRs/GDRs*	*FIIs**	*Offshore Funds*	*Total*
1992-93	240 (—) [99]	1 (—) [0]	3 (—) [1]	244 (—) [100]
1993-94	1,520 (533) [43]	1,665 (1,66,400) [47]	382 (12,633) [11]	3,567 (1,362) [100]
1994-95	2,082 (37) [54]	1,503 (-10) [39]	239 (-37) [6]	3,824 (7) [100]
1995-96	683 (-67) [25]	2,009 (34) [73]	56 (-77) [2]	2,748 (-28) [100]
1996-97	1,366 (100) [41]	1,926 (-4) [58]	20 (-64) [1]	3,312 (21) [100]
1997-98	645 (-53) [35]	979 (-49) [54]	204 (920) [11]	1,828 (-45) [100]
1998-99	270 (-58) [69]	-390 (-140)[-100]	59 (-71) [15]	-61 (-101) [-16]
1999-00	768 (184) [25]	2,135 (647) [71]	123 (108) [4]	3,026 (5,061) [100]
2000-01	831 (8) [30]	1,847 (-13) [67]	82 (-33) [3]	2,760 (-9) [100]
2001-02	477 (-43) [24]	1,505 (-19) [75]	39 (-52) [2]	2,021 (-27) [100]
2002-03	600 (26) [61]	377 (-75) [39]	2 (-95) [0]	979 (-52) [100]
2003-04	459 (-24) [4]	10,918 (2,796) [96]	0 (-100) [0]	11,377 (1,062) [100]
2004-05	613 (34) [7]	8,280 (-24) [93]	16 (—) [0]	8,909 (-22) [100]
Total	10,554	32,755	1225	44,534
Average	812	2,520	94	3,426

Note: (1) * Represents Fresh Inflow of Funds by FIIs.

(2) Figures in (—) indicates Annual Growth Rate.

(3) Figures in [—] indicates Individual Item % to Total.

Source: RBI: Report on Currency and Finance, 2004-05.

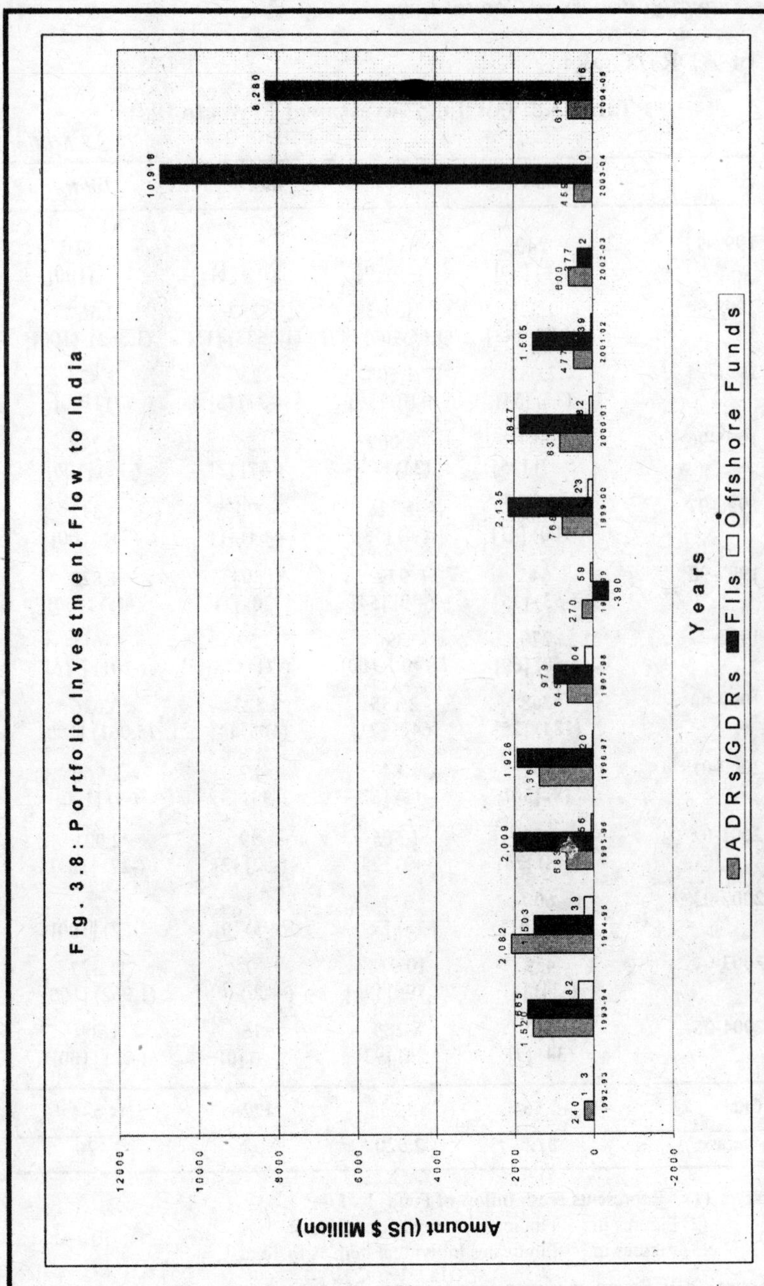

Fig. 3.8: Portfolio Investment Flow to India

The process of liberalization and globalization has created waves of changes leading to higher adoptiveness and responsiveness in the corporate world. The best response since liberalization has mostly come from FIIs in terms of portfolio investments particularly through Euro Issues. The Euro issues have emerged as a source of foreign funds and these have a greater prospective for foreign investors who are generally institutional investors interested mainly in the return for their investment by way of capital appreciation and dividends.

The foreign investment is encouraging, with the majority of equity participation in its portfolio. The Indian companies have been encouraged to access global capital market through the Euro issues GDRs and ADRs. The Euro issues have a brighter scope to access more foreign funds from Global Markets. There should be a national policy on Euro issue to monitor the various government agencies like SEBI, DEA, and RBI etc.

SECTION-III

IPOs THROUGH BOOK-BUILDING SYSTEM

3.14: INTRODUCTION:

The stock market has been acknowledged all over the world as vital for long-term economic growth. Several empirical studies have proved that there is a strong positive correlation between the level of sophistication of a country's stock market and its level of economic growth and development. Countries with well-developed stock markets generally tend to enjoy higher economic growth and development than those with underdeveloped stock markets (Frank). There was a vital need to strengthen the capital market which could only be achieved through structural modifications, introducing new market mechanism, instruments, and by taking steps for safeguarding the interest of the investors through more disclosures and transparency. In this context, an important mechanism named as Book-Building in the system of Initial Public Offerings (IPOs) was introduced by SEBI in India on the basis of the recommendations of the committee constituted under the chairmanship of Y.H. Malegam in October, 1995. Book-Building is the most practical mechanism for the quick and efficient management of mega issues97 (including offers for sale).

3.15: MEANING

SEBI guidelines, 1995 defined book building as "a process undertaken by which a demand for the securities proposed to be issued by a body of corporate is elicited and built up and the price for such securities is assessed for the determination of the quantum of such securities to be issued by means of a notice, circular, advertisement, document or information memoranda or offer document". In general, the word "Book- Building" is a method of marketing the shares of a company whereby the quantum and the price of the securities to be issued will be decided on the basis of the 'bids' received from the prospective shareholders by the lead merchant bankers. According to this method, share prices are determined on the basis of real demand for the shares at various price levels in the market.

3.16: OBJECTIVES

The main objectives of this section are as follows:

* To understand the conceptual frame work of Book-Building.
* To study the regulatory guidelines of SEBI for Book-Building Issues.
* To examine the recent developments in the Book-Building Process.
* To analyze the Trends in the Book-Building Issues in India.

3.17: MALEGHAM PANEL'S RECOMMENDATIONS

The introduction of book-building in India in 1995 was on account of the recommendations of an expert committee appointed by SEBI under Chairmanship of Y.H. Malegham "to review the (then) existing disclosure requirements in offer documents." Two of the terms of reference being "the basis of pricing the issue" and "whether substantial reduction was possible in the time taken for processing applications by SEBI." The committee has submitted its report with several recommendations and the SEBI accepted the same in November 1995. The book-building route should be open to issuer companies, subject to certain terms and conditions. Some of them are presented below:

* The option should be available only to issues exceeding Rs. 100 crore;
* The book-building issuer companies could either reserve the securities for firm allotment or avail themselves of the book- building process;
* Draft prospectus to be submitted to SEBI could exclude information about the offer price;
* A book runner to be nominated from among the lead market bankers, charged with specific responsibilities and the name is to be submitted to the SEBI's approval; and
* The requirement of 25 percent of the securities to be offered to the public will be continued.

There have been several amendments/revisions to the above guidelines; the first one in December 1996 made available the option of book-building to all corporate bodies which were otherwise eligible to make an issue of capital to the public, and in case of under subscription, the spill-over from the public portion could be permitted to the placement area and vice-versa. In 1997, the restriction of the facility to 75 percent of the issue was thought to severely constrain the benefits arising out of price and demand discovery and the facility was extended to 100 percent of the issue, available only if the issue amount was Rs. 100 crore and above, compulsorily offering an additional 10 percent of the issue size to the public through prospectus and reserving at least 15 percent of the issue size to individual investors applying up to ten tradable lots. Further, audited financial ratios had to be disclosed, namely, EPS, P/E, average return on net worth for the last three years and net asset value based on last year's balance sheet.

However, there were no takers for the 100 percent book-building facility. Based on suggestions made by leading merchant bankers, the following amendments were made to the guidelines in 1999:

* The issuer may be allowed to disclose either the issue size or the number of securities to be offered to the public;
* Allotment should be in demat mode only; and
* Reservation of 15 percent of issue amount for individual investors need to the public at a fixed price. Some of the earliest mega issues through the book-building route were those of Larsen & Toubro, ICICI, Tisco and so many others.

3.18: SEBI GUIDELINES

(a) In January 2000, SEBI has issued a compendium of guidelines, circulars and instructions to merchant bankers relating to issue of capital, including those on the book-building mechanism. The compendium includes a model timeframe for book-building: "After the price has been determined on the basis of bidding, statutory public advertisements for a continuous three days containing, inter alia, the price as well as a table showing the number of securities and the amount payable by an investor, based on the price determined, shall be issued and the interval between the advertisement and issue opening date should be a minimum of five days."

(b) The draft prospectus to be circulated has to indicate the price band within which the securities are being offered for subscription. The bids have to be within the price bands. Bidding is permissible only if an electronically-linked transparent facility is used. An issuing company can also fix a minimum bid size. An initial bid can be changed before the final rate is determined. The mega issues such as Petronet LNG and Biocon were successfully launched through the 100 percent book-building route.

(c) The Prospective bidders were advised to read the "Red herring prospectus" carefully. According to the Act, a "Red herring prospectus" means a prospectus that does not have complete particulars on the price and the quantum of securities offered. The Concise Oxford Dictionary gives the meaning of 'red herring' as a misleading clue or distraction, so named from the practice of using the scent of red herring in training hands.

(d) The year 2000, Amendment to the Act gave legal cloak to the book-building route by allowing circulation of the information memorandum and the red herring prospectus. According to the Act, a process is to be undertaken prior to the filing of a prospectus by which a demand for the securities proposed to be issued by a company is elicited, the price and the terms of the issue of such securities are assessed by means of a notice, circular, advertisement or document. Incidentally, the working group on the Comprehensive Companies Bill, 1997 (since lapsed) had advocated introduction of book-building. It defined the term as "an international practice that refers to collecting orders from investment bankers and large investors based on an indicative price range. In capital markets, with sufficient width and depth, such a pre-issue exercise often allows the issue to get a better idea of the demand and the final offer price of an intended public offer."

(e) SEBI (Disclosure and Investor Protection) Guidelines, 2000 contain for book-building under chapter XI which includes guidelines for 75% book-building process, 100% book-building process, disclosure requirements, allocation / allotment procedure and maintenance of books and records.

3.19: TYPES OF BOOK-BUILDING PROCESS

The Companies are bound to adhere to the SEBI's guidelines for book building offers in the following manner:

3.19.1. 75% Book-Building Process

Under this process 25% of the issue is to be sold at a fixed price and the balance of 75% through the Book Building process. Chart-3.1 indicates this process.

3.19.2. Offer to Public through Book-Building Process

The process specifies that an issuer company may make an issue of securities to the public through prospectus in the following manner:

(a) 100% of the net offer to the public through book building process, or

Chart-3.1: 75% Book Building Process

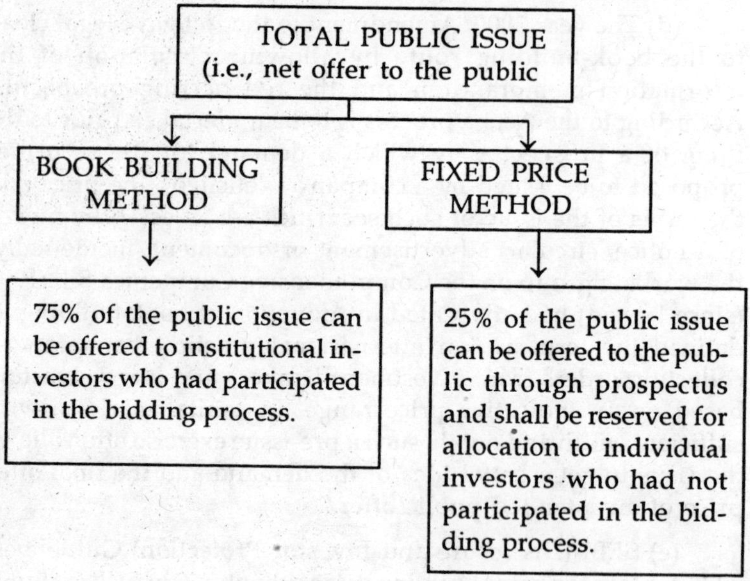

Chart-3.2: 100% of the Net Offer to the Public Through 100% Book Building Process

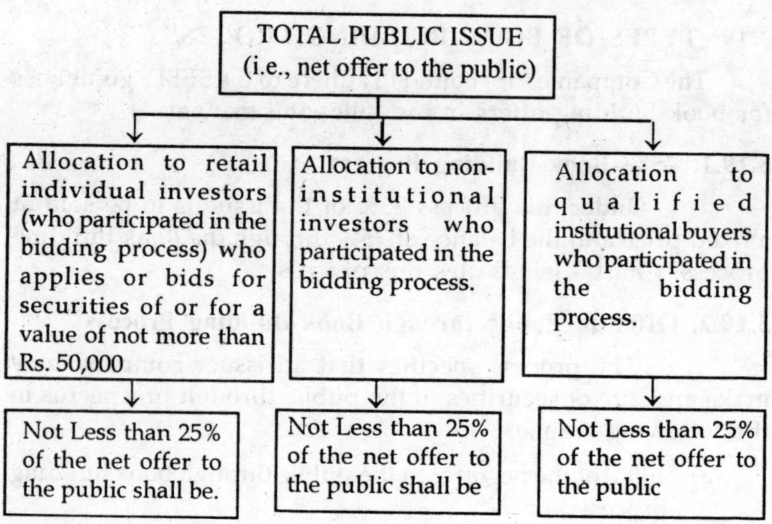

(b) 75% of the net offer to the public through book building process and 25% of the net offer to the public at the price determined through book building process (Chart-3.2 and 3.3).

Chart- 3.3: 75% of the Net Offer to the Public Through Book- Building Process:

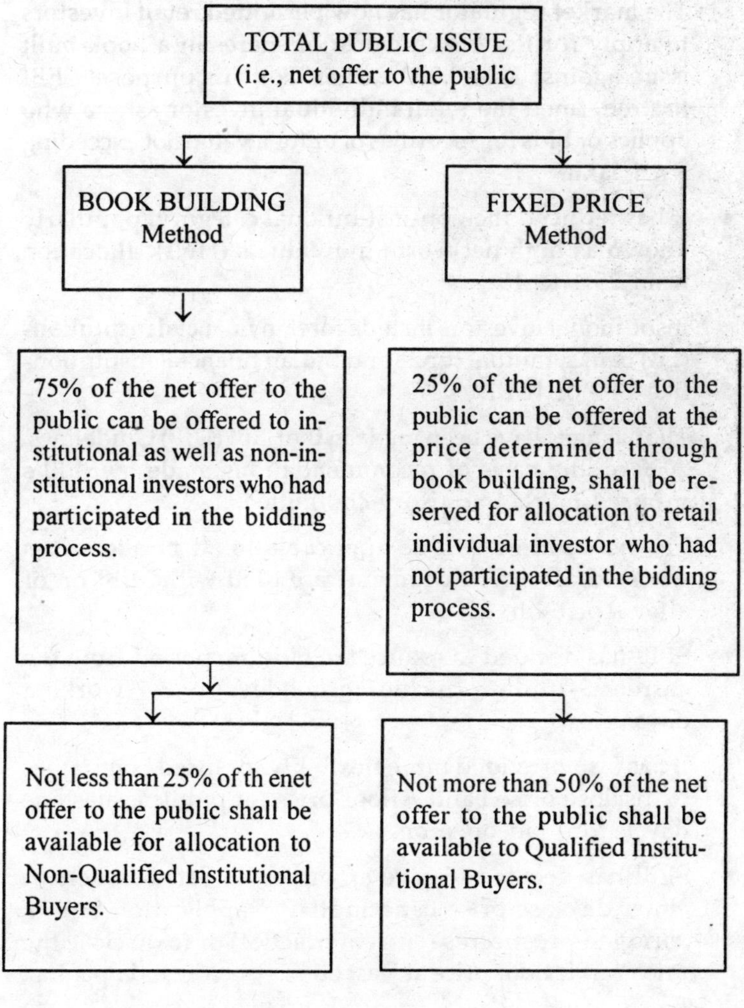

RECENT CHANGES IN BOOK-BUILDING MECHANISM

The Securities and Exchange Board of India on 29th March, 2005 announced sweeping changes in the IPO norms. They are as follows:

- Increased allocation for retail investors in book-built issue from 25% to 35% and has also changed the definition of the retail category.
- The market regulator has now permitted retail investors to apply for Rs. 1 lakh worth of shares in a book-built issue against Rs. 50,000 earlier. For this purpose, SEBI has redefined the retail individual investor as one who applies or bids for securities of or for a value not exceeding Rs. 1 lakh.
- It has reduced the non-institutional category, popularly known as high net worth individuals (HNI), allocation from 25% to 15%.
- Institutional investors include foreign financial institutions (FII) banks, mutual funds and Indian financial institutions like LIC or IDBI.
- The changes have been made in the SEBI (DIP) Guidelines, 2000 on the basis of recommendations made by SEBI's primary market advisory committee.
- The new norms will be applicable to all public issues whose draft offer documents are filed with SEBI on or after April 4th, 2005.
- SEBI has decided to reduce the bidding period from the current 5-10 days (including holidays) to 3-7 working days.
- It has also provided more flexibility for listed companies to disclose price band / floor price for public issues one day before bid opening.
- SEBI has decided to give an option to listed issuers to either disclose price band in RHP / application form / abridged prospectus (current practice) or to disclose the price band/floor price at least one day before bid opening.

- It is proposed to amend the guidelines to improve contents and ensure uniformity in data display on the websites of the stock exchanges. The date will be made available for a further period of three days after the closure of the bids/issue.

3.20: BOOK BUILDING PROCESS IN INDIA

3.20.1. The principal parties / intermediaries involved in a book building process are

* The issuer company,
* The Book Running Lead Manager (BRLM) who is a Category I Merchant Banker registered with SEBI, and
* The Syndicate Members (Chart-3.4) who are intermediaries registered with SEBI and who are permitted to carry on activities as underwriters. Syndicate Members are appointed by Book Running Lead Manager.

3.20.2. The steps for book building process (Chart-3.5) are

(a) Preparation of draft prospectus,

(b) Formation of Syndicate,

(c) Record of orders,

(d) Consolidation,

(e) Closure of order book,

(f) Determination of price,

(g) Agreement with syndicate members,

(h) Payment in advance,

(i) Filling of prospectus,

(j) Two Separate accounts are opened by the issuer company for collection of application money,

(k) Collection of application for securities,

(l) Allotment of placement and public portions,

(m) The placement portion may be used to adjust under subscription,

(n) Rate of allotment, and

(o) Maintenance of records.

Chart-3.4: Book Building Process

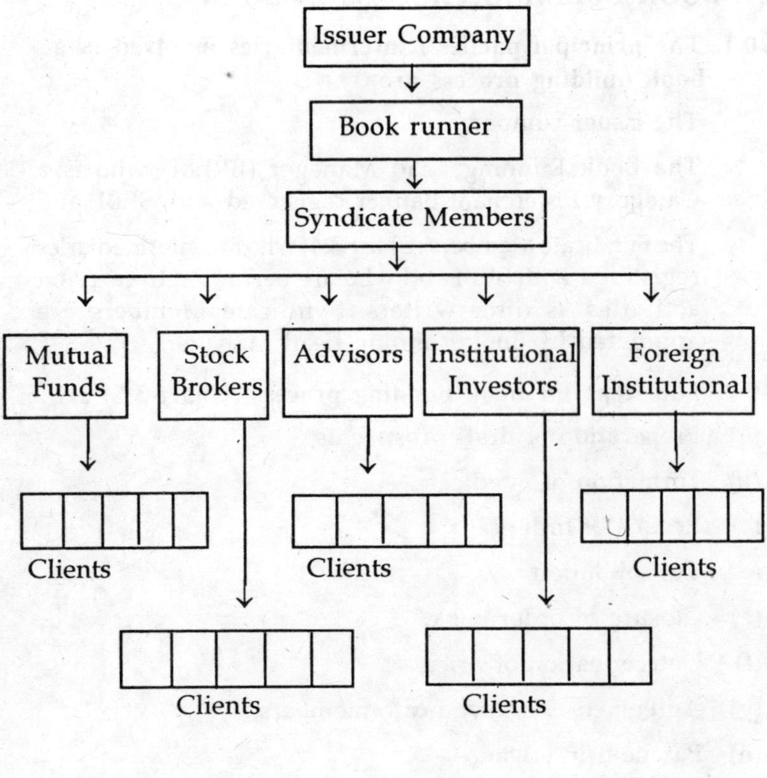

3.21: RECENT TRENDS IN BOOK-BUILDING ISSUES IN INDIA

* The book-building process in India is transparent. All investors (including small investors) can see on an hourly basis where the book is being built before applying. Therefore, no asymmetry as far as information dissemination is concerned.

* The year 2004 was a significant and bumper year because

Chart 3.5: Steps Involved in Book-Building Process

Nominate Book Runner

↓

Form Syndicate of Brokers, Arrangers, Underwriters, Financial Institutions, etc.

↓

Submit Draft Offer Document to SEBI without mentioning Coupon Rate or Price

↓

Circulate Offer Document among the Sydicate Members

↓

Ask for Bids on Price and Quality of Securities

↓

Aggregate and forward all Offers to Book Runner

↓

Run the Book to maintain a record of Subscribers and their Orders

↓

Consult with Issuer and Determine the Issue Price as Weighted Average of the Offers Received

↓

Firm up Underwriting Commitments

↓

Allot Securities Amogn Syndicate Members

↓

Securities Issued and Listed

↓

Trading Commences on Exchanges

Source: Agarwal, Sanjib: Barat's Manual of Indian Capital Market, Bharat Law Huse, New Delhi, 1997, p. 578.

Table 3.9: Pattenr of Meda Issues Durign 1992-93 to 2003-04

Year	*No. of Mega Issues*	*% of Changes*	*Amount Raised Through Mega Issues (Rs. Crores)*	*% of Change*	*Total Amount Raised (Rs. Cores)*	*% of Change*	*Share of Mega Issus in Total Capital Mobilised (%)*
1992-93	34	NA	NA	NA	NA	NA	45..25
1993-94	NA	NA	7,387	NA	19,501	NA	37.88
1994-95	112	NA	33,602	354.9	55,920	186.7	60.09
1995-96	56	–50.0	19,133	–43.1	33,869	–39.4	56.49
1996-97	58	3.6	25,491	33.2	34,737	2.6	73.38
1997-98	128	54.7	43,119	69.2	50,741	46.1	84.98
1998-99	114	–10.9	55,229	28.1	62,633	23.4	88.18
1999.00	192	68.4	62,351	12.9	71,710	14.5	86.96
2000-01	160	–16.7	69,764	11.9	77,710	8.4	89.77
2001-02	155	–3.1	42,858	–38.6	49,852	–35.8	85.97
2003-93	142	–9.4	37,685	–12.1	42,712	–14.3	88.23
2003-04	112	–21.1	51,823	37.5	56,149	31.4	92.30
2004-05	149	33.0	69,669	34.4	74,986	33.5	92.91
Total	1412		518,111		630,513		82.17
Average	118		40,767		50,502		

NA = Not Available.

Source: CMIE Capital Markets Issues, August 2003, June 2004 and 2005, p. 6.

companies have raised Rs. 30,511 crore through public issues and 99% of this being good quality securities from established companies and almost all issues were through book-building. The Pattern of Mega Issues during 1992-93 to 2003-04 was presented in Table-3.9 and large issues were presented in Table-3.10.

* The practice of book building is new to the Indian capital market and the procedure is still evolving. ICICI was the first company to use Book- Building method for its Rs. 1,000 crore bond issue in April 1996 followed by Rs. 4,323 crore Larsen & Toubro issue and Rs. 5,878 crore

Fig. 3.9: Pattern of Mega Issues During 1992-93 to 2004-05

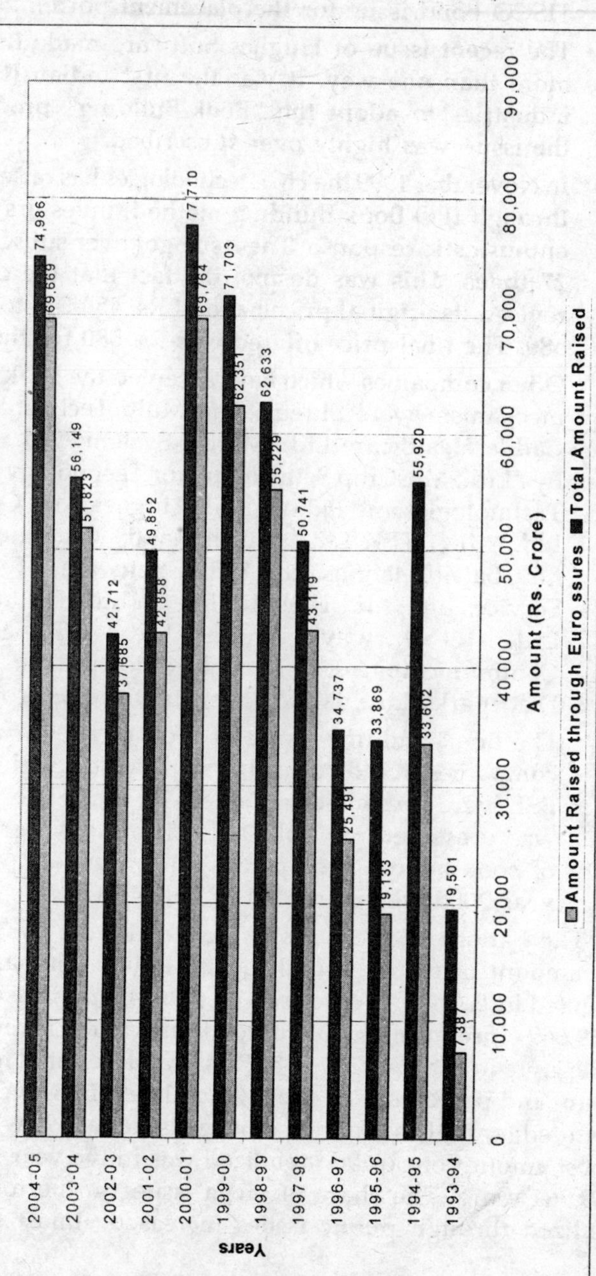

TISCO bond issue for the placement portion.

* The recent issue of Hughes Software made history in more than one way. It was the first Indian IPO in IT industries to adopt the "Book-Building" process and the issue was highly over subscribed.
* In November 1999 the HCL technologies has raised capital through IPO Book Building method, investors gave an enthusiastic response. The issue got over subscribed by 27 times. This was despite the fact that the company revised its original price band of Rs. 450-540 to Rs. 500-580. The final price offered was Rs. 580 for the shares.
* Other companies which have accepted the book building mechanism were Shree Rama Multi Tech Ltd., Zydus Cadila Healthcare Ltd., Mascot Systems Ltd., Creative Eye Ltd., MosChip Semiconductor Technology Ltd., SIP Technologies and Exports Ltd., Hughes Tele. Com India Ltd., MRO TEK Ltd., Pritish Nandy Communications Ltd., Balaji Telefilms Ltd., AZTEC Software & Technology Services Ltd., Mid-Day Multimedia Ltd., D-Link (India) Ltd., Jet Airways (India) Ltd., UTV Software Communications Ltd., Punjab National Bank, Gateway Distriparks Ltd., IVRCL Infrastructure & Projects Ltd.
* The Book-Building issues of IPOs of above mentioned companies in India during 1999-2005 through NSE and BSE were presented in Table-3.13 and its performance was presented in Table-3.11. Listing day performance of book-building companies during first quarter of the year 2005 was presented in Table-3.12.

The Pattern of Mega Issues and their role in relation to total amount of capital mobilized by Indian companies were presented in Table-3.9. We observed that 149 mega issues raised Rs. 69,669 crore forming 93% of total capital mobilized through public issue in the year 2004-05. This year accounted for highest amount and percentage of capital mobilized. However, 1999-00 accounted for highest number of mega issues at 192 whereas the highest amount of capital mobilized was in the year 2000-01 at Rs.69,764 crore. The share of mega issues in the total capital mobilized through public issues increased almost two times from 45.25% in 1992-93 to 92.91% in 2004-05.

If we observe the growth rate in the amount of capital raised during the decade, the year 1997-98 recorded at an increase of 69.2% and the year 2001-02 recorded highest decline at -38.6%. The amount of total capital mobilized from the public issues as shown significantly wide fluctuations from 186.7% in 1994-95 and -35.8% in 2001-02. This indicates there is no clear cut consistency in the number and amount of public issues. Apart from this the amount raised through mega issues as also recorded similar trends. Based on this, we can highlight that through book-building process is highly commendable.

Table 3.10: Large Isues Durign 2003-04

Sl. No.	*Name of the Company*	*Type of Issues*	*Type of Instrument*	*Date of Opening of Issues*	*Offer Size (Rs. Crores)*	*Percentage to Total*
1.	ONGC	Voluntary Offer for Sale	Equity	13-03-04	10,695	54.98
2.	GAIL (India Ltd)	Voluntary Offer for Sale	Equity	27-02-04	1,564	8.04
3.	IPCL	Vountary Offer for Sale	Equity	20-02-04	1,221	6.27
4.	Maruti Udyog Ltd.	Voluntary Offer for Sale	Equity	12-06-04	993	5.10
5.	IDBI	Public Issue	Bond	9-3-04	588	3.02
6.	Patni Comp. Systems Ltd.	Public Issue	Equity	27-12-03	431	2.21
7.	ICICI Bank Ltd.	Public Issue	Bond	30-10-03	343	1.76
8.	IDBI	Public Issue	Bond	19-01-04	797	4.09
9.	Petronet LNG Ltd.	Public Issue	Equity	1-3-2004	391	2.01
10.	IBP Company Ltd.	Voluntary Offer for Sale	Equity	23-02-04	357	1.83
11.	ICICI Ltd.	Public Issue	Bond	2-08-03	486	2.49
12.	IDBI	Public Issue	Bond	17-12-03	1,586	8.15
	Total				19,452	100.00

Source: CMIE Reports.

We observe from the table-3.10, that the total offer size was Rs. 19,452 Crore from 12 companies during 2003-04. Among them, 54.98% was raised by ONGC alone and the remaining was from the rest of 11 companies.

The types of issues are consisting of voluntary offer for sale and public issues. The contribution of voluntary offer for sale is significantly higher than the public offer. Further, types of instruments issued by the companies are equity and bonds. Amount contributed through equity is 80.5% as compared to 19.5% of bonds. Hence, the financial year 2003-04 has claimed highest amount of funds raised through mega as well as large issues in the Indian capital market.

The data relating to mega issues through book-building process is presented in Table-3.11. It is prominent to note that the mega issues have flooded the capital market to capitalize the positive sentiment of the investors due bullish trend in the capital market followed by heavy inflow of funds from FIIs.

The Kotak Mahindra Capital Services Company followed by DSP Merrill Lynch Ltd., has become prominent Book Running Lead Managers (BRLM) of mega issues, since, the former has handled 18 and the later has managed 14 mega issues successfully. JM Morgan Stanley Private Ltd., Enam Financial Consultants Pvt. Ltd., has successfully managed 11 mega issues each and became third highest Book Running Lead Managers. All other merchant bankers have handled few of the mega issues ranging from 1 to 9 each. Therefore it can be said that Kotak Mahindra Capital Services has became most favorable BRLM in India.

As per the data of the table, it is evident that Bharat Shipyard Ltd., was over subscribed by 72 times, Indoco Remedies ltd., by 68 times, Power Trading Corporation of India, Dishman Pharmaceuticals & Chemicals Ltd., by 38 times each, NDTV 37 times, Biocon Ltd., 32 times. All other mega issues have also recorded their over subscription ranging from 6 to 30 times. It is evident that some of the mega issues were over subscribed by many times within couple of minutes from opening of the issue due to enormous support from corporate enterprises, financial institutions and high net worth investors.

Table 3.11: Performance of Book Building Issues

Sl.	Name of the Book Building Issue	Issue Price (Rs.)	Market Price as on 14-04-05	% of Increase/ Decrease
1.	Tata Consultancy Services Ltd.	850.00	1,390.00	63.50
2.	Jet Airways (India) Ltd.	1,100.00	1,270.00	15.40
3.	Divi's Laboratories Ltd.	1,100.00	1,270.00	15.40
4.	ONGC Ltd.	140.00	1,028.00	634.30
5.	Dishman Pharmanceuticals & Chemicals Ltd.	175.00	628.00	258.80
6.	CMC Ltd.	485.00	622.00	28.20
7.	I-Flex Solutions Ltd.	530.00	595.00	12.30
8.	IBP company Ltd.	620.00	537.00	-13.40
9.	Dredging Corporation of India Ltd.	400.00	495.00	23.70
10.	IVRCL Infrastructure & Projects Ltd.	415.00	428.00	3.10
11.	Biocon Ltd.	315.00	425.00	34.90
12.	Maruthi Udyog Ltd.	125.00	410.00	228.00
13.	ICICI Bank Ltd.	280.00	410.00	46.40
14.	Panjab National Bank	390.00	394.00	1.00
15.	Patni Computer Systems Ltd.	230.00	353.00	53.50
16.	Indoco Remedies Ltd	245.00	292.00	19.20
17.	GAIL Ltd.	195.00	215.00	10.30
18.	Bharathi Televentures Ltd.	45.00	210.00	367.00
19.	New Delhi Tele vision Ltd.	70.00	186.00	165.70
20.	India Petro Chemical Corporation Ltd.	170.00	167.00	-1.70
21.	Deccan Chrnoicle Holdings Ltd.	162.00	159.00	-1.80
22.	Bharathi Shipyard Ltd.	66.00	145.00	119.00
23.	UTV Software Communications Ltd.	130.00	141.00	8.50
24.	D-Link(India) Ltd.	300.00	141.00	8.50
25.	Gateway Distriparks Ltd.	72.00	119.00	65.30
26.	Aztec Software & Tech. Services	80.00	116.00	45.00
27.	India Bulls Fin. Services Ltd.	19.00	116.00	510.50
28.	Indraprashantha Gas Ltd.	48.00	101.00	110.40
29.	Data Matics Tech. Ltd.	110.00	101.00	-8.10
30.	NTPC Ltd.	62.00	84.00	35.50
31.	TV Today Network Ltd.	95.00	79.00	-16.80
32.	Midday Multimedia Ltd.	70.00	77.00	10.00
33.	Emami Ltd.	70.00	77.00	10.00

34. SAIL	14.00	64.00	357.10
35. Mochip Semiconductor	10.00	43.00	330.00
36. Petronet LNG Ltd.	15.00	42.00	180.00
37. Creative Eye Ltd.	50.00	10.00	-80.00
38. Verdhman Acrylics Ltd.	10.00	6.00	-40.00

The position of book-building issue companies is presented in Table-3.11. An analysis of current market price of the mega issues after their listing and price at which the shares were allotted shows interesting and thought provoking information. Current market price is significantly higher than that of the cut-off price. Some of the companies' share prices have shown mind boggling arise in the capital market. For instance Divi's Laboratories shows 634.5%, India Bulls Financial Services Ltd., 510.50%, Bharti Televentures Ltd., 367.00%, Moschip Semiconductor 330.0%, and some of the other companies are also shown the positive results. However, some of the mega issues were quoted below their issue price and investors put to heavy losses prominent among them are Creative Eye Ltd., -80.0%, Vardhman Acrylics Ltd., -40.0%, D-Link (India) Ltd., -58.0%, and Today Network Ltd., -16.80% etc.

Table 3.12: Listign Day Performance of IPOs During First Quarter of 2005

Sl. No.	*Company Listing*	*Price (Rs.) Close*	*Differences %)*
1. Dena Bank	33.50	32.50	-2.99
2. Jet Airways	1,155.00	1,305.00	12.99
3. UTV	150.00	168.50	12.33
4. Emami	75.00	76.15	1.53
5. PNB	401.00	387.90	-3.27
6. Gateway Distriparks	88.90	112.50	26.04
7. IVRCL Infrastructure	434.60	412.25	-5.14
8. Jaiprakash Hydro Power	32.00	31.15	-2.66
9. 3i Infotech	118.00	97.80	-17.12
10. Gokaldas Exports	500.00	630.45	26.09

Source: Prime Database.

Listing day Price Trends of book-building companies during first quarter of the year 2005 was presented in Table-3.12. The following observations were made from the above data of the table:

* Gokaldas Exports got listed on the bourses on 27th April 2005 on a premium over its listing price and ended the day on a positive note. However, if one takes the 10 public issues that got listed in the calendar year 2005, 50% (or five) of them ended the first day below the listing price.
* The worst performer of the year was 3i InfoTech that got listed on April 22nd 2005. The listing price of the stock was Rs. 118 and the stock ended its first day at Rs. 97.80, thereby declined more than 17% of its listing price.
* The second spot was occupied by IVRCL Infrastructure & Projects Ltd. that made its debut on the bourses on April 11th 2005. The offer price of the stock was at Rs. 395. The stock that listed at Rs. 434.60 ended at Rs. 412.25. The stock lost more than 5% on the first day itself.
* The Infrastructure major was closely followed by Punjab National Bank (PNB) that got listed at Rs. 401 on March 29th 2005. The banking major also ended the first day on a dismal note, declining 3.27% to end the day at Rs. 387.90. The stock got listed only marginally higher than its offer price that was fixed at Rs. 390.
* Dena Bank, another banking stock whose offer opened in January, 2005 was listed on the bourses on February 23rd 2005. The stock got listed at Rs. 33.50 and ended at Rs. 32.50, thereby shedding nearly 3% on the every first day. The stock got listed at a premium over its offer price of Rs. 27 but couldn't sustain the premium level on the bourses.
* Jaiprakash Hydro Power Ltd., Which was listed on April 18th 2005, also failed to bring smiles on the faces of its investors on first day. The listing price of the stock was

at Rs. 32 and the stock ended the first day marginally lower at Rs. 31.55. The stock, whose offer price was also Rs. 32, ended the first day shedding 2.66%.

* There were five issues that made a sparkling debut on the bourses and leading the pack was the latest entrant-Gokaldas Exports Ltd. The stock gained nearly 26.09% on the very first day of listing. Gateway Distriparks Ltd. closely follows with a gain of 26.04% on the first day closing at Rs. 112.05. The listing price of Gateway that made its debut on March 31St 2005 was at Rs. 88.90.
* Other impressive debutants of the year were the high-profile Jet Airways Ltd., and UTV Software Communications Ltd. Both the stocks gained over 12% on the very first day, when compared with their listing price.
* Emami Ltd. that got listed on March 24th 2005, ended the day at Rs. 76.15 compared with its listing price of Rs. 75, thereby gaining a marginal 1.53% on the first day.

3.22: LIMITATIONS OF BOOK-BUILDING SYSTEM

The book-building system has its various limitations. Some of them are as follows:

* Book-building is appropriate for mega issues only. In the case of the potential investors, the companies can adjust the attributes of the offer according to the preferences of the potential investors. It may not be possible in big issues since the risk-return preference of the investors cannot be estimated easily;
* The issuer company should be fundamentally strong and well known to the investors;
* The book-building system works very efficiently in matured market conditions. In such circumstances, the investors are aware of the various parameters affecting the market price of the securities. But, such conditions are not commonly found in practice;

* There is a possibility of price rigging on listing as promoters may try to bail out syndicate members.

3.23: GREEN SHOE OPTION (GSO):

A Company making an initial public offer of equity shares through the book-building mechanism can avail of the GSO for stabilizing the post-listing price of its shares. The GSO means "an option of allocating shares in excess of the shares included in the public issue and operating a post-listing price stabilizing mechanism through a stabilizing agent (SA)." GSO in the system of IPO using book building method was recognized by SEBI in India through its new guidelines on 14th August 2003 (Vide SEBI/CFD/DIL/DIP/Circular No.11). According to SEBI guidelines, "a company desirous of availing the GSO shall in the resolution of the general meeting authorizing the public issue, seek authorization also for the possibility of allotment of further shares to the management team, as the SA", who will be responsible for the price stabilization process, if required. It owes its origin to the Green Shoe Company which used this option for the first time throughout the world. Recently, ICICI Bank has, perhaps, used GSO in the first time in case of its public issue through book building mechanism in India.

REFERENCES

1. Alexander, G, J, Eun, C S, and Janakiramanan, S: 'International Listings and Stock Returns: Some Empirical Evidence', Journal of Financial and Quantitative Analysis, 23 (2) 839-55.
2. Gupta S.K. and Others: "Financial Institutions and Markets", Kalyani Publishers, New Delhi, 2004, p.21.19.
3. Ravi M. Kishore: "Financial Management", Taxmann's Publications, New Delhi, 2003, p. 24.15.
4. Patil R H: "Capital Market Developments", The Journal of the Indian Institute Bankers, 65 (3), July-September, 1994.
5. Mega Issue is an Initial Public Offer with a capital offered to public exceeds more than Rs. 100 crore.

Table 3.13: Book-Building Issues in India During 1999-2005 at NSE and BSE

Sr. No.	*Name of the Book-Building Issue*	*Book Running Lead Manager*	*Date of Issue*	*No. of Times Over Sub.*	*No. of Members*	*No. of Bidding Centers*	*Issue Size No. of Shares (Lakh)*	*Issue Size Amount (Rs. Lakh)*	*Floor Price (Rs.)*	*Issue Price (Rs.)*
1.	Hughes Software Systems Ltd.	Kotak Mahindra Capital Company	22.09.1999 to 28.09.1999	-	-	8	39.37	-	-	-
2.	HCL Technologies Ltd.	Kotak Mahindra Capital Company	16.11.1999 to 24.11.1999	-	173	12	127.80	-	-	-
3.	Shree Rama Multi Tech Ltd.	DSP Merrill Lynch	15.01.2000 to 21.01.2000	-	9	10	99.37	-	-	-
4.	Zydus Cadila Healthcare Ltd.	JM Morgan Stanley Ltd	09.02.2000 to 16.02.2000	-	17	11	133.97	-	-	-
5.	Mascot Systems Ltd.	Kotak Mahindra Capital Company	10.04.2000 to 18.04.2000	-	1	3	22.50	-	-	-
6.	Creative Eye Ltd.	HSBC Securities and Capital Market (India)	30.06.2000 to 06.07.2000	-	2	1	18.76	-	-	-
7.	SIP Technologies and Exports Ltd.	Jardine Fleming	12.07.2000 to 18.07.200	-	13	8	11.26	-	-	-
8.	Hughes Tele. Com India Ltd.	Kotak Mahindra Capital Company	29.08.2000 to 05.09.2000	-	44	16	674.10	-	-	-
9.	MRD TEK Ltd.	DSP Merrill Lynch	04.09.2000 to 09.09.2000	-	10	10	45.98	-	-	-

10.	Pritish Nandy Communications Ltd.	JM Morgan Stanley Ltd.	04.09.2000 to 11.09.2000	-	8	9	23.55	-	-	-
11.	Balaji Telefilms Ltd.	JM Morgan Stanley Ltd.	06.10.2000 to 12.10.2000	-	12	12	25.20	-	-	-
12.	AZTEC Software & Technology Services	JM Morgan Stanley Ltd.	12.10.2000 to 18.10.2000	-	15	13	46.80	3,744.00	80	80
13.	Creative Eye Ltd.	HSBC Securities and Capital Market (India)	03.11.2000 to 09.11.2000	-	4	8	45.04	2,252.00	50	50
14.	Mos Chip Semiconductor	Karvy Investor Services India Ltd.	14.12.2000 to 19.12.2000	-	7	11	20.09	20.90	10	10
15.	Mid-Day Multimedia Ltd.	IL&FS Merchant Banking Services Ltd.	12.02.2001 to 16.02.2001	-	3	13	45.00	3,150.00	70	70
16.	D-Link (India) Ltd	Tata Finance Merchant Bankers Ltd.	20.022001 to 27.02.2001	-	9	16	13.71	4,113.00	300	300
17.	Bharati Tele Ventures Ltd.	JM Morgan Stanley Private DSP Merrill Lynch Ltd.	20.02.2001 to 02.02.2002	-	28	59	1,853.37	83,401.52	45	45
18.	I-Flex Solutions Ltd.	JM Morgan Stanley Private Merrill Lynch Ltd. Kotak Mahindra Capital Co. Ltd. Solomon Smith Barney India Pvt. Ltd.	05.06.2002 to 11.06.2002	-	97	30	39.62	20,997.01	530	530
19.	Divi's Labories Ltd.	M/s. Investsmart India Ltd., M/s Kotak Mahindra Capital Company Ltd.	17.02.2003 to 21.02.2003	-	34	27	32.05	4,486.56	130	140

(Contd.)

Table 3.13: Book-Building Issues in India During 1999-2005 at NSE and BSE *(Contd.)*

20.	Maruti Udyog Ltd.	Kotak Mahindra Capital Company	12.06.2003 to 19.06.2003	-	106	64	794.68	99,334.50	115	125
21.	Vardhman Acrylics Ltd.	HSBC Securities and Capital Market (India) Ltd.	15.09.2003 to 19.09.2003	-	4	52	27.13	271.30	10	10
22.	Indraprastha Gas Ltd.	Jardine Fleming	28.11.2003 to 05.12.2003	-	5	20	400.00	19,200.00	40 to 48	48
23.	T.V. Today Network Ltd.	Kotak Mahindra Capital Company	18.12.2003 to 27.12.2003	-	110	74	145.00	13,775.00	80 to 95	95
24.	Patni Computer Systems Ltd.	DSP Merrill Lynch	27.01.2004 to 05.02.2004	22	93	200	187.24	43,065.20	200 to 230	230
25.	CMC Ltd.	HSBC Securities and Capital Market (India) Ltd. Enam Securities	23.2.04 to 28.02.2004	10	71	36	39.76	19,285.41	485	485 &460.75 for RI
26.	India petrochemicals Corporation Ltd.	SBI Capital Markets Ltd., Mahindra Capital Company Ltd.	20.02.2004 to 27.02.2004	5	113	36	718.50	122,145.10	170	170&161.5 for RI
27.	IBP Company Ltd	ICICI Securities Ltd., Kotak Mahindra Capital Company	23.02.2004 to 01.03.2004	3	88	45	57.58	35,701.40	620	620&589 for RI
28.	Dredging Corporation of India Ltd.	Enam Financial Consultants Pvt. Ltd., Kotak Mahindra Capital Company Ltd.	26.02.2004 to 04.03.2004	18	95	37	56.00	22.400.00	385 to 400	400&380 for RI

29.	Gas Authority of India Ltd.	HSBC Securities & Capital Markets (India) Ltd., ICICI Securities Ltd.	27.02.2004 to 05.03.2004	7	58	36	845.65	164,902.06	195	195&185.25 for RI
30.	Power Trading Corporation of India Ltd.	SBI Capital Markets Ltd., Enam Financial Consultants Pvt. Ltd.	01.03.2004 to 08.03.2004	43	80	43	585.00	9,360.00	15 to 16	16
31.	Petronet LNG Ltd.	DSP Merrill Lynch Ltd., ICICI Securities Ltd., JM Morgans Stanley Pvt. Ltd.	01.03.2004 to 09.03.2004	3	92	56	2,609.80	29,145.99	13 to 15	15
32.	Oil& Natural Gas Corporation Ltd.	JM Morgan Stanley Private Ltd. DSP Merrill Lynch Ltd.	05.03.2004 to 13.03.2004	2	128	.62	1,425.939	69,632.40	680 to 750	750 & 712.5 for RI
33.	Biocon Ltd.	DSP Merrill Lynch Ltd. Kotak Mahindra Capital Co. Ltd.	11.03.2004 to 18.03.0224	32	105	20	100.00	31,500.00	270 to 315	315
34.	ICICI Bank Ltd.	DSP Merill Lynch Ltd., JM Mahindra Capital Company Ltd.	02.04.2004 to 7.4.04	5	153	64	1,196.083	34,902.40	255 to 295	280
35.	Dishman Pharmaceuticals & Chemicals Ltd.	Enam Financial Consultants Ltd., IL&FS Investsmart Ltd.	29.03.2004 to 07.04.2004	38	110	54	34.34	5,322.70	155 to 175	175
36.	Datamatics Technologies Ltd.	Enam Financial Consultants Pvt. Ltd.	12.04.2004 to 19.04.2004	27	74	68	103.00	11,330.00	101 to 110	110
37.	New Delhi Television Ltd.	JM Mrgan Stanley Ltd., Kotak ICICI Securities Ltd.	21.04.2004 to 28.04.2004	37	110	40	173.02	12,111.40	63 to 70	70
38.	Tata Consultancy Services Ltd.	JM Morgan Stanley Pvt. Ltd. DSP Merrill Lynch Ltd., JP Morgan India Pvt. Ltd.	29.07.04 to 05.08.2004	8	178	109	554.53	471,350.50	775 to 900	850

(Contd.)

Table 3.13: Book-Building Issues in India During 1999-2005 at NSE and BSE *(Contd.)*

39.	India Bulls Financial Services Ltd.	SBI Capital Markets Ltd., DSP Merill Lynch Ltd.	06.09.2004 to 10.09.2004	18	106	54	271.88	5,165.72	16 to 19	19
40.	National thermal Power Corporation Ltd.	ICICI Securities Ltd., Enam Financial Consultants Pvt. Ltd., Kotak Mahindra Capital	07.10.2004 to 14.10.2004	13	170	54	8,658.30	536,814.60	52 to 62	62
41.	S.A.L. Steel Ltd.	SBI Capital Markets Ltd., IL & FS Investsmart Ltd.	01.11.2004 to 05.11.2004	19	89	43	420.00	5,880.00	12 to 14	14
42.	Deccan Chronicle Ltd.	ICICI SEcurities Ltd.	25.11.2004 to 02.12.2004	9	97	35	80.13	12,981.06	162 to 194	162
43.	Bharati Shipyard Ltd.	SBI CAPTAL Market Ltd., Enam Financial Consultants Pvt. Ltd.	01.12.2004 to 08.12.2004	72	123	62	125.00	8,250.00	55 to66	66
44.	Indoco Remedies Ltd.	Enam Financial Consultants	17.12.2004 to 23.12.2004	61	136	35	40.00	7,350.00	220 to 245	245
45.	Jet Airways (India) Ltd.	Deutsche Equities India Pvt. Ltd. HSBC Securities and Capital Markets (India) Pvt., UBS Securities India Pvt. Ltd., Citigroup Global Markets India Pvt. DSP Merrill Lynch Ltd., Kotak Mahindra Capitla Company Ltd.	18.02.05 to 24.02.2005		149	62	172.67	189,937.00	950 to 1125	1100
46.	UTV Software Communications Ltd.	Enam Financial Consultants Pvt. Ltd.	21.02.2005 to 24/02/2005	-	155	67	69.99	9,098.70	115 to 130	130

47.	Enami Ltd.	Anand Rathi Securities Pvt. Ltd. ICICI Securities Ltd.	4.3.05 to 10.03.2005	-	89	37	50.00	3,000.00	60 to 70	-
48.	Punjab National Bank	ICICI Securities Ltd., DSP Merrill Lynch Ltd., Enam Financial Consultants Pvt. Ltd., JM Morgan Stanley Pvt. Ltd., Kotak Mahindra Capital Company Ltd.	07.03.2005 to 11.03.2005	-	161	79	800.00	312,000.00	350 to 390	390
49.	Gateway Distriparks Ltd.	IL&FS Investmart Ltd., Kotak Mahindra Capital Company Ltd.	9.3.05 to 14.03.05	-	135	38	210.00	15,120.00	60 to 72	72
50.	IVRCL Infrastructure & Projects Ltd.	Enam Financial Consultants Pvt. Ltd.	18.03.05 to	-	117	41	to be	-	385 to 415	-
Total Amount Raised through Book-Building Issues								397,287.99		

* = Not Known.RI = Retail Investors.

Source: www.nseindia.com

CHAPTER-IV

SECONDARY MARKETS

4.1: INTRODUCTION

The Government of India introduced economic reforms in the field of trade, industry and commerce so as to bring about the integration of the Indian economy with the global economy. Capital market in India has experienced remarkable developments in the past few years. The growth of the economy has capitalized the changes in the capital market along with the regulation of secondary market in India. In this process the size of investors has increased rapidly and the role played by the stock exchanges were also increased. The secondary market developments, regional stock exchanges -threats and opportunities and investors protection in the Indian capital market were presented in Section-I, Section-II and Section-III of this chapter respectively.

4.2: OBJECTIVES

The chapter "Secondary Markets" is aimed at examining the following objectives:

* To examine the new bench marks in the secondary market in India.
* To study the selected secondary market development indicators in India.
* To analyze the trading intensity in the world stock exchanges.
* To explore opportunities for the growth of RSEs in India.

* To learn the threats for the growth of RSEs in India.
* To suggest the ways to overcome the threats for the growth of RSEs in India.
* To examine the Present Disclosure Standards for the protection of investors in the India capital market.
* To analyze the Powers of SEBI to take Punitive or Preventive Measure for the protection of investors.
* To study the Role of SEBI for the Redressal of Investor Grievances in the Indian Capital Market.
* To explain the Investor Awareness / Assistance / Education Programmes Arranged by SEBI.
* To suggest the Recommendations for Strengthening Investor Confidence in the Indian Capital Market.

SECTION-I

DEVELOPMENTS IN THE SECONDARY MARKET

4.3: INTRODUCTION

Change has become a ubiquitous phenomenon. Indeed, the intensity and speed of change in the market place is rendering all veterans, conventional and orthodox organizations and people redundant at an amazing speed. Unambiguously, markets have become merciless without any respect for the long standing and accumulated expertise. Amidst such choppy waves, market participants are virtually left with two choices - either change or perish. Apparently, nothing but change is stable in the world, which interestingly offers both - opportunities and challenges. The changes have been taken place in the administration of stock exchange, securities trading, settlement, delivery versus payment, securities transfer, ownership mode, trading in derivatives, risk containment measures, screen based trading, investor protection fund and many more.

4.4: MEANING

Secondary market (stock exchange) is one in which an investor purchases an asset from another investor, rather than an issuing corporation. The defining characteristic of the secondary market is that investors' trade among themselves on previously issued securities without the involvement of the issuing companies (except in the case of buy-back). The investors could be institutions like FIIs, Mutual Funds, Insurance Companies or individuals. The trading system differs, albeit marginally, depending upon investor status.

4.5: DEFINITIONS

Some of the important definitions are presented below:

According to Hastings, "Stock Exchange or Securities Market comprises all the places where buyers and sellers of stocks and bonds or their representatives undertake transactions involving the sale of securities."

According to Husband and Dockery, "Securities or Stock Exchanges are privately organized markets which are used to facilitate trading in securities."

According to Derek Honeygold, "Stock Exchanges can be described as the place where a marriage of convenience is enacted between those who wish to raise capital, such as companies, governments and local authorities, and those who to invest - largely households through the medium of institutions acting upon their behalf."

According to Section 2(3) of the Securities Contract (Regulation) Act 1956, "The stock exchange has been defined as any body of individuals whether incorporated or not, constituted for the purpose of assisting, regulating or controlling the business of buying, selling or dealing in securities." Under the said Act, the following securities can be traded at the stock exchange: (a) Shares, scrips, stocks, bonds, debentures, debenture stocks or other marketable securities of a like nature in or of any incorporated company or other body corporate; (b) Government securities; and (c) Rights or interest in securities.

4.6: CHANGING REGULATIONS OF SECONDARY MARKET

The Indian securities market is in transition. Several important changes were brought for the smooth and effective functioning of stock exchanges from the time to time by the SEBI. The revolutionary changes have been taking place over a period of time. In fact, on almost all the operational and systematic risk management parameters, settlement system, disclosures, accounting standards, the Indian securities market is at par with the global standards. Indeed, on a few paradigms, it is ahead of the global benchmarks. Some of those initiatives taken place in the secondary market are discussed below:

4.6.1. Overall Administration, Supervision and Control of the Stock Exchanges

The Central government for the first time in April 1988 constituted an administrative body Viz. Securities and Exchange Board of India and in January 1992, the Central Government enacted an Act granting a statutory recognition to the Securities and Exchange Board of India as a regulator of the securities/ markets. The Governing Board of the Council to be consisting of total 10 members, 4 from stock exchanges, 4 from government, corporate finance, commerce, accountancy, management and law and 2 from investment and development finance institutions.

4.6.2. Membership of the Stock Exchange

Minimum basic educational qualification is 12th standard or equivalent and graduation after 5 years. Members to have reasonable background in economics, corporate finance, taxation, etc. The stock exchanges have to approve members (trainers) to impart adequate knowledge and training to aspirants for membership. Financial institutions, commercial banks and companies are also eligible for membership of stock exchanges. Membership is to be open to a qualified person at any time. Multiple memberships are allowed to members to encourage provision of better services to the investing public and to further the healthy development of capital market.

4.6.3. Listing of Securities

Listing of securities means permission to trade by quoting shares and debentures officially on the trading floor of the stock exchange. Every security issued by companies cannot be traded at a stock exchange. The stock exchanges fix certain standards which the company must fulfill before getting the securities listed. Recently changed listing agreements are: (i) On 29th October,

2004 SEBI directed all the stock exchanges to amend the existing Clause 49 of the listing agreement in areas pertaining to composition of board of directors, audit committee, subsidiary companies, disclosures, CEO/CFO certification, report on corporate governance and compliance. It also clarified that the provisions would be implemented for entities seeking listing for the first time, at the time of seeking in- principle approval for such listing and for existing listed entities having a paid- up share capital of Rs. 3 crore and above or net worth of Rs. 25 crore or more at any time in the history of the company, by April 1st, 2005. (ii) On 2nd November, 2004 new model listing agreement for debt securities was finalized. (iii) On 8th December, 2004 Clause 16 of the Listing Agreement was instructed that the company on whose stocks, derivatives are available or whose stocks form part of an index on which derivatives are available, should give a notice period of 30 days to stock exchanges for corporate actions like mergers, de-mergers, splits and bonus shares. (iv) On 29th March, 2005 SEBI extended deadline for ensuring conformity by companies with the revised Clause 49 of the listing agreement up to December 31st, 2005.

4.6.4. Public Issues

The companies eligible to make a public issue can freely price their equity shares or any security convertible into equity at a later date in cases of public/rights issues by listed companies and public issue by unlisted companies. In addition, eligible infrastructure companies can freely price their equity shares subject to compliance of disclosure norms of SEBI. The public and private sector banks can also freely price their shares subject to approval by RBI. A company may issue shares to applicants in the firm allotment category at higher price than the price at which securities are offered to public. Further an eligible company is free to make public/rights issue in any denomination determined by it in accordance with sub-section (4) of section 13 of the Companies Act, 1956 and SEBI norms.

4.6.5. Trading related Issues

All stock exchanges in India follow screen-based trading system, NSE being the first stock exchange in the country to provide nation-wide order-driven, screen-based trading system.

Exchanges have fully automated screen based trading system where a member can punch into the computer quantities of securities and the prices at which he likes to transact and the transaction is executed as soon as it finds a matching order from the counter party. The electronically matching orders operate on a strict price/time priority and hence cuts down on time, cost and risk of error, as well as on fraud resulting in improved operational efficiency. It allows faster incorporation of price sensitive information into prevailing prices, thus increasing informational efficiency of the market. It enables the market participants to see the full market on real time, making the market transparent. It allows a large number of participants, irrespective of their geographical locations, to trade with one another simultaneously, improving the depth and liquidity of the market. It ensures full anonymity by accepting orders, big or small, from members without revealing their identity, thus providing equal access to everybody. It provides perfect audit trail which helps to resolve disputes by logging in the trade execution process in entirety. The trading system provides tremendous flexibility to the users in terms of kinds of orders that can be placed on the system.

SEBI also allowed use of internet as an order routing system for communication clients' orders to the exchanges through brokers. SEBI- registered brokers can introduce internet-based trading after obtaining permission from respective stock exchanges. SEBI has stipulated the minimum conditions to be fulfilled by trading members to start internet based trading and services. NSE was the first exchange in the country to provide web-based access to investors to trade directly on the exchange. It launched internet trading in February 2000. It was followed by the launch of internet trading by BSE in March 2001. The orders originates from the PCs of investors are routed through the internet to the trading terminals of the designed brokers with whom they have relations and further to the exchange for trade execution. Soon after these orders get matched and result into trades, the investors get confirmation about them on their PCs through the same internet route.

4.6.6. Price Bands or Circuit Breaks

Stock market volatility is generally a cause of concern for

both policy makers as well as investors. To curb excessive volatility, SEBI has prescribed a system of price bands. The price bands or circuit breaks bring about a coordinated trading halt in all equity and equity derivatives markets nation-wide. An index-based market-wide circuit breaker system at three stages of the index movement either way at 10%, 15% and 20% has been prescribed. The breakers are triggered by movement of either S&P CNX Nifty or Sensex, whichever is breached earlier. As an additional measure of safety, individual scrip-wise price bands have also been fixed. No price bands are applicable on scrips on which derivative products are available or on scrips included in indices on which derivatives products are available. For auction market the price bands of 20% are applicable. In order to prevent members from entering orders at non-genuine prices in such securities, the Exchanges have fixed operating range of 20% for such securities.

4.6.7. Trading and Settlement Cycle

The trades accumulate over a trading cycle of one day and at the end of the day, these are clubbed together, and positions are netted and payment of cash and delivery of securities settle the balance after 2 working days. All trades executed on a day 'T' are settled on T+2 day. The clearing corporation of the exchange notifies the consummated trade details to the clearing members/ custodians on the trade day. The custodians affirm back the trades to the clearing corporation by T+1 day. Based on the affirmation, the clearing corporation nets the positions of counterparties to determine their obligations. A clearing member has to pay-in / pay-out funds and/or securities. A member has security-wise net obligations to receive/deliver a security. The obligations are netted for a member across all securities to determine his fund obligations and he has to either pay or receive funds. Members' pay-in/pay-out obligations are determined latest by T+1 day and are forwarded to them on the same day so that the obligations can be settled on T+2 day. The securities/funds are paid-in/paid-out on T+2 day and the settlement is complete in 2 days from the end of the trading day.

4.6.8. Risk Management

To pre-empt market failures and protect investors, the

regulator/exchanges have developed a comprehensive risk management system, which is constantly monitored and upgraded. It encompasses capital adequacy of members, adequate margin requirements, limits on exposure and trading, indemnity insurance, on-line position monitoring and automatic disablement, etc. they also administer an efficient market surveillance system to curb excessive volatility, detect and prevent price manipulations. Exchanges have set up trade/settlement guarantee funds for meeting shortages arising out of non-fulfillment/partial fulfillment of funds obligations by the members in a settlement. A clearing corporation assures the counterparty risk of each member and guarantees financial settlement in respect of trades executed on NSE.

4.6.9. Investor Protection Fund

All the stock exchanges are required to set up a fund called "Investor Protection Fund". The purpose of the fund is to provide compensation, arising out of defaults of the member brokers of the exchange, to investors. The contribution to investor protection fund is from members as a fraction of transaction charges, part of listing fees, and interest on security deposits to be made by companies at the time of public issues etc. The amount of compensation available against a single claim of an investor arising out of default by a member broker of a stock exchange is Rs. 1,00,000 in case major stock exchanges , Rs. 50,000 in case of medium-size stock exchanges and Rs. 25,000 in case of smaller stock exchanges. However, BSE provides compensation up to Rs 10,00,000 from this fund.

For ensuring smooth completion of settlements the stock exchanges have set up Trade Guarantee Fund/Settlement Guarantee Fund. Twelve stock exchanges established Trade/ Settlement Guarantee Fund. NSE is having a clearing corporation for settlement purpose. The existing trades guarantee funds set up by stock exchanges provide counter party guarantee for all the transactions which take place on stock exchanges and met the payment obligations of the brokers immediately without waiting to declare them as defaulters. This means that the settlement (pay-in and payout) is effected immediately and investors get their money without delay.

4.6.10. Systems Audit

Trading, settlement and risk management systems of stock exchanges are almost completely automated. For this reason, it becomes very important that the systems do not have deficiencies which can impair their efficacy. It also becomes important to ensure that the stock exchanges have suitable Disaster Recovery Sites and Business Continuity Plans and that the systems are adequately secure. Active stock exchanges have been asked to carry out systems audit through external agencies competent to carry out systems audit exercise. SEBI does follow-up for rectification of deficiencies pointed out in the systems audit reports. In 2004-05 too, such follow-up was done through off-site analysis of compliance reports from stock exchanges and meetings with the senior management of stock exchanges.

4.6.11. Dematerialization of Securities

A depository holds securities in dematerialized form. It maintains ownership records of securities in a book entry form and also effects transfer of ownership through book entry. SEBI has introduced some degree of compulsion in trading and settlement of securities in dematerialized form. While the investors have a right to hold securities in either physical or demat form, SEBI has mandated compulsory trading and settlement of securities in select securities in dematerialized form. Two depositories in India, Viz., NSDL and CDSL, maintain ownership records of dematerialized securities in a book entry form and transfer ownership of securities electronically without making the securities move from person to person. 4,761 and 4,628 companies were connected to NSDL and CDSL respectively at the end of March 2003, when 76.9 billion securities with a value of Rs. 5,875 billion were held in demat form with the depositories. Demat settlement accounts for nearly 100% of turnover settled by delivery. This has almost eliminated the bad deliveries and associated problems.

4.6.12. Implementation of STP

The Straight Through Processing (STP) was launched in India on November 30, 2002. SEBI mandated the use of the STP system for all institutional trades with effect from July 1st, 2004. SEBI had prescribed a detailed system flow and the regulatory framework of the STP system by issuing the SEBI (STO Centralized Hub and STP Service Providers) Guidelines, 2004. SEBI also outlined the transaction work flow for the system of STP and prescribed the messaging formats based on internationally accepted ISO 15022 messaging standards. There are currently four STP service providers and STP centralized hub has been set up by NSE. There has been a steady increase in number of messages passing through STP network with approximately 2,500 STP users registered in the system.

4.6.13. Institutionalization

Capital markets are said to be more efficient when they have more participants, instruments, processes and other alternatives. Indian capital market was dominated by individual investors till early part of the 1990's. Earlier institutional investors such as Life Insurance Corporation of India, General Insurance Corporation of India and its four subsidiaries, Development Financial Institutions, Banks, etc., used to take minor role in the capital market activity. Unit Trust of India, the only mutual fund then, used to play active role in the primary market and secondary capital market. 1990s saw entry of many new participants to the capital market. SEBI permitted private sector and joint sector (Indian as well as Foreign), mutual funds. Government of India and SEBI allowed Foreign Institutional Investors, Non-resident Indians and Overseas Corporate Bodies to trade in securities. Additionally, non-banking finance companies also have been taking interest in dealing in securities. Thus, the variety of participants taking interest in the Indian capital market substantially increased and the current variety is as large as is available in any other developed market. Of the above mentioned only three classes of investors are very active: individuals, mutual funds and FIIs. Large variety of investors is very important for broadening and deepening of the market. Variety infuses counter balance impact in the market i.e. when one class sells another class buys so that the market is in balance.

4.6.14. Development of Financial Infrastructure

Development of financial infrastructure could involve many aspects. It involves development of informed sophisticated investor class, adequate legal and regulatory environment, institutions/

institutional investors such as mutual funds, venture capital funds, insurance companies, pension funds, FIIs etc., world class securities trading and payment and settlement systems, adequately capitalized and professionally run capital market intermediaries. It also includes promoting investor associations, self-regulatory organizations. Setting up of depositories, surveillance system, and another step towards this SEBI has introduced new financial instruments (derivatives). SEBI is also a member of IOSCO. Information regarding technology, surveillance, trading system, risk management etc. is shared among members of IOSCO. SEBI has benefited immensely from the knowledge and inputs thus received.

Derivatives markets can and do play a vital role in promoting market efficiency through better price discovery, risk transfer and transaction integrity. Innovations in new instruments in developed markets cannot be isolated from emerging market. In fact, the growth of derivative markets in the industrial world has spurred derivatives market developments in emerging market. All the developed economies and capital markets have financial derivatives trading on their exchanges that provides risk management tool to hedge the risk in the underlying market.

Only two exchanges, namely the NSE and BSE, offer platform for trading of derivatives of securities (interest rate derivatives such as FRAs / IRSs are traded on OTC). The derivatives trading system at NSE provides a fully automated screen-based trading for Nifty futures and options and stock futures and options and the recently launched interest rate derivatives on notional government security with a 10 year maturity and a notional treasury bill with maturity of 91 days or three months, on a nationwide basis as well as a online monitoring and surveillance mechanism. It supports an anonymous order driven market, which operates on a strict price/time priority. It provides tremendous flexibility to users in terms of kinds of orders that can be placed on the system.

4.6.15. Global Linkages

The pace of transformation and change in the securities markets has been rather rapid. With global linkages being established in the domestic securities markets at a fairly good pace, it becomes important that skills and expertise are updated on a continuous basis on the entire range of activities that cover product design and distribution, process and practices, and other related aspects. Training and certification assume significance in this background.

The BSE lays emphasis on this aspect and has invested sizable sums in creating the infrastructure for capital market training and certificate which are carried out by the BSE Training Institute. Despite the regional stock exchanges not having been able to generate business in the background of recent reforms, there exists a possibility for using their infrastructure to promote new business segments or to cater to the emerging requirements of investors. In addition to the emerging requirements of investors in addition to the options of consolidation of exchanges, their infrastructure can be put to use better for investor services and support and also for carrying out investor related programmes and projects.

4.6.16. Integrated Market Surveillance System

Effective surveillance is the sine qua non for a well functioning capital market. As an integral part in the regulatory process, effective surveillance can achieve investor protection, market integrity and capital market development. According to IOSCO, "the goal of surveillance is to spot adverse situations in the markets and to pursue appropriate preventive actions to avoid disruption to the markets."

In India, the stock exchanges hitherto have been entrusted with the primary responsibility of understanding market surveillance. Given the size, complexities and level of technical sophistication of the markets, the tasks of information gathering, collection and analysis of data / information are divided among the exchanges, depositories and SEBI. Information relating to price and volume movements in the market, broker positions, risk management, settlement process and compliance pertaining to listing agreement are monitored by the exchanges on a real time basis as part of their self regulatory function. However, regulatory oversight, exercised by SEBI, extends over the stock exchanges through reporting and inspections. In exceptional circumstances, SEBI initiates special investigations on the basis of reports received from the stock exchanges or specific complaints received from stakeholders as regards market manipulation and insider trading.

SEBI is now on the verge of providing final touches to Integrated Market Surveillance System (IMSS) that would help identify unusual market behavior on a real-time basis. The system envisages integration of data available from stock exchanges (cash and derivative segments), clearing corporations and depositories into a single integrated market surveillance system. The IMSS is expected to generate alerts that will help SEBI identify and detect serious market violations such as market manipulations, insider trading and other types of frauds that undermine market integrity. The proposed IMSS solution is expected to be operational by March 2006. The system would be implemented across exchanges and segments and would integrate the surveillance systems of BSE, NSE, CDSL, NSDL and other stock exchanges with that of market regulator in phases. The new surveillance system would focus on real time reports from exchanges pertaining to abnormalities and suspicious transactions in terms of price, volume, big brokers, scrips and intermediaries who constitute about 80-85 percent of the trading volumes.

4.6.17. Corporate Governance

SEBI constituted a Committee on Corporate Governance headed by Shri N.R. Narayana Murthy, which submitted its report on February 8th, 2003 for the maximization of shareholder value and increase investor confidence. Taking a signal from the same, SEBI amended Clause 49 of the Listing Agreement to revise the requirements of corporate governance as mandated by the listing agreement. For entities seeking listing for the first time, the corporate governance requirements are to be complied at the time of seeking in-principle approval for such listing. However, for listed entities having a paid-up share capital of Rs. 3 crore and above or net worth of Rs. 25 crore or more at any time in the history of the company, corporate governance requirements were proposed to be complied by April 1st, 2005. Taking into account the fact that many companies are still not in a state of preparedness to be fully complaint with the requirements, the date for ensuring compliance with the corporate governance requirements of the listing agreement has been extended up to December 31st, 2005.

4.6.18. Corporatization and Demutualization (C and D) of Stock Exchanges

The stock exchanges world over have been generally formed as 'mutual' organizations. The trading members not only provide broking services, but also own, control and manage such exchanges for their mutual benefit. They don't generally distribute profit among themselves and therefore, termed as 'not-for-profit' organizations. Stock exchanges owned by members may work towards the interest of members alone which may be detrimental to the rights of other stakeholders. There could also be conflict of interest between ownership and management. In order to eliminate conflict of interest, there is a need to segregate the management functions from ownership and trading rights through demutualization. Moreover, stock exchanges should ideally work as body corporate similar to any other 'for-profit' corporate entity.

The announcement made by the Honorable Finance Minister in the Parliament on March 13th, 2001 that the stock exchanges would be corporatised and demutualised, SEBI constituted a Group on Corporatization and Demutualization of Stock Exchanges under the Chairmanship of Justice M.H. Kania, former Chief Justice of India, for advising SEBI on Corporatization and demutualization of exchanges and to recommend the steps that need to be taken to implement the same. Based on the recommendations of the Group, all the stock exchanges were advised to submit their proposals for C and D to SEBI for approval.

4.6.19. Transparency

Market transparency refers to the availability to market participants' information on the trading process. Information can include prices, volume, and source of order and identification of counterparty to the trade. If all trade-related data are publicly made available, brokers/investors need not fear that they are trading with someone having superior information. Markets that are highly transparent attract more buyers/sellers because of inherently higher safety level of the system. Informational symmetry is paramount to ensure quality in trading. Quality information reinforces an investor's confidence in the market place. As result, the markets remain liquid. Transparency allows an investor to compare the price at which his/her deal is executed with the reported market price. Thereby he/she is aware of any mark-up on the transaction.

4.6.20. BSE IndoNext Trading Platform

In the Union Budget 2004-05, the Central Government proposed to set up a trading platform to enable the small and medium enterprises (SMEs) to raise capital, both debt and equity, as well as provide liquidity to the securities. This trading platform is expected to provide the much needed avenue for financing SMEs and help redress the present imbalance in this regard. SEBI took the initiative to encourage the BSE and the Regional Stock Exchanges (RSEs) to set up this market. The government also amended Section 13 of the Securities Contract (Regulations) Act, 1956 to facilitate trading by brokers of RSEs on this market.

4.6.21. Securities Transaction Tax (STT)

In the Union Budget 2004-05, Government proposed a package of tax measures relating to securities transactions. The tax on long term capital gains from securities transactions was abolished while the short-term capital gains tax was reduced to a flat rate of 10 percent. Moreover, it was proposed to levy a tax on buyers at the rate of 0.15 percent of the value of securities transacted on the stock exchanges in the form of securities transaction tax. Pursuant to the representations received from the market participants, the STT was modified by the Government in consultation with SEBI. The revised STT includes (i) the delivery-based transactions would attract STT of 0.15 percent (i.e., 15 basis points) and the seller; (ii) for day traders and arbitrageurs, the STT of 0.015 percent (1.5 basis points) would be imposed on sellers of equities and settled on net basis; (iii) for units of equity oriented mutual funds, the STT of 0.15 percent (15 basis points) would be imposed on sellers; (iv) the rate of STT on sale of derivatives (Futures and Options) would be 0.01 percent (1 basis points) ; and (v) no STT would be levied on buying and selling of bonds, including government bonds, units of MFs other than equity oriented funds. The STT was notified on September 28th, 2004. The stock exchanges have been advised to levy and collect STT on all transactions done by their members and remit the same to the Government of India with effect from October 1st, 2004. In the Union Budget 2005-06, the STT was further revised as under (Table-4.1).

Table 4.1: Securities Transaction Tax in India

(Percent)

Type of Transactions	*2004-05 (Old Rate)*	*2005-06 (Revised Rate)**
A. Equity		
1. Delivery-based Transactions**	0.1500	0.2000
2. Non-delivery based Transactions	0.0150	0.0200
B. Derivative Transactions	0.0100	0.0200

* The revised STT became effective from June 1st, 2005.

** To be equally sahred by both buyers and sellers.

Source: CMIF Capital Market 2004-05, p. 13.

4.6.22. The MAPIN Database

SEBI is developing a database about market participants and investors, called the MAPIN database, to give a Unique Identification Number (UIN) to individuals and entities participating in the capital market. Once the database is built, SEBI will mandate that transactions of concerned participants (Primary Market, Secondary Market, etc.) are identified with the UIN. The MAPIN database utilizes fingerprints as an identifier, apart from traditional identifiers such as photographs, name and address. Fingerprints are photographs of fingers, and are a good tool in the effort of establishing uniqueness, and preventing the opening of benami accounts. Present day technology makes it possible to collect such data in an affordable and convenient manner. The use of fingerprints is not unique to MAPIN; fingerprints are currently used in the registration of sale of real estate also. This unique identity will be critical to the ability of SEBI to rapidly investigate market misbehavior. The stock exchanges (for secondary market trades) have digitized information. Such information can be analyzed very easily if each transaction is linked to the UIN.

4.6.23. Policy Initiatives for Market Intermediaries

The following are some of the important policy initiatives taken by SEBI for market intermediaries are presented below:

* In order to bring about uniformity in documentary requirements across different segments and exchanges and also to avoid duplication and multiplicity of documents, SEBI in consultation with stock exchanges (BSE and NSE) has formulated uniform set of broker client registration and agreement documents. The same have been made applicable from April 1st, 2005.
* In order to disseminate information regarding cancellation of registration of brokers and cautioning the investing public not to deal with 70 brokers whose registration has been cancelled by SEBI during 2003-04, a public notice was published in the news papers. In the interest of investors, it has been decided to publish such information at periodic intervals.
* In order to promote greater disclosure of information in the interest of investors and from the point of view of measuring the adequacy of systems and controls to meet internal as well as external compliance requirements, a draft concept paper on the professional rating of market intermediaries was placed on SEBI website for public comments.
* SEBI has requested credit rating agencies to develop an appropriate rating model for stock brokers, based on the parameters set out in the concept paper read with public comments. Considering the public response and market acceptance to the rating concept for stock brokers, the concept may be extended gradually to other intermediaries as well.
* A review of the existing net worth requirements for stock brokers was taken up and report of the sub-group on Secondary Market Advisory Committee (SMAC) formed for the purpose was uploaded on SEBI website for public

comments. The comments received on the paper are being analyzed.

* Guidelines were issued for allowing SEBI registered market intermediaries to float overseas subsidiaries so as to undertake financial services activities/capital market related activities abroad which have been approved by the SEBI Board.

4.6.24. Other Initiatives

Detailed guidelines have been issued specifying the disclosures to be made by listed companies which resort to changing of names frequently. The stock exchanges have been advised to include the value of the membership card as liquid assets for the purpose of net worth calculation of members. The Mutual Funds and FIIs have been advised to enter the Unique Client Code for the parent entity at the order entry individual schemes/sub-accounts in the post closing session.

4.7: SECONDARY MARKET - SELECTIVE INDICATORS

Secondary Market development like the economic development is a complex and multi-faceted concept and no single measure will capture all aspects of secondary market development. It has become necessary to examine a broad array of secondary market development indicators. Specifically, we analyze different measures of secondary market like, number of stock exchanges, number of brokers, number of listed companies, turnover, FII net investment, stock market indices and P/E ratio. The relevant data is presented in Table-4.2.

4.7.1. Number of Stock Exchanges

Stock exchanges are the pivot of the capital market. They serve as the channels through which primary issues are offered to the investing public and they provide the mechanism through which outstanding securities are traded, while there are only 7 stock exchanges in 1946, 9 in 1980 and 11 in 1990. As on March 31, 2005, 23 stock exchanges were operating, of them, National Stock Exchange of India Ltd. (NSE), the Stock Exchange, Mumbai (BSE), OTC Exchange of India Ltd. (OTCEI) and Inter-Connected Stock Exchange Ltd. (ISE) fall under the category of national

Table 4.2: Secondary Market-Selective Indicators

(Amount Rs. Crore)

Year	No. of Stock Exchanges	No. of Brokers *	No. of Listed Companies: NSE	No. of Listed Companies: BSE	No. of Listed Companies: Total *	Turnover *	FII Net Investment in India	S&P CNX Nifty: Index **	S&P CNX Nifty: P/E Ratio	BSE Sensex: Index **	BSE Sensex: P/E Ratio
1992-93	22	...	...	2,861	6,925	92,461	13.4	822	...	2,884	29.30
1993-94	23	...	...	3,583	7,811	210,029	5,126.2	908	...	2,961	46.80
1994-95	23	6,711	415	4,702	9,077	179,380	4,796.3	1,093	...	4,029	30.40
1995-96	23	8,476	422	5,603	9,100	252,024	6,942.0	955	...	3,265	17.30
1996-97	23	8,867	550	5,832	9,890	670,622	8,574.5	993	...	3,433	14.60
1997-98	23	9,005	612	5,853	9,833	910,971	5,957.5	1,092	...	3,808	15.20
1998-99	23	9,069	645	5,849	9,877	1,020,719	–1,584.4	951	16.53	3,277	14.60
1999-00	23	9,192	673	5,815	9,871	2,053,699	10,121.9	1,362	24.60	4,613	22.70
2000-01	23	9,782	785	5,869	9,954	2,874,238	9,934.0	1,319	17.21	4,212	19.70
2001-02	23	9,687	793	5,782	9,644	883,459	8,755.2	1,074	18.10	3,323	16.23
2002-03	23	9,519	818	5,650	9,413	968,955	2,688.9	1,023	13.36	2,918	14.26
2003-04	23	9,368	909	5,528	...	1,620,932	45,764.5	1,455	20.70	4,582	18.57

** : Indicates that the combined total of all I the stock exchanges. ... : Indicates Not Available. ** : Indicates the Yearly average.*

Source: Complied from SEBI Annual Reports, SBI Bulletins, BSE Annual Reports and NSE Fact Book.

exchanges, while the balance 19 stock exchanges fall under the category of regional stock exchanges.

The stock exchanges are granted recognition by SEBI under Section 4 of Securities Contracts (Regulation) Act, 1956. There are twenty two[1] stock exchanges recognized under Securities Contracts (Regulation) Act, 1956. Eight stock exchanges have been granted permanent recognition, there were granted a tenure period renewal and remaining exchanges have been granted yearly renewal. During 2004-05, SEBI has granted renewal of recognition to 13 stock exchanges, of which 11 were granted recognition for one year and the other two were granted recognition for 2 years. All the exchanges are fully computerized and offer 100 percent on-line trading. The trading platform of the stock exchanges was accessible to 9,128 members and 13,684 sub-brokers from over 358 cities on 2004-05.

4.7.2. Number of Brokers

The Indian broking industry has undergone structural changes during the recent years. Greater emphasis has been given on consolidation and restructuring in the broking segment. Brokers and sub-brokers are the two major intermediaries in the secondary market. The trading platform of an exchange is accessible only to brokers. The broker enters into trades in exchanges either on his own account or on behalf of clients. No stock broker or sub-broker is allowed to buy, sell or deal in securities, unless he or she holds a certificate of registration granted by SEBI. A broker / sub-broker comply with the code of conduct prescribed by SEBI. Over time, a number of brokers-proprietor firms and partnership firms have converted themselves into corporates. Out of 9,128 brokers registered with SEBI at the end of March 2005, 3,773 brokers, accounting for 41.33 percent of total, were corporate entities. At the end of March 2005, there were 13,684 sub-brokers registered with SEBI. The standards for admission of members stress on factors, such as corporate structure, capital adequacy, track record, education, experience, etc. and reflect a conscious endeavor to ensure quality broking services.

4.7.3. Number of Listed Companies: The basic norms for listing of securities on the stock exchanges are uniform across all the exchanges. They may, however, prescribe additional norms over and above the minimum norms. These norms are part of the byelaws of the stock exchanges. The number of primary listings of companies on various stock exchanges has been on a decreasing trend. At the end of March 2003, the primary listing of companies on stock exchanges was 9,413. The number of companies listed on the NSE was increased from 415 to 970 over a period of study. But in the case of BSE first six years showed the increasing trend and last six years showed the decreasing trend. Finally it is not recovered from the decreasing tendency of number of companies listed. BSE is dominating all the other stock exchanges including NSE over the period of time in the form of number of companies listed. The proportion is loosing from the time to time by the BSE.

4.7.4. Turnover

The total turnover in all stock exchanges rose modestly by 2.86 percent in 2004-05 as compared with 67.25 percent in the previous year. The NSE and BSE combine accounted for more than 99 percent of the total turnover in 2004-05. The turnover at BSE and NSE rose by 3.2 percent and 3.7 percent, respectively in 2004-05 on top of 60.0 percent and 77.9 percent in the previous year. Month-wise, the BSE recorded the highest turnover in March 2005 (Rs. 59,528 crore) while the NSE recorded the highest turnover in December 2004 (Rs. 1,15,055 crore) followed by March 2005 (Rs. 1,13,055 crore). In percentage term, the highest increase in turnover over the previous month was observed in December 2004 in case of both the major exchanges.

4.7.5. FII Net Investment

Strong macro-economic fundamentals of the Indian economy coupled with other positive factors like good corporate results, low inflation, abolition of long-term capital gains tax, transparent regulatory system, etc., were the major factors which influenced the FII investment in India during 2004-05. The total number of FIIs registered with SEBI went up from 540 as on March 31st, 2004 to 685 as on March 31st 2005, an increase of 145 over the year. The FIIs continued to remain bullish on the Indian securities for the second year in succession. The net FII investment in 2004-05 was Rs. 45,881 crore which was marginally higher than

Rs. 45,764.5 crore in 2003-04.

4.7.6. Stock Market Indices

The Indian stock market, which witnessed a strong rally in 2003-04, continued to maintain its momentum during 2004-05 except subdued condition witnessed in the first quarter of the year. Barring a temporary phase of turbulent condition around the middle of May 2004, the stock market in India gradually gathered momentum with benchmark BSE Sensex crossing 6000-mark on November 17, 2004 and reached an all time high of 6915.05 on March 8th , 2005 before closing at 6492.82 on March 31st, 2005. The market reached a crescendo when the Sensex zoomed past 7000- mark for the first time in its history in June 2005 and 8800 points in October 2005. The similar trend is observed on the NSE S&P CNX Nifty.

In essence, it has been a rollicking performance during the last two years after the Sensex breached the psychological barrier of the 5000-mark. As optimism runs high, with bulls appearing in total command, a section of the market pundits expect the Sensex to zoom past the 10,000-mark in two year's time. Whether this is wishful thinking only time will tell, but one thing is for sure, the Sensex, in particular, and the Indian stock market, in general, are on a solid footing. The key drivers for the growth of the Sensex are:

* The Indian economy is one of the fastest growing economies along with China;
* Extremely low level of investments by Indian and foreign investors;
* The Indian economy is growing at 7.5 percent in the current year and the expected growth for the coming year is 6 to 8 percent;
* There are few markets outside India and China, where growth is taking place and where global players can participate;
* Enhanced visibility of Indian companies with major corporate restructurings and cleaning up of their balance sheets;

* Very low interest rates limiting other investment avenues and contributing in a small way to the liquidity seen in the financial markets; and
* Areas like engineering, auto components, designing apart from IT and pharma are making their presence felt globally.

4.7.7. P/E Ratio

The P/E ratio is an indicator of the returns left for shareholders after providing for liabilities of a company. During the upswing of a business cycle, P/E ratio has a general tendency to fall. Following global recovery, the P/E ratio, in fact, declined in most of the countries despite higher security prices. Similar to the international trend, the P/E ratio relating to benchmark indices also declined in India. This is an indication that market has the potential to grow further. However, the P/E ratios relating to major indices such as BSE Sensex and NSE S&P CNX Nifty were lesser than those in the previous year (2003-04). The P/E ratio on the NSE S&P CNX Nifty shows the continuous up and down trend from 1998-99 to 2004-05. The BSE Sensex is also recorded the ups and down trends by taking more time than the NSE S&P CNX Nifty.

4.8: SECONDARY MARKET - TRADING INTENSITY:

The equity market capitalization in India has grown from Rs. 7.25 trillion in March 2003 to Rs. 13.77 trillion in March 2004. This equity market capitalization works out to US $ 310 billion. This has pushed Indian equity market into a significant one among those of the emerging economies. The equity market capitalization is around 49 percent of 2003-04 GDP which places the equity market on par with the banking system in terms of financial intermediation (Economic Survey 2003-04). However, given the fact that India is the second largest equity market in the world in terms of the number of listed companies, and one of the important goals of our economic and financial reforms is to obtain the deep and liquid stock market, we cannot possibly satisfy ourselves with the current level of market capitalization.

The data of the Table-4.3 shows the top exchanges of the world, according to the World Federation of Exchanges (FIBV), sorted by the number of transactions per year. While the mean

Table 4.3: Trading Intensity in the World

(Number of Traders in Million)

Exchange	Country	1999		2000		2001		2002		2003		2004	
		Trades	Rank	Trades	Rank	Trades	Rank	Trades	Rank	Trades	Rank	Trades	Rank
NASDAQ	US	290	1	724	1	603	1	601	1	733	1	...	1
NYSE	US	169	2	221	2	339	2	546	2	723	2	...	2
NSE	INDIA	87	5	146	5	172	4	234	3	336	3	...	3
SHANGAI	CHINA	...	...	...	...		3	179	5	206	4	...	4
BSE	INDIA	61	6	125	6	133	8	148	7	180	5	...	5
KOREA	KOREA	161	3	160	3	158	6	193	4	139	7	...	6
TAIWAN	TAIWAN	159	4	161	4	141	7	170	6	164	6	...	7
SHENZHEN	CHINA	...	...	...	...	...	5	130	8	132	8	...	8
DEUTSCHE	GERMANY	37	7	68	7	84	9	73	9	75	9	...	9
LONDON	LONDON	17	13	25	14	33	14	...	12	...	11	...	10

... : Not Available.

Source: Ministry of Finance, Economic Survey 2003-04.

transaction value varies enormously across countries, the number of transactions conveys something about the vitality of trading and the complexity of the IT systems required. One international ranking in the area of finance, where India figures, is the size of securities exchanges, as measured by the number of transactions. While the average value of transaction in India is small by world standards, India has a very large number of transactions, which are required to be implemented by commensurately large and yet low-cost IT systems. In 2002, NSE appeared at rank 3 and BSE appeared at rank 7. This was the first time that India fared well in any international ranking connected with finance. In the 2003 ranking, NSE retained the 3rd rank and BSE improved to 5th rank. In 2002, NSE displaced Shanghai to take 3rd place, and BSE moved up from 8th rank in 2001 to 5th rank in 2003. NSE and BSE were stable at rank 3rd and 5th respectively in 2003 and 2004.

SECTION-II

REGIONAL STOCK EXCHANGES -THREATS AND OPPORTUNITIES

4.9: INTRODUCTION

The Regional Stock Exchanges (RSEs) have been very popular in India. They flourished due to theoretical and practical anomalies in the pre-liberalization period. But, in the post-liberalization era the RSEs have seen their demise. Many of them are virtually on non-operational. The National Stock Exchange (NSE) since 1994 has drastically changed the method of trading and settlement of securities in this country. From 'open-outcry system to electronic trading and settlement on computer screens -the Indian capital markets have come a long way. RSEs lost their relevance due to their own investor-unfriendly practices and the changes in regulatory approach in the years following the creation of the NSE. There are 19 RSEs in India. Table-4.4 gives a brief profile of the RSEs.

Profile of the stock exchanges were presented by considering the data on turnover, number of listed companies, market capitalization and total number of members for the period of 1995-96. From the Table-4.4, we can draw the following lines:

- Out of the total turnover (Rs. 2,26,519 crore) the national stock exchanges' contribution was Rs. 1,17,569 crore (52%) and the regional stock exchanges' contribution was Rs. 1,08,950 crore (48%) for this period.
- Number of companies listed was 12,696, out of this 5,346 (42.10%) companies on the national stock exchanges and 7,350 (57.90%) companies on the regional stock exchanges respectively.
- Market capitalization from the national and regional stock exchanges are Rs. 9,65,849 crore (80.27%) and 2,37,431 crore (19.73%) respectively.
- The total number of members registered in national and regional stock exchanges are 2,266 (26.73%) and 6,210 (73.275) respectively.
- From this profile, we can point out that the regional stock exchanges are also playing an important role in the Indian capital market.

4.10: OPPORTUNITIES FOR THE GROWTH OF REGIONAL STOCK EXCHANGES IN INDIA

- Corporate Laws in India require a company issuing securities to list them at a stock exchange closest to its Registered Office and also at a stock exchange having a national presence. While only BSE and NSE satisfy the latter criteria, companies are forced to get their shares listed on at least one RSE which is closest to their Registered Office. Table-4.5 and Table 4.5(a) shows the number of companies listed as primary listing on various stock exchanges and its annual growth rate respectively. Out of the 19 regional stock exchanges 12 stock exchanges recorded the positive and 7 stock exchanges recorded a negative annual growth rate in the number of companies listed. Hence, we can say that the regional stock exchanges have the opportunities to grow further in the future also.
- The anomalies in the trading and settlement system earlier followed by stock exchanges in India were also a cause for the creation and flourishing of so many RSEs. Until recently, stock exchanges used to follow a

five day settlement period. In simple words, is meant that transactions were effected for a given period of five days (say, from Monday to Friday) and then they were settled i.e. shares and money actually changed hands with buyers and sellers, through the exchange. The punters at all exchanges taking advantage of this anomaly kept their trades 'open' (unsettled) for full five days. Here, it is emphasized that settlement pattern (Table-4.6) across exchanges suggests that most of the transactions on the stock exchange are effected to take speculative advantage and not with the intention to take delivery of the shares. A logical conclusion that can be drawn is that the speculators are dominant in all stock exchanges and sincere investors are still a minority in the market. To make more profit, punters simultaneously traded in same scrip across multiple exchanges.

- The above anomaly was aggregated by the fact that the settlement periods of different stock exchanges ended on different days of the week. For example, Friday used to be the last day on BSE and Tuesday on NSE. Add to this the fact the 'carry forward of trades' was allowed on exchanges. The usual modus-operandi of punters was to transfer 'open' trades from one exchange to other exchanges at approximately the same price and take more time advantage to carry the trades forward till they were actually settled or closed with an opposite and matching transaction. In this shifting of trades from one exchange to other the RSEs made their killing and witnessed large volumes.
- A theoretical philosophy prevalent in socialist India's mindset according importance to RSEs was that the RSEs are the agents of regional economic development and led to better allocation of regional capital. According to the theory RSEs facilitated in more people getting investment opportunities closer to their homes.
- Most companies in a bid to make trading in their shares available to the largest possible number of investors also got their securities listed on more than one RSE. As business across all stock exchanges soared, companies opted to list their securities on multiple exchanges.

Table 4.4: Stock Exchanges in India—A Profile

Sl. No.	*Stock Exchange*	*Turnover (Rs. Crore)*	*No. of Listed Companies*	*Market Capitalisation (Rs. Crore)*	*Total Members*
	National Stock Exchange				
1.	Mumbai	50,064	3,990	563,748	608
2.	USEIL	67,287	422 846	217,721 183,737	873
3.	OTCEI	218	88	643	785
4.	ICSEIL	—	—	—	—
A	Total	117,569	5,346	965,849	2,266
	% to Total	52.00	42.10	80.27	26.73
	Regional Stock Exchanges				
5.	Ahemdabad	8,786	551	7,651	285
6.	Bangalore	890	253	17,812	230
7.	BHubaneshwar	226	43	887	222
8.	Calcutta	62,128	1,962	77,131	861
9.	Cochin	1,803	90	7,244	488
10.	Coimbatore	2,503	86	1,233	192
11.	Delhi	10,076	1,579	30,465	379
12.	Gauhati	619	175	786	206
13.	Hyderabad	1,286	520	11,917	304
14.	Jaipur	1,048	145	4,004	587
15.	Ludhiana	4,849	227	7,198	275
16.	Madhya Pradesh	205	229	6,645	188
17.	Madras	1,594	593	28,604	200
18.	Magadh	1,629	29	246	193
19.	Mangalore	39	18	3,183	147
20.	Pune	7,072	121	12,533	197
21.	SKSE	564	36	1,999	437
22.	Uttar Pradesh	2,373	321	7,260	507
23.	Vadodra	1,260	372	10,633	312
B	Total	108,950	7,350	237,431	6,210
	% to Total	48.00	57.90	19.73	73.27
C	Grand Total	226,519	12,696	1,203,280	8,476

Note: In case of NSE the figures in bold represnet the "permitted equities."
Source: SEBI Annual Report, 1995-96.

Table 4.5: Primary Listign of Companies on Stock Exchanges

Sl. No.	Stock Exchange	No. of Companies					
		1997-98	1998-99	1999-00	2000-01	2001-02	2002-03
1.	Ahemdabad	692	693	687	692	671	669
2.	Bangalore	255	253	256	269	278	279
3.	Bhubaneshwar	46	46	46	46	46	46
4.	Calcutta	1,892	1,907	1,903	1,900	1,865	1,857
5.	Cochin	94	95	95	93	94	92
6.	Coimbatore	95	95	95	108	93	91
7.	Delhi	1,669	1,672	1,968	1,692	1,687	1,681
8.	Gauhati	196	196	161	153	152	1
9.	Hyderabad	624	629	632	680	675	674
10.	ICSEIL			0	1	1	12
11.	Jaipur	186	181	188	198	193	191
12.	Ludhiana	296	295	296	291	290	286
13.	Madhya Pradesh	248	249	251	251	93	249
14.	Madras	649	665	643	674	640	7
15.	Magadh	34	34	33	34	24	0
16.	Manglore	23	23	26	26	26	26
17.	Mumbai	1,811	1,808	1,810	1,512	1,774	1,726
18.	NSEIL	11	11	16	6	6	7
19.	OTCEI	115	116	115	114	113	113
20.	Pune	176	181	187	193	198	196
21.	SKSE	46	46	46	46	48	47
22.	Uttar Pradesh	346	352	352	334	332	816
23.	Vadodra	329	330	335	336	345	347
	Total	9,833	9,877	9,871	9,954	9,644	9,413

Note: The Primary Listing of Company represents the company in the region of stock exchange where it is listed.

Source: SEBI Various Annual Reports.

Table 4.6: Delivery Pattern Across Stock Exchanges

Sl. No.	Stock Exchange	Delivery Ratio (As a Percentage of Value) 1998-99	1999-00	2000-01	2001-02	2002-03	2003-04	2004-05
1.	Ahemdabad	1.0	5.0	7.0	3.0	0.6	0.0	0.6
2.	Bangalore	3.0	6.0	4.0	29.0	0.0	0.0	0.0
3.	Bhubaneshwar	0.0	0.0	0.0	0.0	0.0	0.0	0.0
4.	Calcutta	2.0	5.0	7.0	7.0	6.1	13.8	46.5
5.	Cochin	5.0	0.0	6.0	6.0	0.0	0.0	0.0
6.	Coimbatore	2.0	3.0	0.0	0.0	0.0	0.0	0.0
7.	Delhi	3.0	9.0	12.0	32.0	18.2	4.7	0.0
8.	Gauhati	0.0	0.0	100.0	10.3	0.0	0.0	0.0
9.	Hyderabad	9.0	33.0	17.0	20.0	40.0	100.0	65.0
10.	ICSEIL	1.0	2.0	4.0	17.0	0.2	0.0	0.0
11.	Jaipur	2.0	50.0	0.0	0.0	0.0	0.0	0.0
12.	LUdhiana	3.0	3.0	3.0	6.0	0.0	0.0	0.0
13.	Madhya Pradesh	6.0	0.0	30.0	60.0	0.0	0.0	0.0
14.	Madras	10.0	30.0	13.0	9.0	0.0	0.2	101.2
15.	Magadh	0.0	0.0	0.0	0.0	0.0	0.0	0.0
16.	Managlore	48.0	0.0	0.0	0.0	0.0	0.0	0.0
17.	Mumbai	20.0	16.0	17.0	20.0	16.0	25.7	27.0
18.	NSEIL	15.0	10.0	8.0	14.0	14.2	20.0	24.2
19.	OTCEI	12.0	1.0	31.0	0.8	0.0	0.0	0.0
20.	Pune	2.0	3.0	2.0	3.0	0.0	0.0	0.0
21.	SKSE	0.0	0.0	0.0	0.0	0.0	0.0	0.0
22.	Uttar Pradesh	2.0	2.0	2.0	1.0	1.6	0.6	0.5
23.	Vadodra	1.0	3.0	0.0	0.0	0.0	0.0	0.0
Total		13	11	11	15	20	22	25

Note: The Primary Listing of Company represents the company in the region of stock exchange where it is listed.

Source: SEBI Various Annual Reports.

Table 4.7: Distribution of Turnover on Cash Segment of Stock Exchanges (Rs. Crore)

Sl.No.	Stock Exchange	1992-93	1993-94	1994-95	1995-96	1996-97	1997-98	1998-99	1999-00	2000-21	2001-02	2002-03	2003-04	2004-05
1.	Ahmedabad	22,183	23,540	12,452	20,626	41,065	31,117	29,928	37,566	54,036	14,644	15,459	4,544	8
2.	Bangalore	730	2,316	712	897	4,389	8,637	7,749	1,115	600	70	0	0	0
3.	Bhubaneshwar	1,899	814	303	211	231	203	74	68	0	0	0	0	0
4.	Calcutta	NA	57,641	52,872	62,149	105,481	178,779	172,818	357,167	355,035	27,075	6,523	1,928	2,715
5.	Cochin	65	382	614	287	152	164	96	66	26	2	0	0	0
6.	Coimbatore	27	2,052	3,192	5,007	4,798	4,274	769	78	0	0	0	0	0
7.	Delhi	7,413	12,099	9,144	10,083	48,992	67,936	50,651	94,528	82,997	5,526	11	3	0
8.	Guhati	443	452	285	616	484	120	52	0	0	0	0	0	0
9	Hyderabad	676	984	1,160	1,107	480	1,861	1,270	1,236	978	41	5	2	14
10.	ICSE	NA	NA	NA	NA	NA	NA	NA	274	237	70	53	0	0
11.	Jaipur	296	616	879	1,048	1,519	453	63	2	0	0	0	0	0
12.	LUdhiana	1,050	3,150	4,975	4,849	5,274	8,316	6,070	6,872	9,154	964	0	0	0
13.	Madhya Pradesh	356	132	118	202	5	1	1	10	2	16	0	0	0
14.	Madras	3,407	4,618	6,117	3,259	3,912	2,458	739	500	218	48	76	101	27
15.	Magadh	NA	1,938	797	1,629	2,755	323	1	9	2	0	0	0	0
16.	Mangalore	12	108	62	39	380	314	11	0	0	0	0	0	0
17.	Mumbai	45,696	84,536	67,79	50,064	124,190	207,112	310,750	686,428	1,000,032	307,292	314,073	503,053	518,716
18.	NSE	NA	NA	1,805	67,287	295,403	370,193	414,474	839,052	1,339,510	513,167	617,989	1,099,534	1,140,072
19.	OTCEI	2	38	365	224	219	283	198	3,603	126	4	0	16	0
20.	Pune	752	3,459	3,672	7,096	10,084	8,624	4,827	6,090	6,171	1,171	0	0	0
21.	SKSE	265	614	329	452	395	17	0	0	0	0	0	0	0
22.	Uttar Pradesh	5,508	6,789	7,923	12,373	16,070	15,209	18,429	23,876	25,112	13,349	14,763	11,751	5,343
23.	vadodara	1,681	3,751	3,855	2,519	4,344	4,577	1,749	159	2	20	3	0	0
	Total	92,461	210,029	179,380	252,024	670,622	910,971	1,020,719	2,058,699	2,874,238	883,459	968,955	1,620,932	1,666,895

NA: Not Available *Source*: SEBI Annual Report (Various Issues)

4.11: THREATS FOR THE GROWTH OF RSEs IN INDIA

From the above presentation we observed the following reasons as the cause for the redundancy of the RSEs:

4.11.1. Technological Changes

The RSEs have failed to technologically upgrade themselves with the time. Post 1994, the year of creation of NSE the working and dynamics of stock exchanges in India has undergone a sea change. NSE introduced in India, computer based trading as against the open-outcry system. In the new technologically advanced version of trading on stock exchanges, the focus shifted from broker domination to investor supremacy. The transparent practices and policies of NSE attracted the mass of investors to its flock. Investors now prefer to trade on 'order driven quotes' rather than 'order forced or forced quotes'.

Once the investors recognized the benefits of trading on the technologically superior and transparent NSE, the RSEs began to loose their relevance. Table-4.7 and 4.7(a) suggests that during the last five years trading on BSE and NSE grew rapidly while those on RSEs tumbled. In 2004-05 trades on BSE and NSE accounted for 99 percent of the total trades across all exchanges. This is because of the establishment of online trading centers by the national stock exchange (NSE) thought the country by selecting the major towns/cities.

4.11.2. Dis-intermediation

One of the greatest advantages of the technology is that promotes dis-intermediation i.e. either totally doing or reducing the number of intermediaries required to effect and complete a transaction or reducing the number of intermediaries involved in a transaction. In case of stock exchanges it led to latter. With the advent of NSE's computer based trading investors got a better deal in terms of correct prices and lower commissions. This was especially possible as brokers' expenses on overhead on operations as 'Trading Floor' and allot office exchanges within the exchange premises to all its brokers and the brokers freed of their liability to play the rent for such spaces. The earlier 'investor-sub-broker-broker-exchange' channel which hampered faster settlement of trades and also added to the cost of transaction borne by the investor was done away with.

4.11.3. Satellite Based Trading

NSE's computer and satellite based trading spreads the brokers to places other than the location of the stock exchange. Brokers were no longer to operate from the city where the NSE located. They can carry operations from various cities and towns where the sub-brokers of RSEs are recognized. It dented the business of sub-broker-broker combine of the RSEs and by extension business of RSEs got affected. Investors got a better option and moved to NSE/BSE brokers instead of with RSEs brokers. Thus the levels of intermediation in trades on stock exchanges decreased long with reduced cost of transactions.

4.11.4. Management and Operational Practices

Management and operational practices of RSEs was not investor friendly. The brokers' interests dominated their policy making and dispute settlement. Short-delivery, bad-delivery, arbitrary auctions and carry-forward etc. were the areas of constant conflict between the brokers/sub-brokers and the investors. Investor's complaints against the brokers were high and compliances were too low. Whereas the NSE's investor friendly policies and transparent dispute settlement mechanism were an instant hit amongst investors to attract them towards BSE and NSE.

4.11.5. Commercial Failure

Commercial failure of RSEs was fuelled due to regulatory changes. The stock exchanges followed different settlement cycles ending on different days of the week. Armed with the earlier allowed facility of carry-forward of trades, the brokers, mainly punters abused this facility to transfer their 'open' positions on one exchange to other as the settlement cycle and maximum time of carry-forward on one exchange ended. This 'created false trades' on all exchanges including the RSEs. When SEBI banned the carry-forward of trades, there was a sharp fall in volumes across all exchanges but the RSEs with their shrinking investor base and eroded public confidence were the worst hit as their commercial utility in keeping these false trades alive, vanished overnight. With curbed punter interest and eroded public confidence the business of the RSEs nosedived.

New settlement system of 'T+3' and 'T+2', where each trading day (T) is a complete settlement cycle in itself and the trades are to be compulsorily settled on second (+2) or third (+3) day also added to the commercial failure of RSEs. Punters/ brokers interest diminished leaving the RSEs bleeding.

4.11.6. Depository Operations

One of the tenets of creation of RSEs was their physical proximity to investors of their region. The advent of trading and settlement in dematerialized (Demat) securities rendered this concept redundant. As no longer are the investors required to deliver shares in physical (Paper) form. As the bulk of trading and settlement moves in Demat (Electronic) mode, for investors and brokers alike physical proximity lost relevance. The brokers of NSE and BSE, scattered all over the country comfortably settled their trades from their offices and need not visit the exchange as shares in Demat get transferred to exchanges and vice-versa.

4.11.7. Over-confident Attitude

Complacency of RSEs and over-confident attitude in handling the crisis emerging from expanding presence of NSE/BSE and decreasing volumes due to multitude of factors is also responsible for their pathetic conditions. When they were unquestionable irrespective of the fact their killing was made by financially killing the investors and keeping him disadvantaged. When NSE/BSE decided to expand trading terminals to various cities and towns, the RSE brokers resorted to demonstration and opposing the move. Little efforts were made to improve their own working. Clamor for protection through regulatory mechanism dominated their survival/revival strategy. No concrete efforts matched their rhetoric.

4.12: MEASURES TO OVERCOME THE THREATS/ PROBLEMS OF REGIONAL STOCK EXCHANGES

As RSEs are presently virtually out of business it is time they introspect to make their prospects of survival track and also garner good public footage.

4.12.1. To Float the Membership

RSEs can be enrolled as members of BSE/NSE and the members of RSEs by extension become their sub-brokers. Although some of the members of RSEs may have acquired independent memberships of BSE and NSE, many may not have become so, due to financial and regulatory constraints, as both NSE and BSE prescribed stringent conditions to become members. This will save cost of establishment and also cost of operations to the numerous members of NSE/BSE. Beyond monetary involvement, the RSEs would be able to bring back investors to their fold. As these members of RSEs, they are located in interior/semi-urban areas there is an immense opportunity in bringing them technologically superior BSE/NSE to small towns. Some RSEs have already done this exercise but few are still there to take this measure.

This can lead to increase in total investor population of the country. Rural/Semi-urban areas have a lot of savings but a very few investment avenues are available to them. Further, not only, these members of RSEs can carry their business in such areas with an eye on protecting investor's interest but they also can become real conduits for channeling rural ingestible surplus to the industrial sector. In this process they may even bridge the gab between agricultural and industrial sectors.

4.12.2. To Convince the Management of Unlisted Companies

A RSE may approach all those financially sound and good public limited companies situated in its area and offer to list their shares. This will not be an easy task to convince managements of all such closely held companies to bring them into Stock Exchanges folds. But, if a RSE approaches professionally and the benefits of listing are to be explained to them, chances of some of them agreeing to the idea cannot be ruled out. In the area of falling interest rates and fluctuating market valuation of stocks such companies with stable source of business and revenue can also make a good investment opportunity even for the conservative investors.

Prior to listing such companies will require much managerial help in restructuring of the companies with regard to finances, accounts, compliance etc. The RSEs can vend professional help for restructuring such companies functioning. Given, Central Listing around the corner these closely held companies shall in due course reap the benefits of nation-wide corporate presence and trading across all exchanges. Inherent benefits of access to large and diversified capital and bigger investor base shall naturally follow.

4.12.3. To Disseminate the Information

One of the functions of a stock exchange is to disseminate information on capital market prices, functioning and educate, inform and update various constituents of the market. This is one area where no stock exchange except the NSE has done commendable job. Thus, it remains an acknowledged fact that the stock exchanges across India including the BSE (except for some fragmented efforts in recent times) have largely been laggards in discharging this function. It is a well-known fact that a large chunk of investors in India are ignorant of market basics and dynamics. More number of investors is investing on hearsay, rumors and tips of the brokers. The RSEs by virtue of their scattered presence all over the country can act as catalyst for providing information to various investors.

4.12.4. To Educate the Investors

The RSEs have a rich experience in nitty-gritty of stock trading, procedures and even the pitfalls of the game. They are information super-houses which can be put to varied uses. The RSEs can use their knowledge, expertise and experience in educating and training the public about investment opportunities in the stock market. This can help in adding a large number of new investors and benefit the economy and market as a whole. For this purpose, the RSEs can design their own short term course modules or use the established training material of the NSE's Certification in Financial Markets (NCFM) which interalia is available in Basic Capital Markets, Dealers, Depositories and Derivatives modules.

4.12.5. To Upgrade the Skills of Market Operators

The resources, skill, and knowledge of RSEs can also be productively utilized to provide orientation, training and skill up-gradation of the manpower in the financial sector. The existing manpower in this market is ill-trained and intellectually ill-equipped to handle many procedures and systems prevalent in the markets. This is one area where the RSEs can really deliver the goods. As even today the market operators scattered all over the country need a lot of training and orientation on the functioning of the market.

4.12.6. To Monitor the Compliances

Monitoring of compliance by the companies is another weak area in India. Rules are framed but their actual implementation by the people and parties concerned, is a matter of concern. The RSEs can play a role in this by monitoring the compliance for various agencies. In a way, a number of departments and agencies involved in the regulation and control of the corporations in India can outsource them. Department of Company Affairs, Company Law Board, SEBI, RBI etc., can get a lot of their compliance related work done through the help of RSEs. The RSEs can also act as contact point for such regulators and can dispense both information and services on their behalf. As the staff of RSE is already somewhat equipped with working of regulatory organizations a small amount of training will render them fit for discharging the envisaged multiple functions.

SECTION-III

INVESTORS PROTECTION

4.13: INTRODUCTION

Investors are the backbone of the securities market. Protection of their interests is paramount important. They are expected to alert and active, at the time, after and even continue to make an investment. Technically, an investor is also a buyer, therefore, buyer's beware or the caveat emptor; the principle that a person who buys is responsible for finding any faults in the thing that he buys is also applicable to him.[2] But the problem, in a crucial manner, is that the financial products of investment in capital market never be in terms of physical assets like Land & Building. In fact, the products are Shares and Securities; either purchased from primary or secondary market. Therefore, a number of regulatory authorities in the financial market (i.e. capital and money market) such as Department of Company Affairs, Company Law Board, Ministry of Finance, Securities and Exchange Board of India, Reserve Bank of India, etc. are functioning towards investors' protection, developing a number of measures, specially giving stress upon disclosures under the powers given by the Companies Act, 1956, the Securities (Contracts) Regulation Act, 1956 the Securities and Exchange Board of India Act, 1992, the Reserve Bank of India Act, 1938, the Banking Regulation Act, 1949 etc.

4.14: PRESENT DISCLOSURE STANDARDS IN INDIA

The disclosure provisions of the securities laws involve three issues: (i) Who should disclose; (ii) What and in which manner must be disclosed; and (iii) Where and when must be disclosed. The said three issues were solved by three important parties involved in the disclosure provisions of the securities in Indian Capital Market. They are: (A) Issuers; (B) Intermediaries; and (C) Overseeing Authority.

4.14. (A). Disclosure by Issuers

A review of disclosure guidelines, regulations and requirements in some of the emerging securities market reveals that the disclosure requirements are the same with minor differences and they include disclosure prior to issue, prior to listing and post-listing requirements. Now, there are various provisions to ensure that the adequate information is disclosed on corporate governance.

4.14. A (i). Prior to Issue Disclosures in India

The principle of full and fair disclosure to investors prior to issue, in the case of India, is set out in the SEBI Regulations for Merchant Bankers and in the SEBI Guidelines for Disclosure and Investor Protection (DIP). The offer document / prospectus generally are required to contain information on:

* The description of the securities offered and details of the transaction in which the securities are being offered.
* Audited financial statements updated to 6 months prior to the date of opening of the issue.
* The issuer's business and property and the legal

environment in which the company operates.

* The company's financial condition and results of operations as approved by the Board of management.
* Company formation.
* Objects for which the issuer was formed.
* The identity of substantial (top 10) shareholders of the company by number of shares for the periods of 2 years prior to filing of the prospectus with the regulator, 10 days prior to filing of the prospectus of the with the regulator and as on the date of filing of the prospectus with the regulator.
* The internal regulations of the company (Articles of Association).
* Rights of shares.
* Minimum subscription to be received.
* Mode of payment for the securities etc.

4.14. A (ii). Prior to Listing Disclosure

Prior to listing the issuer must prepare and file a listing document containing information on the records of dividends, bonus etc. for the last 10 years. The listing document requires disclosing specific information on the rights attached to shares, charges or fees for sub-division, consolidation of shares and other procedural matters which do not find a place in detail in the prospectus. The stock exchanges are vested with the authority to enforce listing document disclosure by delaying or refusing a listing. Since the listing document is a material document pertaining to the offering it is available for public inspection.

4.14. A (iii): Post Listing/Ongoing Disclosures

In India, like in other jurisdictions, the disclosure requirements on continuous basis for the companies' are prescribed under Companies Act and Listing Agreement. Companies are required to file information required under Companies Act on continuous basis to Registrar of Companies (RoCs). The listed companies are required to file information on the following on a continuous basis to stock exchanges under the listing agreement:

Annually:

* Complete & full balance sheet and profit & loss account.
* Directors report to shareholders.
* Announcements regarding name change indication any new line of business.
* Cash flow statements.
* Consolidated financial statements.
* Related party disclosures.

Half-yearly:

* Half-yearly results approved by the board of directors and subjected to a limited review by the auditors of the company within 2 months after the close of the half year.
* Explanation if the sum total of First and Second quarterly un-audited results in respect of any item varies by 20 percent or more from the respective half yearly results.
* The aggregate non-promoter shareholding along with the half financial results.

Quarterly:

* Un-audited results within one month from the end of the quarter.
* Change in the name of the company and any new line of business suggested.
* Segment-wise revenue, results and capital employed along with the quarterly un-audited financial results.
* Shareholding pattern on a quarterly basis within 15 days of the end of the quarter.
* Statement of variation between projected utilization of funds and/or projected profitability statement made by it in the Prospectus/Letter of Offer and the actual utilization of funds/profitability on a quarterly basis etc.

4.14. A (iv). Disclosures on Corporate Governance

In India Clause 49 of the listing agreement for companies mandates requirements intended at promoting corporate governance of listed companies. Under this clause information required to be disclosed in the Corporate Governance Report includes:

* All pecuniary relationships or transactions of the non-executive directors.
* All elements of remuneration package of all the directors i.e. salary, benefits, bonuses, stock options, pension etc.
* Details of fixed component and performance linked incentives, along with the performance criteria; service contracts, notice period, severance fees.
* Stock option details, if any - and whether issued at a discount as well the period over which accrued and over which exercisable.
* Industry structure and developments
* Opportunities and threats.
* Segment-wise or product-wise performance.
* Outlook, risks and concerns.
* Internal control systems and their adequacy.
* Discussion on financial performance with respect to operational performance.
* Material developments in Human Resources / Industrial Relations front, including number of people employed.

4.14. (B). Disclosures by Intermediaries

The securities market requires services of a large variety of intermediaries like merchant bankers, brokers, etc. to bring the suppliers of funds and suppliers of securities together for a variety of transactions. To ensure that there is accurate and timely flow of information among the intermediaries, investors and the supervising and oversight authorities, intermediaries are required to make periodical disclosures as required by the rules and regulations prescribed for them.

* The permitted activities that a registered intermediary can undertake on behalf of the investors are disclosed on the registration certificate issued by SEBI.

* There is a regulatory obligation on the part of the intermediaries to keep the supervising authority informed of any deviation from the prescribed capital requirements.

* Every investment manager keeps records of the balance sheet, profit and loss account and such other documents including the transaction details of each client separately as are mentioned in the regulations and after the end of each accounting period, furnish to the oversight authority copies of such documents.

* Intermediaries are requested to submit their financial positions. These are to be certified an auditor.

* Intermediaries and their employees cannot give advice to the clients or in public media unless they make proper disclosure of their interest in the security.

* Every market intermediary is required to appoint a compliance officer who is responsible for monitoring the compliance of the Act, rules regulations, notification, guidelines, instructions etc. issued by SEBI and Central Government and for redressal of grievances.

4.14. (C). Disclosure by Overseeing Authority

The SEBI Act, 1992 established the SEBI and clothed it with responsibilities to protect the interests of investors in securities and to promote the development of, and to regulate the securities market and for matters connected therewith or incidental thereto by such measures as it thinks fit. The SEBI's regulatory jurisdiction extends over corporates in the issuance of capital and transfer of securities, in addition to all intermediaries and persons associated with securities market. SEBI discloses information through its Websites, manual, monthly bulletin and annual reports. The SEBI normally disseminate information on the following:

* Rules, Regulations, Guidelines, Schemes and Circulars.

* Committee and group reports.

* Offer documents, listing agreements, takeovers and buybacks offers.
* Addresses of registered intermediaries.
* Permitted activities of intermediaries (available on the registration certificate).
* Action, if any, taken against them.
* Market activity and Statistics (SEBI Bulletin).

4.15: POWERS OF SEBI TO TAKE PUNITIVE / PREVENTIVE MEASURES

The SEBI Act gives powers to SEBI to take punitive/ preventive action ranging from the power to issue directions under section 11B, power to issue cease and desist orders under section 11D, several powers under section 11(4), power to cancel or suspend registration under section 12(3), and power to levy penalties under Chapter VIA. The Act also gives power to SEBI to file prosecutions under section 24 for contravention of provisions of the Act or Regulations.

The powers to take action under these sections and the procedural safeguards provided in each type of action are presented below:

4.15. (A). Directions under Section 11 B / 11 (4)

Section 11 B provides that actions may be taken after making or causing an enquiry to be made. Although the Act here does not specifically mention that opportunity of hearing is to be given unlike in sections 11(4) and 12(3), in keeping with the principles of natural justice, orders under section 11B are passed mostly after giving a hearing. The hearing is held before Chairman/ Member. The enquiry referred to in the section may be done through an investigation/ inspection ordered by the Board for fact finding and gathering evidence. Action under section 11B is taken against entities and registered intermediaries mentioned in section 11 B (iii).

Section 11 (4) introduced in the year 2002 amendment which gives additional powers to SEBI for issuing directions has a specific provision that hearing shall be given "before or after passing such orders". The action can be taken pending investigation or enquiry or on completion of investigation or enquiry.

4.15. (B). Suspension / Cancellation of Registration

Section 12 (3) under the Chapter-V on Registration Certificate states that "the Board may, by order, suspend or cancel a certificate of registration in such manner as may be determined by regulations and Provided that no order under this sub-section shall be made unless the person concerned has been given a reasonable opportunity of being heard".

4.15. (C). Monetary Penalties

Chapter VIA of the SEBI Act lays down the conditions and procedure for levy of monetary penalty on persons related to securities market or registered intermediaries. The Act states that "the Board shall appoint any of its officer not below the rank of a Division Chief to be an adjudicating officer for holding an inquiry in the prescribe manner after giving any person concerned a reasonable opportunity of being heard for the purpose of imposing any penalty".

4.15. (D). Inquiry/Enquiry/Investigation

Investigations are undertaken with a view to examine alleged or suspected violations as well as to gather evidence and identify persons/entities behind irregularities and violations such as: (i) price manipulation; (ii) creation of artificial market; (iii) insider trading; and (iv) public issue related irregularities, takeover violations and other misconducts, etc. SEBI has undertaken over 900 investigation cases since 1992-93. The experience gained during investigations has contributed to evolution of policies and procedures in the regulatory and enforcement environment. Investigation is conducted at three stages. They are: (i) Preliminary Investigation, (ii) Formal Investigations and (iii) Post Investigative Proceeding.

From the Table-4.8, we observed that during 2004-05, 130 new cases were taken up for investigation as against 121 in the previous year. Over the years, SEBI has undertaken 908 investigation cases of which 755 cases have been completed.

During 2004-05, 130 new cases were taken up for investigation and 179 cases were completed. The average number of cases taken up for investigation and cases completed are 70 and 58 respectively. The average number of cases completed by SEBI was at 83 percent. The cases completed as a percentage of cases taken up ranges among 26.13 percent to 137.69 percent. The ratio was above 100 percent in the last two years of the study. This is also proved by the Correlation (0.774) analysis. The calculated value of t at 5 percent level of significance is much higher than the table, the correlation is significant.

Table 4.8: No. of Cases Investigated and Completed by SEBI

Year	*Cases Taken up for Investigation*	*Cases Completed*	*Cases Completed as a % of Cases Taken Up*
1992-93	2	2	100.00
1993-94	3	3	100.00
1994-95	2	2	100.00
1995-96	60	18	30.00
1996-97	122	55	45.08
1997-98	53	46	86.80
1998-99	55	60	109.09
1999-00	56	57	101.79
2000-01	68	46	67.65
2001-02	111	29	26.13
2002-03	125	106	84.80
2003-04	121	152	125.62
2004-05	130	179	137.69
Total	908	755	83.15
Average	70	58	82.86
Correlation			0.774
t-Test			6.400
t0.05			1.796

Note: The pending cases are of the nature of preliminary scutiny as well as of formal investigations.

Source: SEBI Annual Report 2004-05, p. 74.

Fig. 4.1: No. of Cases Investigated and Completed By SEBI

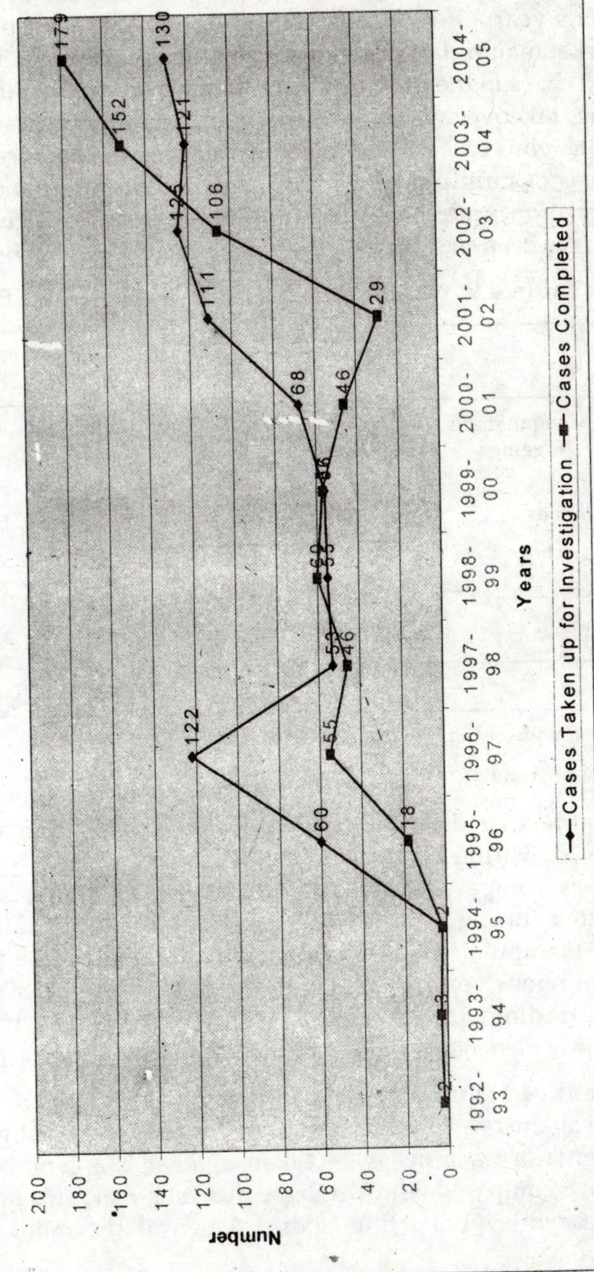

From the Table-4.9, we observed that, during 2004-05, 130 new cases were taken up for investigation as against 121 in the previous year. Of total cases taken up, 84.6 percent pertained to market manipulation and price rigging as against 79.3 percent of such cases in the previous year. Other cases pertain to insider trading, takeover violations, irregularities in public issues, and miscellaneous cases. Many investigation cases were taken up on the basis of multiple allegations of violations and hence, strict classification under specific category becomes difficult. Such cases have been classified on the basis of main charge/ violations.

Table 4.9: Nature of Cases investigated by SEBI

Particulars	*No. of Cases 2003-04*	*% to Total*	*No. of Cases 2004-05**	*% to Total*
Market Manipulations and Price Rigging	96	79.3	110	84.6
"Issue" Related Manipulations	2.	1.7	2	1.5
Insider Trading	14	11.6	7	5.4
Take-overs	2	1.7	1	0.7
Miscellaneous	7	5.8	10	7.7
Total	121	100.0	130	100.00

* Data ofor the current year are provisional

Source: SEBI Annual Report 2004-05, p. 97.

Table-4.10 shows that the nature of investigation cases completed. During 2004-05, number of cases completed increased to 179 as compared with 152 in 2003-04. Of the total cases completed during 2004-05, 82.6 percent of cases pertaining to market manipulations and price rigging as against 80.3 percent in the previous year. Other cases completed were pertaining to insider trading, public issue related irregularities, takeover violations, misleading advertisements, unfair practices, etc.

Table-4.11 presents details of regulatory action initiated by SEBI against various companies on the basis of investigations. The regulatory actions were taken against 232 companies in 2004-05 as compared with 174 in the previous year. This indicates an increased level of action against the enrolling companies by

SEBI in 2004-05. Under SEBI Act, 1992, prohibitory orders were issued against 134 entities in 2004-05 as compared with 106 in 2003-04. Similarly, warnings were issued to 53 entities in 2004-05 as against 22 entities in 2003-04. In addition, a total of 42 intermediaries were suspended for varying periods during the year as against 43 suspensions in the previous year. 712 show cause notices were issued to non-intermediaries in 2004-05 which were found to have committed various violations, as against 438 in the previous year indicating an increase of 63 percent.

Table 4.10: Nature of Investigated and Completed Cases

Particulars	*No. of Cases 2003-04*	*% to Total*	*No. of Cases 2004-05*	*% to Total*
Market Manipulations and Price Rigging	122	80.3	148	82.7
"Issue" Related Manipulations	3	2.0	2	1.1
Insider Trading	9	6.0	10	5.6
Take-overs	3	2.0	2	1.1
Miscellaneous	15	9.9	17	9.5
Total	152	100.0	179	100.0

Source: SEBI Annual report 2004-05, p.98.

4.15. (E). Prosecution: section 24(1) of the SEBI Act provides that "without prejudice to any award of penalty by the Adjudicating Officer under this Act, if any person contravenes or attempts to contravene or abets the contravention of the provisions of this Act or of any rules or regulations made hereunder, he shall be punishable with imprisonment for a term which may extend to ten years, or with fine, which may extend to twenty-five crore rupees or with both".

Table-4.12 shows the prosecutions launched. The number of prosecutions launched against companies, persons and entities have declined substantially in 2004-05 as compared to 2003-04. In 2004-05, prosecution was launched in respect of 83 cases as compared with 464 cases in 2003-04. In 2003-04, SEBI launched prosecution against all CIS entities who had failed to comply with directions issued under Section 11 B of SEBI Act, 1992. Total number of such cases was 332. This resulted in a substantial rise in the number of cases filed in the year 2003-04. Prosecution was launched against 410 persons / entities in 2004-05 as against 2,375 in 2003-04. Up to 2004-05, prosecution was launched in 969 cases and against 4,806 persons/entities.

Table 4.12: Prosecutions Launched

Year	*No. of Cases in which Prosecution has been Launched*	*% to Total*	*No. of Persons/Entities Prosecution has been Launched*	*% to Total*
Up to and including 1995-96	9	0.9	58	1.3
1996-97	10	1.0	57	1.2
1997-98	11	1.1	81	1.7
1998-99	15	1.6	145	3.0
1999-00	19	2.0	121	2.5
2000-01	20	2.1	98	2.0
2001-02	109	11.2	613	12.8
2002-03	229	23.6	848	17.6
2003-04	464	47.9	2375	49.4
2004-05	83	8.6	410	8.5
Total	969	100.0	4806	100.0
Average	97		481	

Source: SEBI Annual Report 2004-05, p. 106.

Table 4.13: Region-wise Data on Prosecution

Region	*No. of Cases*	*Percentage to Total*
Northern	322	33.23
Western	465	47.98
Southern	105	10.84
Eastern	77	7.95
Total	969	100.00

Source: SEBI Annual Report 2004-05, p. 106.

Table-4.13 shows that 48 percent of the cases belonged to the western region while 33 percent cases related to the northern region. The percentage shares of southern and eastern regions were 11 percent and 8 percent, respectively.

Table-4.14 depicts the nature of prosecutions launched under various sections of different Acts. The prosecutions have been launched under the Companies Act, SEBI Act, Depositories Act, Securities Control (Regulation) Act and the Indian Penal Code. Of the 969 cases, 875 have been launched under the SEBI Act and 5 under the Indian Penal Code. Prosecutions are launched to communicate a tough approach for implementation of regulatory penalties. Different sections of SEBI Act, Securities Control (Regulation) Act and relevant sections of Companies Act were also invoked to impose penalties on defaulting parties.

Table 4.14: Nature of Prosecutions Launched During 2004-05

Nature of Prosecuton Launched	*No of Cases*	*Percentage to Total*
Sec. 63, 68 of Companies Act, 1956	18	1.86
Sec. 73, 77 and 113 of companies Act, 1956	42	4.33
Indian Penal Code, 1860	5	0.52
SEBI Act, 1992	875	90.30
Depositories Act, 1996	13	1.34
Securities Contracts (Regulation) Act, 1956	16	1.65
Total	969	100.00

Source: SEBI Annual Report 2004-05, p. 106.

4.16: ROLE OF SEBI FOR THE REDRESSAL OF INVESTOR GRIEVANCES IN THE INDIAN CAPITAL MARKET

SEBI has a comprehensive investor grievances processing mechanism. The Office of Investor's Assistance and Education (OIAE) is the single window interface of SEBI with the investors. The OIAE accepts grievances of all investors who prefer to file their complaints with SEBI for matters falling within its jurisdiction.

A standardized complaint format is available at all SEBI offices and on the SEBI website for the convenience of investors. Complaints are taken up with the concerned entities either directly by OIAE or by the Investor Complaint Cell of the concerned department. SEBI officers also hold meetings with the company officials to impress upon them their obligations to redress the grievances of investors. Action under Section 11B & 15C of SEBI Act is initiated against recalcitrant companies.

Table 4.15: Redressal of Investor Grievances by SEBI

Year	*Grievances Received Druing the Year*	*Grievances Redressed During the Year*	*Grievances Redressed as % of Grievances Received*
1991-92	18,794	4,061	21.6
1992-93	110,317	22,946	20.8
1993-94	584,662	339,517	58.1
1994-95	516,080	351,842	68.2
1995-96	376,478	315,652	83.8
1996-97	217,394	431,865	198.7
1997-98	511,507	676,555	132.3
1998-99	99,132	127,227	128.3
1999-00	98,605	146,553	148.6
2000-01	96,913	85,583	88.3
2001-02	81,600	70,328	86.2
2002-03	37,343	38,972	104.1
2003-04	36,744	21,531	58.6
2004-05	54,435	53,361	98.0
Total	2,840,095	2,686,993	1,295.6
Average	202,864	191,857	92.5
Correlation		0.84	
t-Test	5.36		
t0.05	1.78		

Source: SEBI Annual Report 2004-05, p. 24.

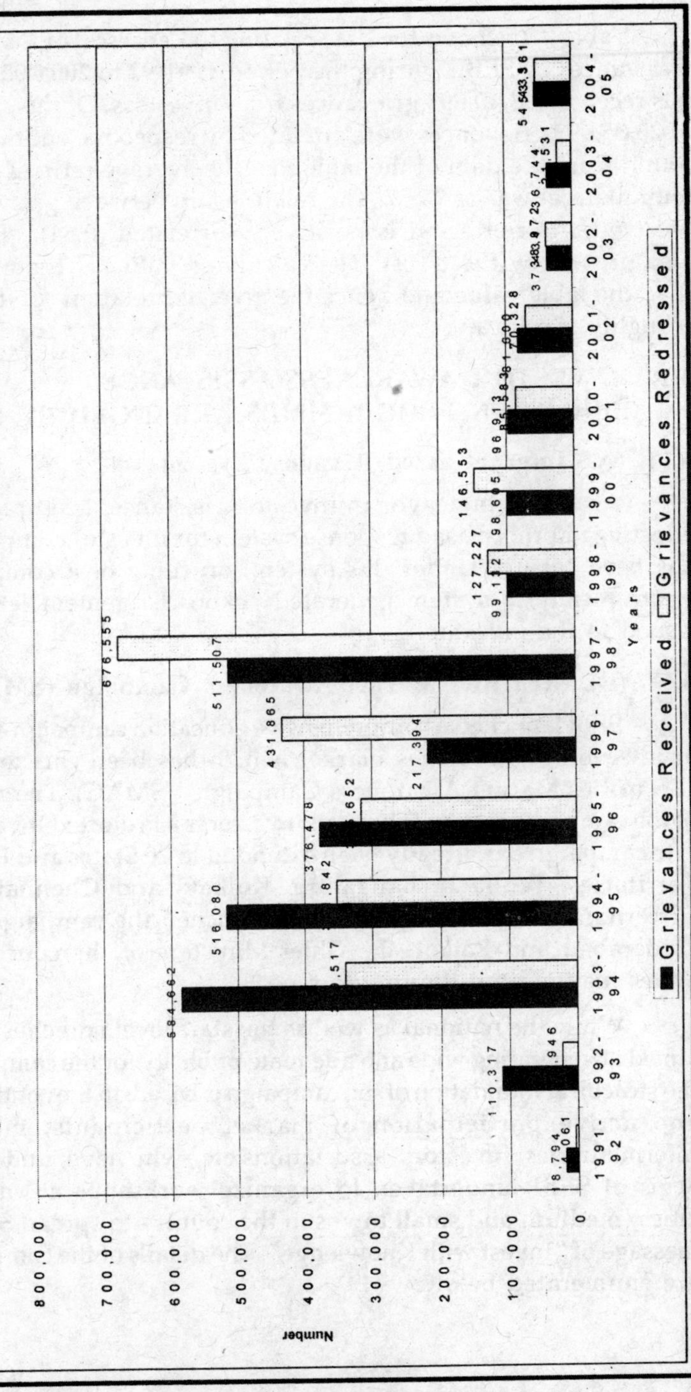

Fig. 4.2: Redressal of Investor Grievances by SEBI

Table-4.15 shows the data relating to Redressal of Investors Grievances by SEBI. During the period 1991-92 to 2004-05, SEBI has received 28,40,095 grievances from investors. Of this, a total of 26,85,993 grievances were attended by respective entities. We found from the data of the table that the average redressal rate (cumulative) was at 94.57. The relationship between grievances received and redressed is positively correlated (0.84). This is also proved by the t-Test. The calculated value of t is greater than the table value and hence the given correlation coefficient is highly significant.

4.17: INVESTOR AWARENESS/ASSISTANCE/ EDUCATION PROGRAMMES ARRANGED BY SEBI

4.17. (A). Internet-based Response System

As a new endeavor in investor assistance, a simple and effective internet-based response system for investor complaints has been set up. Under this system, on filing of a complaint electronically, a system generated acknowledgement letter is issued to the investor.

4.17. (B). Securities Market Awareness Campaign (SMAC)

SEBI launched a comprehensive education campaign aimed at investors in securities market, which has been christened - "Securities Market Awareness Campaign" (SMAC). The motto of the campaign is - 'An Educated Investor is a Protected Investor'. The campaign has already been extended to 20 States and Union Territories. While in Bangalore, Kolkata and Chennai, the Governors of the respective States launched the campaigns, in Hyderabad and Rajkot, the Chief Ministers of the concerned States inaugurated the programme.

While the national as well as the state level launches were aimed at generating wide and adequate publicity for the campaign, the structural foundation of the campaign is based on the continued and active participation of market participants, market intermediaries, investors' associations etc., who have, under the aegis of SEBI, undertaken to organize workshops at various cities/medium and small towns in the country to spread SEBI's message of "Invest with Knowledge". The details of the campaign are enumerated below:

4.17. B. (i). *Workshops*: The workshops are aimed at reaching out to the common investors and are being held primarily in small and medium towns and cities all over the country. At the workshops, the aim is to educate the investors about the functioning of the securities market, the basic fundamentals of investment and risk management and the rights and responsibilities of an investor. The message is made simple, with lectures and discussions conducted in the local/regional language. Till April 2005, 1949 workshops were conducted in around 480 cities/towns in the country.

4.17. B. (ii). *Audio-Visual Clip*: At the times of the national level launch, SEBI had prepared a 4 1/2 minute audio-visual clip depicting some of the concerns of the common investor and detailing the theme of the Securities Market Awareness Campaign. The thematic audio-visual is played at the various workshops being organized across the country.

4.17. B. (iii). *Distribution of Educative Materials*: SEBI has prepared standardized reading materials and presentation materials for the workshops. In addition, reference guides on the various topics like: (a) Rights and responsibilities of investors, (b) Substantial acquisition of Shares and Takeovers, (c) Simple "dos and don'ts" relating various aspects of the securities market, and (d) Mutual funds are distributed.

4.17. B. (iv). *Investor Website*: In order to make the information relevant to the investors and available at one place, a dedicated investor website (http://investor.sebi.gov.in) has been operationalised and the information content on this website is augmented on a periodic basis.

4.17. B. (v). *Advertisements*: SEBI has prepared simple "dos and don'ts" for investors relating to various aspects of the securities market. While these simple messages have been put on the investor website and have been printed in the form of leaflets to be distributed across the country, it was felt that these messages could be spread across the investor base by way of advertisements in newspapers, especially in the regional newspapers. Till date, over 700 advertisements relating to various aspects of securities market appeared in 48 different newspapers/ magazines, covering approximately 111 cities and 9 regional languages, apart from

English and Hindi.

4.17. B. (vi). *All India Radio*: With regard to educating investors through the medium of radio, All India Radio was requested to allot free slots to SEBI on their various programmes. AIR allotted 5 free slots in the month of January 2004 in its programme "People's Corner". Further, 8 free slots were allotted in the programme- Business Pulse - in the months of May and June 2004. These progrmmes are aimed at creating awareness among the common public regarding the functioning of various public service departments. SEBI officials participated in this live, interactive (with "phoned in" queries from investors) progrrame covering topics such as mutual funds, secondary market, risk management, derivatives, issues and listing in the primary market, investor education and grievances redressal mechanism etc.

4.17. (C). MAPIN

SEBI, which has asked securities market participants to register to Central Database of Securities Market Participants' and Investors' Identification Numbers (MAPIN), has extended the deadline to December 31, 2005. MAPIN is the Market Participants and Investors Integrated Database, which is being created by SEBI to enhance investor protection. Intermediaries and key personnel who facilitate dealing in securities are a critical link between the 'market' and 'investors'. Therefore, it is necessary to create an inventory of these functionaries working in the market place. The MAPIN Database will allot a Unique Identification Number (UIN), which would be required to be quoted by all market participants and investors while carrying out securities transactions. The unique client code, which investors obtain currently, will be replaced by the UIN given by the MAPIN database. As of date, the total number of registrants under this database is 2,00,000 comprising 1,48,000 individuals and 52,000 corporates and intermediaries.

4.18: RECOMMENDATIONS

Capital market is the backbone of any country's economy. It facilitates conversion of savings to investments. Globally, there are increased evidences to suggest that investor confidence has assumed an important role in the economic development of a country. The following are some of the important recommendations for strengthening investor confidence in the Indian capital market:

4.18.1. Information Related Measures

These include- the latest and easy availability information, public information should be available, education of investors, transparency in the system, improve awareness of investors in the primary as well as secondary markets, sensitive information should be made available to everyone at the same time, action against issue managers, analysts and company for providing over optimistic and wrong information, information related to promoters background and project implementation experiences should be available, and advertisements on the improvements taking place in the market should be released regularly.

4.18.2. Scandals and Irregularities

Regarding the irregularities and scams in the Indian financial market, the publication India Abroad has commented: "Since the beginning of reforms in 1991, there has been a spurt in financial crimes. The first major scandal that made newspaper headlines was the 1992 multi-billion dollar securities fraud that centered on Mumbai stock exchange broker Harshad Mehta... Other major white collar offences reported since 1991 are those concerning the Calcutta based blue chip company, ITC Ltd., the share switch charges against Reliance Industries, questionable transactions by the Shaw Wallace Company, The MS shoes scandal masterminded by Pawan Sachdeva, the Indian Bank fraud and the CRB Capital Market case... White collar crimes have become so common that the CBI, which started an economic offenses wing after the securities scandal, recently strengthened the division by recruiting specialists with background in banking and finance". India Abroad "How Liberalization Spawned a String of Scandals" June 27, 1997, page 28. So that the same story is not being continued, to take the initiation to regulate scandals, prevent corporate frauds, disallow bogus companies to raise funds from the market, tighter regulations, market price control, stability of market, transparency in operations, more power to take action against frauds, post listing performance of company to be monitored, autonomy to regulatory authorities, better means of project appraisal, minimum standards for companies to enter market, improve quality of paper, and black list brokers, underwriters and merchant bankers.

4.18.3. Government

The central government has to take some of the following initiations for the protection of interests of investors. They are: improve infrastructure and economic conditions, promote and attract investors, corruption to be checked at various levels, appoint independent nominees with good character, introduce rating of equity, take steps to protect small investors, insurance of stock market investments should be developed, grievance redressal machinery should be more efficient, reduce political interference in markets, pension and provident funds should be allowed to invest in primary markets.

4.18.4. Intermediaries

They are classified into primary market intermediaries and secondary market intermediaries. The intermediaries in the primary market are merchant bankers, underwriters' bankers to an issue, portfolio managers, debenture trustees and registrars to an issue and share transfer agents - they play an important role in the mobilization of capital and investment formation in the primary capital market. The secondary market intermediaries are stock brokers and sub-brokers - they play a significant economic role in the secondary securities market of the capital market. They bring investors, both buyers and sellers, together to make aggregate demand and supply at any point of time. For the increasing confidence in the brokers the following initiations has to be taken. They are: Honesty and fair and fair dealing in brokers should be encouraged, lower brokerage, improve relationship with customers, broker activities are to be regulated, reduce number of brokers, take action against brokers with bad conduct, brokers with good research facilities to be allowed, banks and financial institutions to play a leading role.

4.18.5. Markets

The market form of measurements are:-Improve trust of small investors, transparency of markets, volatility to be checked, market vigilance is important, proper audit of exchanges should take place, improve liquidity, allow good issue managers to manage issues, delisting of companies should be avoided, proper information on post listing activities should be made available by stock exchanges to investors, compulsory listing after completion of requirements only, market making activity to be improved, renew faith in the long-term, ensure new investors' confidence in the market, small investors to get firm allotment, more margin to be taken from brokers, and liquidity should be improved.

REFERECES

1. The application for renewal of recognition of Mangalore stock exchange was refused vide Order dated August 31st, 2004 under Section 4(4) of the Securities Contracts (Regulation) Act, 1956,.the matter is sub-judice as on March 31st 2005.
2. Hornby, A. S.: Oxford advanced learner's dictionary of current English, New York: Oxford University Press, 2000.

CHAPTER-V

STOCK MARKET VOLATILITY AND LIQUIDITY

5.1: INTRODUCTION

This chapter is divided into three sections and these sections are aimed at examining: (I) the varying perceptions of stock price volatility of Indian capital market along with identifying possible reasons for volatility and measures the degree of volatility; (II) the relationship between volatility and liquidity in the Indian stock market by taking sample of BSE and NSE indices; and (III) the investment trends and patterns of FIIs and their impact on stock market liquidity and volatility.

5.2: CONCEPTS OF STOCK MARKET VOLATILITY AND LIQUIDITY

The term Volatility is the most basic statistical risk measure. It can be used to measure the market risk of a single instrument or an entire portfolio. While, volatility can be expressed in different ways, statistically, volatility of a random variable is its standard deviation. In day-to-day practice, volatility is calculated for all sorts of random financial variables such as stock returns, interest rates, the market value of a portfolio, etc. Stock return volatility measures the random variability of the stock returns. Simply put, stock return volatility is the variation of the stock returns in time. More specifically, it is the standard deviation of daily stock returns around the mean value and the stock market volatility is the return volatility of the aggregate market portfolio. The high volatility is the reflection of high risk, because the security values are not dependable and the capital markets are not regarded as efficient. When examining the issue of stock market volatility, it is relevant to measure percentage of volatility of stock return. This reflects the percentage change in the value of the amount invested in the stock market.

Furthermore, Liquidity is an important feature of any financial market. Liquidity is the lubricating agent that facilitates a frictionless smooth functioning of the financial markets. Liquidity is an essential and efficient part of a stock market. While liquidity refers to the ease with which the buyers and sellers promptly transact with minimal impact on the price of a stock, efficiency refers to the speed with which the prices in the market move to reflect the information flows. In general, the term liquidity refers to the easy convertibility of assets into cash and when we talk about scrips i.e. shares, debentures, bonds etc. their liquidity is directly related to the technicalities, depth and speculative tendencies in the market. Liquidity of an asset is very precisely defined by Keynes that an asset is more liquid than another, 'if it is more certainly realizable at short notice without loss' (1930). The variations in the degree of liquidity affect the price discovery process and efficiency of the market. If the price difference is less, then it indicates more liquid or the reverse position is less liquid. The liquidity of the market is the situation in which large quantities of shares are traded without having any material impact on the price of such shares.

5.3: OBJECTIVES

The chapter "Stock Market Volatility and Liquidity" is aimed at examining the following objectives:

* To understand the varying perceptions about the volatility of Indian stock prices.
* To analyze the reasons for the volatility.
* To compare the degree of volatility of indices of NSE and BSE, with a view to identify attributable common factors as well as to suggest the measures for reduction of their volatility.
* To explain the concepts of stakeholders in the stock market volatility and liquidity.

* To present the theoretical relationship between Volatility and Liquidity.
* To study the volatility and liquidity in the Indian stock markets by taking the sample of BSE and NSE indices.
* To present the regulatory frame work initiated by SEBI and Government of India for the FIIs.
* To examine the investment trends and pattern of FIIs in order to bring out the relative diversities in their investment.
* To study the impact of FII's investment on stock market liquidity and volatility.

SECTION-I

STOCK MARKET VOLATILITY

5.4: INTRODUCTION

In the past few years the Indian Capital Market has undergone metamorphic reforms. Every segment of Indian Capital Market viz., primary and secondary markets, derivatives, institutional investment and market intermediation has experienced impact of these changes. The capital market, today, is being recognized as one of the most transparent, efficient and clean market (C.N.Bajpai 2004). In the recent past there have been perceptions that volatility in the market has gone up. Volatility is an important indicator of the dynamic fluctuation of stock market prices. Sometimes, wide fluctuations in prices of stock can scarce away the investor from the market place. However, they have to know the variations in the stock market from time to time in order to understand the changing pattern of the capital market prices for their decisions to buy/sell the securities. Therefore, this section "Stock Market Volatility" is aimed at examining the pattern, trends, causes and impact of volatility on stock market in particular and investors in general.

5.5: CAUSES OF STOCK PRICE VOLATILITY

The empirical studies evidencing that the factors which have caused the markets to become more volatile are many Viz; (i) the low P/E effect, (ii) low-priced stocks, (iii) the small firm and neglected firm effects, (iv) market over-reaction, (v) computerized tools have made it easier to trade large amounts of stocks continuously, (vi) increasing political uncertainty is unnerving the market; (vii) round the clock trading has reduced wait and watch reflex on the part of investors, (viii) the existence of asymmetric information problem, (ix) runs on financial intermediaries, (x) herd behavior on the part of investors, (xi) excessive speculation, (xii) fluctuations in the prices of real assets, (xiii) changes in exchange rate more than justified by changes in economic fundamentals, (xiv) instability of commodity prices, (xv) the January effect, (xvi) the weekend effect and (xvi) the persistence of technical analysis. Turn of the year, month, week, and holidays are reported to have consistently generated abnormal equity returns, unrelated to the attendant risks, at the developed stock markets and are identified as calendar anomalies. Fama (1965) reported Monday's variance to be 20 percent greater than other daily returns. Later, many fascinating studies by French (1980), Gibbons and Hess (1981), Lakonishok and Levi (1982), Gultekin and Gultekin (1983), Keim and Stambagh (1984), Theobald and price (1984), Jaffe and Westerfield (1985), Santesmases (1986), Board and Sutcliffe (1988) and Lakonishok and Smidt (1988) presented ample evidence for stock market volatility as to the developed economies. Taxation at the year-end, cash flows at the month-end, unfavorable news releases at the weekend and over-reactions due to human psychology are attributed to be the causes for such calendar anomalies.

5.6: MEASUREMENT

Stock market volatility is often classified as historical (actual) volatility or implied volatility. The most common measure of historical or actual stock market volatility is the standard deviation. In simple terms, standard deviation measures the deviation of the returns of equity from its mean return. It is an absolute measure i.e. standard deviation of stock returns in one period can be compared with standard deviation of another period to understand which period has been more volatile. Volatility is calculated as the standard deviation of the rates of return (r). The rate of return is the change in price during the period, divided by the price of the investment at the beginning of the period. The rate of change in the return may be calculated as:

$$r_t = \ln (I_t/I_{t-1})$$

Where rt is the rate of return for the period t, ln is natural logarithm, It and I_{t-1} are the beginning and closing prices for the two successive periods t-1 and *t*.

The standard deviation of return *r* from a sample of *n* observations is the square root of the average squared deviation of returns from the average in the sample.

$$\alpha = \sqrt{(1/n\text{-}1)\ \Sigma\ (r_t - \bar{r})^2}$$

Donald E. Fisher and Ronald J. Jordan (1993) suggested the easy way of estimation of volatility for the securities by using past data is as follows:

Volatility = (High – Low)/½(High + Low)

5.7: COMPARISON OF STOCK MARKET VOLATILITY OF NSE AND BSE

It is proposed to analyze stock price volatility of NSE and BSE. For this purpose we have chosen the following Indices of NSE (i) S&P CNX NIFTY (ii) CNX NIFTY JUNIOR (iii) CNX MIDCAP 200 and (iv) S&P CNX 500. Further the BSE Indices include (i) SENSEX (ii) 100 INDEX (iii) 200 INDEX and (iv) 500 INDEX.

5.7.1. Stock Index Volatility

The data relating to such Indices are presented in the Tables-5.1(a) and 5.1(b). The Nifty was at 607 points in the year 1991-92 and rose to 1093 in 1994-95 and declined to 952 points in 1998-99 then onwards it has gradually increased and reached to highest position during the period under review at 1450 points in 2003-04. This trend indicates a bullish position in the Indian capital market, since 1991-92 onwards, on account of Liberalization Privatization and Globalization policies of government of India as well as permitting FIIs to invest in Indian capital markets. The similar pattern is evident in Indices such as Nifty Junior and other Indices. The average of Nifty was stood at 1050.31, Nifty Junior 2028 and the other two Indices varied between 719 to 795 points. The volatility of stock Indices is measured by using Standard Deviation and Coefficient of

Variation. When we compare both the measures for different Indices of NSE, it is observed that Nifty is highly consistent and less volatile followed by S&P CNX 500, whereas Nifty Junior was highly volatile followed by CNX Midcap 200. Thus it shows that there was volatility in the stock Indices of Nifty. However this was relatively less volatile in Nifty as compared to other Indices of NSE.

The BSE Sensex was 2009 points in 1991-92 and increased to 4029 points in 1994-95, then onwards declined for couple of years and reached the highest of 4613 in 1999-2000. However it has witnessed significant fluctuations in Index and then reached to 4582 points at 2003-04. The averages of BSE Sensex were at 3485.7, 100 Index at 1754.3, 200 Index at 374.5 and 500 Index at 1295.8. The volatility of BSE stock prices has reflected by Standard Deviation is highest in the case of BSE Sensex followed by BSE 100 Index with 745.0 and 496.2 respectively. On the other hand the BSE 200 Index has shown more consistent and less volatile since its Co-efficient of Variation value is 66.5 points. The value of Coefficient of Variation reflects a relative volatility of stock Indices. We find that BSE 200 Index followed by BSE Sensex were less volatile as compared to BSE 500 Index and BSE 100 Index. Thus we conclude that all the Indices of BSE are volatile during the period of review; however such position is relatively consistent in the case of BSE Sensex[1] and BSE 200 Index.

A comparative analysis of stock Indices volatility at BSE Sensex and NSE Nifty followed by other Indices of the stock exchanges reveals that the volatility of BSE Sensex and Nifty as shown similar pattern because the Coefficient of Variation of them was 21.37 and 21.80 respectively. But when we observe the values of Standard Deviation it is clearly evident that the BSE prices were more significantly higher volatile than NSE. This position was reversed in the case of other Indices of BSE and NSE. Whereas percentage of volatility has moved around 22 in the case of BSE 500 and S&P CNX 500 Indices. The other Indices of NSE were widely volatile when compared to BSE. It is prominently evident that the Nifty Junior and CNX Midcap 200 have shown more than double the volatility of BSE 100 Index and BSE 200 Index.

Table 5.1(a): NSE Stock Indices

Year	*S&P CNX NIFTY*	*% of Change* 200	*CNX NIFTY Junior*	*% of Change* 500	*CNX MIDCAP*	*% of Change*	*S&P SNX*	*% of Change*
1991-92	607.00	NA	NA	NA	NA	NA	NA	NA
1992-93	822.00	35.42	NA	NA	NA	NA	NA	NA
1993-94	908.00	10.46	NA	NA	NA	NA	NA	NA
1994-95	1093:00	20.37	NA	NA	NA	NA	NA	NA
1995-96	955.00	–12.63	NA	NA	535.00	NA	664.00	NA
1996-97	993.00	3.98	3154.00	NA	472.00	–11.78	669.00	0.75
1997-98	1092.00	9.97	1206.00	–61.76	453.00	–4.03	695.00	3.89
1998-99	951.00	–12.91	1210.00	0.33	563.00	24.28	650.00	–6.47
1999.00	1362.00	43.22	2948.00	143.64	942.00	67.32	1044.00	60.62
2000-01	1319.00	–3.16	2382.00	–19.20	837.00	–11.15	856.00	–18.00
2001-02	1074.00	–18.57	1374.00	–42.32	630.00	–24.73	698.00	–18.46
2002-03	1023.00	–4.75	1410.00	2.62	739.00	17.30	734.00	5.16
2003-04	1455.00	42.23	2540.00	80.14	1301.00	76.05	1148.00	56.40
Mean	1050.31		2038.00		719.11		795.33	
SD	228.97		815.58		274.01		182.87	
CV	21.80		40.22		38.10		22.99	

NA = Not Available/Applicable

Source: CMIE/Capital Market Issues, July 2002, August, 2003 and June 2004, p. 275-278, 248-25` & 270-273.

Table 5.1(b): BSE Stock Indices

Year	*BSE Sensex*	*% of Change*	*BSE 100 Index*	*% of Change*	*BSE 200 Index*	*% of Change*	*BSE 500 Index*	*% of Change*
1991-92	2009.00	NA	948.00	NA	255.00	NA	NA	NA
1992-93	2884.00	43.55	1289.00	35.97	347.00	36.08	NA	NA
1993-94	2961.00	2.67	1408.00	9.23	345.00	-0.57	NA	NA
1994-95	4029.00	–36.07	1883.00	33.74	453.00	31.30	NA	NA
1995-96	3265.00	–18.96	1513.00	–19.65	338.00	–25.38	NA	NA
1996-97	3433.00	5.44	2726.00	80.17	342.00	1.18	NA	NA
1997-98	3808.00	10.92	1653.00	–39.36	369.00	7.89	NA	NA
1998-99	3277.00	–13.94	1453.00	–12.10	335.00	–9.21	1067.00	NA
1999.00	4613.00	40.77	2281.00	56.98	514.00	53.43	1393.00	30.55
2000-01	4212.00	–8.69	2128.00	–6.71	457.00	–11.08	1368.00	–1.79
2001-02	3323.00	–21.10	1584.00	–25.56	350.00	–23.41	1030.00	–24.71
2002-03	2918.00	–12.18	1577.00	–0.44	377.00	7.71	1125.00	9.22
2003-04	4582.00	57.03	2363.00	49.84	386.00	2.38	1792.00	59.29
Mean	3485.69		1759.31	374.46		1295.83		
SD	745.04		496.20		66.49		287.42	
CV	21.37		28.28		17.76		22.18	

NA = Not Available/Applicable

Source: CMIE/Capital Market Issues, July 2002, August, 2003 and June 2004, p. 275-278, 248-25` & 270-273.

Thus we conclude that BSE Sensex and NSE Nifty have shown the volatility of stock prices around 21%, the BSE 500 Index, S&P CNX 500 were around 22% and have similar pattern of stock price volatility. However this position is reversed in the case of CNX Nifty Junior and CNX Midcap 200 which was highly volatile when compared to BSE 100 and 200 Index. This volatility was more than two times.

5.7.2. Volatility of Daily Returns in a Month

The data pertaining to the volatility of daily return is presented in Table- 5.2(a), 5.2(b), 5.2(c) and 5.2(d) for the purpose of identification of highest volatile month in various Indices of NSE and BSE respectively. We found that the April month in every year has experienced the highest average volatility of 2.17, 2.43, 2.09, 2.05, 2.22, 3.23, 1.98 and 2.28 on S&P CNX Nifty, CNX Nifty Junior, CNX Midcap 200, S&P CNX 500, BSE Sensex, BSE 100 Index, BSE 200 Index and BSE 500 Index respectively. The main reasons for such volatility are: (i) More number of companies declares their financial results in the first week of April, (ii) The investors' decision to buy/sell of a particular company's scrip depends on the financial position registered by the companies and (iii) The budget implications are start working from this month of every year. Thus the month of April of every year has witnessed in short rate of volatility.

5.7.3. Top Twenty Volatile Months

The top twenty volatile months of NSE and BSE Indices were presented in Table-5.3(a) and 5.3(b) for the purpose of identification of highest volatile year in the study period. NSE CNX Nifty and BSE Sensex shows the highest volatile year is the 1992. These two Indices are oldest Indices in the Indian capital market. The important causes are: (i) The Indian economy is moved from controlled to decontrolled economy by the introduction of New Industrial Policy in 1991, (ii) The introduction of market friendly Union Budget for the financial year 1992-93, (iii) The RBI Governor asks mutual funds to offload stocks to arrest the runaway boom, (iv) The lifting of curbs on the Calcutta stock Exchange, (v) The modest relaxation of trading restrictions on the NSE, (vi) The BSE authorities call for a confidential report from SEBI on the alleged involvement of the leading operator in the market on 29th April 1992, (vii) The multi-crore Securities Scam was erupted, (viii) The RBI sets up a committee to inquire into securities transactions of banks and financial institutions on 6th May, 1992, (ix) BSE initiates a probe into several transactions of Harshad Mehta on 6th May, 1992, (x) The Government orders a CBI enquiry into the involvement of three banks-SBI, United Commercial Bank and National Housing Bank in the stock market scam, (xi) BSE bans forward sales in 15 specified stocks and cuts margins (xii) Sharp recovery on short sales, ban and cut in the daily margins on purchases, and (xiii) Market was officially closed for three days on account of the developments at Ayodhya. Fresh outbreak of violence triggered by the demolition of the Babri Mosque in Ayodhya on 6th December, 1992.

The Indices other than S&P CNX Nifty and BSE Sensex shows that the year 2000 is the highest volatility. The important reasons are: (i) Presentation of the Union Budget causes disappointment due to doubling of dividend tax levy of progressive tax on export earnings etc, (ii) Reports of the Income Tax Department for issuing notices to FII who have to route investments through Mauritius. Also, NASDAQ Composite Index fell sharply on the previous day i.e., 4th April, 2000, (iii) The Government decides to withdraw notices served earlier to the FIIs, (iv) SEBI raises margins on net sales positions, bans payment of carry-forward charges to naked short-sellers and relaxes daily circuit limit to 12%, (v) RBI hiked bank rate by 1% on 24th July, 2000, and (vi) The recent meltdown of the Information Technology (IT) Stocks is likely to have negative impact on the market. The RBI Annual Report 1999-00 points out that the CNX IT Index has declined by 47.0% between end March 2000 and end July 2000. Another feature that has come up lately is that the movement in stock prices in India (particularly IT stocks) seems to have become correlated with international stock price movements, and (vii) The increased volatility of the Indian currency in the foreign exchange market is likely to affect the stock markets in India.

5.7.4. Market Capitalization

The market capitalization at NSE and BSE is presented

Table 5.2(a): Volatility of NSE Indices of Daily Returns in a Month (Percent)

	1991-92	*1992-93*	*1993-94*	*1994-95*	*1995-96*	*1996-97*	*1997-98*	*1998-99*	*1999-00*	*2000-21*	*2001-02*	*2002-03*	*2003-04*	*Average*
NSE : S&P CNX NIFTY														
April	NA	5.31	2.20	0.93	1.23	1.63	1.61	1.67	3.26	3.51	2.23	1.10	1.36	2.17
May	NA	5.52	1.69	1.07	1.50	1.54	0.85	1.49	2.17	2.64	0.90	1.35	0.75	1.79
June	NA	2.24	1.62	1.25	0.82	1.10	0.86	3.06	1.35	1.48	1.27	1.13	0.94	1.43
July	NA	2.56	1.44	0.65	1.23	1.37	1.38	1.84	1.59	1.76	1.01	1.01	1.05	1.41
August	NA	2.33	1.69	1.04	0.71	1.05	1.54	1.62	1.39	1.07	0.57	0.84	1.51	1.28
September	NA	1.69	1.62	0.81	0.65	1.09	0.93	1.40	1.30	2.04	2.52	0.72	1.81	1.38
October	NA	1.67	1.00	0.67	0.79	1.70	2.99	2.46	2.50	1.59	1.21	0.84	1.53	1.58
November	NA	2.33	1.45	1.09	1.57	1.26	1.66	1,19	1.68	1.44	1.25	0.69	1.30	1.41
December	NA	2.51	2.07	0.97	1.05	1.81	1.37	1.46	1.43	1.42	1.22	0.96	0.97	1.44
January	NA	1.63	2.30	1.47	0.97	2.22	1.49	2.02	2.55	1.21	0.99	0.80	2.18	1.65
February	NA	1.63	2.3	1.47	0.97	2.22	1.49	2.02	2.55	1.21	0.99	0.80	2.18	1.65
March	NA	2.07	1.63	1.48	1.27	2.64	1.61	1.53	1.98	2.90	1.18	1.09	1.48	1.74
NSE: CNX NIFTY JUNIOR														
April	NA	NA	NA	NA	NA	NA	1.26	2.99	3.45	4.55	2.62	0.95	1.16	2.43
May	NA	NA	NA	NA	NA	NA	0.87	2.57	2.06	4.33	1.21	1.74	1.22	2.00
June	NA	NA	NA	NA	NA	NA	0.81	3.85	1.24	2.15	1.30	1.35	1.46	1.74
July	NA	NA	NA	NA	NA	NA	1.50	1.78	1.87	2.07	1.17	1.47	1.48	1.62
August	NA	NA	NA	NA	NA	NA	1.14	1.24	1.59	1.86	0.58	1.03	1.67	1.30
September	NA	NA	NA	NA	NA	NA	0.84	1.06	1.59	2.77	2.68	1.35	1.66	1.71
October	NA	NA	NA	NA	NA	NA	2.43	2.58	2.94	2.30	0.98	1.03	1.65	1.98
November	NA	NA	NA	NA	NA	NA	1.33	1.00	2.31	1.82	0.96	0.61	1.13	1.31
December	NA	NA	NA	NA	NA	NA	1.10	1.31	2.05	2.35	1.82	1.13	1.03	1.54
January	NA	NA	NA	NA	NA	1.81	1.49	1.77	3.34	1.67	0.91	1.05	2.57	1.83
February	NA	NA	NA	NA	NA	1.07	1.38	2.09	2.57	2.41	2.14	1.21	1.78	1.83
March	NA	NA	NA	NA	NA	2.9	2.7	1.84	3.27	3.35	1.11	1.15	1.55	2.18

NA= Not Available/Applicable *Source*: CMIE Markets Issues, July 2002, August 2003 and June 2004, p. 256-259-278; 248-251, 269-272; 248-251, 270-273.

Table 5.2(b): Volatility of NSE Indices of Daily Returns in a Month (Percent)

	1991-92	1992-93	1993-94	1994-95	1995-96	1996-97	1997-98	1998-99	1999-00	2000-21	2001-02	2002-03	2003-04	Average
NSE : S&P CNX MIDCAP 200														
April	NA	NA	NA	NA	NA	1.15	1.69	2.82	3.36	3.4	2.2	0.89	1.22	2.09
May	NA	NA	NA	NA	NA	0.96	0.77	2.66	2.05	2.78	0.94	1.81	0.89	1.61
June	NA	NA	NA	NA	NA	0.99	0.91	3.38	1.22	1.35	1.27	1.48	0.94	1.44
July	NA	NA	NA	NA	NA	0.94	1.31	1.81	1.76	1.79	0.9	1.57	1.28	1.42
August	NA	NA	NA	NA	NA	0.94	1.61	1.37	1.56	1.3	0.38	0.84	1.78	1.22
September	NA	NA	NA	NA	NA	0.62	0.97	1.16	1.58	1.75	2.3	0.83	1.51	1.34
October	NA	NA	NA	NA	NA	1.73	1.14	2.53	2.56	1.42	0.77	0.7	1.46	1.54
November	NA	NA	NA	NA	NA	0.6	1.25	1.02	2.08	1.16	0.78	0.61	1.27	1.09
December	NA	NA	NA	NA	NA	1.35	0.86	1.17	1.96	1.77	1.57	1.04	1.12	1.36
January	NA	NA	NA	NA	NA	2.16	1.54	1.71	2.47	1.05	0.95	1.09	2.63	1.51
February	NA	NA	NA	NA	NA	1.4	1.33	1.84	2	2.38	1.9	1.14	1.79	1.75
March	NA	NA	NA	NA	NA	2.63	2.22	1.64	2.3	3.93	1.09	1.	1.51	1.87
NSE: S&P CNX 500														
April	NA	NA	NA	NA	NA	1.45	1.33	1.95	3.3	3.68	2.53	1.02	1.17	2.05
May	NA	NA	NA	NA	NA	1.12	0.53	2.02	2.03	3.23	1.05	1.5	0.77	1.53
June	NA	NA	NA	NA	NA	0.99	0.82	2.97	1.23	1.64	1.4	1.23	0.87	1.4
July	NA	NA	NA	NA	NA	1.25	0.93	1.75	1.6	2.17	1.05	1.14	1.02	1.36
August	NA	NA	NA	NA	NA	1.02	1.7	1.35	1.36	1.34	0.62	0.75	1.59	1.22
September	NA	NA	NA	NA	NA	0.67	0.91	1.19	1.31	2.28	2.68	0.67	1.89	1.45
October	NA	NA	NA	NA	NA	1.74	1.15	2.36	2.31	1.91	1.32	0.9	1.52	1.65
November	NA	NA	NA	NA	NA	0.83	1.42	1.11	1.95	1.49	1.23	0.54	1.21	1.22
December	NA	NA	NA	NA	NA	1.59	1.09	1.37	1.38	1.89	1.53	1.02	0.92	1.35
January	NA	NA	NA	NA	1.07	2.12	1.38	1.87	2.53	1.42	1.03	0.77	2.55	1.64
February	NA	NA	NA	NA	2.02	1.52	1.23	1.83	2.34	2.18	1.61	0.83	1.8	1.71
March	NA	NA	NA	NA	0.77	2.67	1.79	1.5	2.38	3.6	1.13	0.91	1.48	1.8

NA= Not Available/Applicable *Source*: CMIE Markets Issues, July 2002, August 2003 and June 2004, p. 256-259-278; 248-251, 269-272; 248-251, 270-273.

Table 5.2(c): Volatility of BSE Indices of Daily Returns in a Month (Percent)

	1991-92	1992-93	1993-94	1994-95	1995-96	1996-97	1997-98	1998-99	1999-00	2000-21	2001-02	2002-03	2003-04	Average
						BSE : Sensex								
April	2.04	6.16	2.46	0.82	1.33	1.4	1.46	1.67	3.07	3.83	2.41	0.99	1.21	2.22
May	1.25	5.16	1.89	1.1	1.61	1.39	0.72	1.85	2.14	3.12	0.94	1.55	0.72	1.8
June	1.86	2.21	1.77	1.46	0.88	1.23	0.89	3.09	1.44	1.6	1.28	1.17	1.02	1.53
July	1.8	2.98	1.58	0.72	1.32	1.67	1.09	2.07	1.58	2.14	1.18	1.07	1.04	1.56
August	2.03	2.25	1.83	1.06	0.89	1.25	1.91	1.61	1.34	1.16	0.71	0.91	1.37	1.41
September	2.12	1.98	1.69	0.91	0.67	1.14	1.1	1.64	1.18	2.26	2.73	0.82	1.69	1.52
October	2.08	1.96	0.99	0.71	0.86	1.87	1.34	2.59	2.07	1.61	1.44	0.97	1.44	1.52
November	1.25	2.4	1.47	1.29	1.58	1.29	1.61	1.32	1.79	1.55	1.29	0.68	1.31	1.52
December	1.09	2.77	2.13	1.02	1.15	1.92	1.32	1.52	1.43	1.49	1.33	0.84	0.91	1.45
January	1.72	1.78	2.3	1.43	0.93	2.44	1.52	1.88	2.5	1.32	0.92	0.71	2.05	1.65
February	2.6	2.04	2.48	1.58	2.27	1.91	1.46	1.59	2.43	1.65	1.51	0.79	1.5	1.83
March	8.28	2.4	1.67	1.42	1.29	2.62	1.75	1.88	1.91	2.83	1.32	1.12	1.45	2.3
						BSE 100 INDEX								
April	1.89	2.8	1.93	0.93	1.12	1.2	1.38	1.72	20.01	3.89	2.77	1.07	1.28	3.23
May	0.9	4.89	1.72	0.87	1.15	1.11	0.64	1.91	2.12	3.33	1.07	1.42	0.77	1.68
June	1.3	2.21	1.32	1.12	0.7	0.9	0.9	3.17	1.29	1.78	1.44	1.11	0.92	1.39
July	1.48	2.03	1.31	0.58	1.1	1.19	1.03	1.92	1.61	2.32	1.1	1.09	1	1.37
August	1.88	1.87	1.53	0.9	0.69	1.04	1.82	1.48	1.41	1.34	0.69	0.85	1.62	1.32
September	1.58	1.53	1.38	0.64	0.51	0.66	1.06	1.33	1.25	2.26	2.82	0.71	20.01	1.37
October	1.58	1.31	0.94	0.49	0.78	1.74	1.07	2.53	2.27	2.02	1.37	0.85	1.59	1.42
November	0.96	1.99	1.32	0.89	1.35	1.11	1.65	1.24	1.88	1.59	1.27	0.58	1.24	1.31
December	1.04	2.01	1.75	0.85	0.94	1.8	1.21	1.53	1.3	1.92	1.52	1.06	0.9	1.37
January	1.19	1.41	2.04	1.04	0.84	4.33	1.45	1.93	2.49	1.53	1	0.73	2.56	1.73
February	2.32	1.51	2.03	1.38	2.04	1.79	1.43	1.58	2.7	1.88	1.69	0.84	1.79	1.73
March	8.85	2.12	1.55	1.13	0.98	2.42	1.81	1.8	2.48	3.23	1.13	1.04	1.5	2.31

NA= Not Available/Applicable *Source*: CMIE Markets Issues, July 2002, August 2003 and June 2004, p. 256-259-278; 248-251, 269-272; 248-251, 270-273.

Table 5.2(d): Volatility of BSE Indices of Daily Returns in a Month (Percent)

	1991-92	*1992-93*	*1993-94*	*1994-95*	*1995-96*	*1996-97*	*1997-98*	*1998-99*	*1999-00*	*2000-21*	*2001-02*	*2002-03*	*2003-04*	*Average*
						BSE 200 Index								
April	NA	3.77	1.77	1.23	0.98	1.26	1.36	1.78	2.92	3.7	2.66	1.21	1.17	1.98
May	NA	5.75	1.34	1.09	1.66	1.57	0.55	1.99	2.09	3.16	1.03	1.3	0.78	1.82
June	NA	2.49	1.28	1.16	0.68	1.02	0.86	3.02	1.26	1.65	1.39	1.18	0.9	1.41
July	NA	2.21	1.16	0.55	1.11	1.32	0.98	1.78	1.61	2.16	1.06	1.15	1.02	1.34
August	NA	2.17	1.29	1.08	0.63	1.03	1.72	1.34	1.44	1.31	0.66	0.77	1.62	1.25
September	NA	1.56	1.5	0.63	.051	0.8	0.93	1.24	1.23	2.22	2.77	0.62	1.96	1.35
October	NA	1.39	0.78	0.56	0.75	1.68	1.01	2.38	2.29	1.94	1.26	0.92	1.56	1.37
November	NA	1.79	1.18	0.8	1.31	0.93	1.52	1.14	1.85	1.54	1.17	0.55	1.22	1.25
December	NA	1.9	1.45	0.89	0.77	1.61	1.12	1.4	1.21	1.87	1.47	1.04	0.88	1.3
January	NA	1.25	2.31	1.01	0.73	2.16	1.38	1.78	2.38	1.44	0.96	0.72	2.53	1.55
February	NA	1.16	1.99	1.32	2.07	1.65	1.35	1.47	2.43	2.82	1.84	0.79	1.77	1.64
March	NA	2.41	6.31	1.02	0.09	2.43	1.79	1.71	2.36	3.16	1.21	0.92	1.47	2.14
						BSE 500 INDEX								
April	NA	NA	NA	NA	NA	NA	NA	NA	2.89	3.59	2.6	1.18	1.16	2.28
May	NA	NA	NA	NA	NA	NA	NA	NA	2.07	3/06	1	1.39	0.79	1.66
June	NA	NA	NA	NA	NA	NA	NA	NA	1.23	1.63	1.37	1.21	0.9	1.27
July	NA	NA	NA	NA	NA	NA	NA	NA	2.34	2.08	1.04	1.19	1.05	1.54
August	NA	NA	NA	NA	NA	NA	NA	NA	1.48	1.32	0.64	0.77	1.66	1.17
September	NA	NA	NA	NA	NA	NA	NA	NA	1.22	2.26	2.73	0.64	1.89	1.75
October	NA	NA	NA	NA	NA	NA	NA	NA	2.34	1.9	1.21	0.9	1.55	1.58
November	NA	NA	NA	NA	NA	NA	NA	NA	1.84	1.51	1.17	0.54	1.24	1.26
December	NA	NA	NA	NA	NA	NA	NA	NA	1.3	1.87	1.47	1.04	0.9	1.32
January	NA	NA	NA	NA	NA	NA	NA	NA	2.35	1.41	0.94	0.74	2.59	1.61
February	NA	NA	NA	NA	NA	NA	NA	1.56	2.36	1.81	1.82	0.83	1.77	1.69
March	NA	NA	NA	NA	NA	NA	NA	1.71	2.37	3.13	1.19	0.92	1.48	1.8

NA= Not Available/Applicable *Source*: CMIE Markets Issues, July 2002, August 2003 and June 2004, p. 256-259-278; 248-251, 269-272; 248-251, 270-273.

in Table-5.4. The Mean Market Capitalization of NSE and BSE are Rs. 65,22,127.90 and Rs. 75,75,690.00 respectively. We observed that the BSE Mean Capitalization is greater than the NSE. The capitalization of stock market is influenced by price movements in the market. If the stock prices are bullish the Market Capitalization will increase proportionately in relation to the price changes. The Market Capitalization of NSE has increased by 6.32times in 2003-04 when compared to 1994-95. Whereas the Market Capitalization of BSE has increased by 2.4 times for the same period. The increased Market Capitalization in NSE may be on account of greater volatility of stock prices coupled with coverage of companies.

It is also evident from the values of Co-efficient of Variation and Standard Deviation that the Market Capitalization of NSE was highly volatile or less consistent when compared to BSE.

5.7.5. Turnover

Turnover of NSE and BSE is presented in Table 5.5. It is observed that the Turnover of stock exchanges directly and indirectly influences for greater volatility of stock prices. The Turnover of stock exchange transactions will also indicate depth of the market. So, that the market can absorb increased selling pressure as well as demand for buying securities. Turnover will also add for increased business activity in the stock exchange. The dynamic capital market will always have increased Turnover over a period of time. If there was decline in the Turnover due to bear hammering in the stock market. Prices will fall abnormally and causes for greater volatility and creates risk to the investors.

The Turnover of NSE was at Rs. 10,99,533.00 crores and that of BSE Rs. 5,03,290.00 crores in the year 2003-04 as compared to Rs. 1,806 crores and Rs. 66,576.00 crores in 1994-95. On the other hand the BSE Turnover has risen nearly 7.5 times during the same period. A significant feature is that in both the stock exchanges the Turnover was highest in 2000-02 when compared to rest of the period. There was greater crash in the market prices and caused for lowest amount of Turnover indicating -78.7 and -69.7 decline in Turnover of NSE and BSE respectively in 2001-02. This crash in the market prices was on account of Kethan Parekh Stock Market Scam, coupled with bearish trend in the markets along with various other factors. Moreover the Turnover of BSE was more inconsistent when compared to NSE. However, both of them have shown wide fluctuations in the Turnover under the influence of various Economic, Political factors and Scams etc.

5.7.6. Number of New Listings:

The listing of securities will provide the investors not only the market-ability but also liquidity. On account of listing of securities the floating stock and number of listed companies will increase and facilitates for increased demand for buying of securities. The data relating to listing of securities and the annual growth rate is presented in Table-5.6.

The number of companies listed in National Stock Exchange was 1565 in the year 1994-95 of which around 72% were listed in BSE as against 28% in NSE. However there was a perceptible decline in total listed companies to 232 in the year 2003-04 of which 54% were listed in BSE and 46% were listed in NSE. The share of NSE in total listed companies has increased from 28.31% to 45.76% as against a steep fall from 73% to 54% in BSE.

Thus it indicates that the numbers of companies listed have declined abnormally over a decade and the share of NSE as increased significantly and equating with that of BSE listed companies. The analysis of data relating to Standard Deviation and Co-efficient of Variation reveals that both the values are reflecting wider fluctuations in listed companies. But relatively less inconsistency is evident in the case of NSE rather than BSE.

5.7.7. Number of Scrips and Shares Traded Daily

Table-5.7 and5.8 shows the volatility of number of scrips and shares traded daily on NSE and BSE respectively. Volatility of scrips on NSE recorded at 1.20 times to 0.22 times over a period of 1994-95 to 2003-04. The highest volatility of 1.68 times recorded at NSE in the year 2000-01. The various reasons for the highest volatility in that year were already discussed in the previous sections of the study. The volatility rate varied in between 1.80 to 0.46 at BSE over the same study period. This trend represents that the number of scrips traded daily recorded higher fluctuations in BSE over the NSE.

Table 5.3(a): NSE Indices-Top 20 Volatile Months (Percent)

Rank	S&P CNX NIFTY		CNX NIFTY Junior		CNX Midcap 200		S&P CNX 500	
	Month	Volatility	Month	Volatility	Month	Volatility	Month	Volatility
1	May-92	5.52	Apr-00	4.55	Mar-00	3.93	Apr-00	3.63
2	Apr-92	5.31	May-00	4.33	Apr-00	3.40	May-01	3.60
3	Apr-00	3.51	Jun-98	3.85	Jun-98	3.38	Apr-99	3.30
4	Apr-99	3.26	Apr-99	3.45	Apr-99	3.36	May-00	3.23
5	Jun-98	3.06	Mar-01	3.35	Apr-98	2.82	Jun-98	2.97
6	Oct-97	2.99	Jan-00	3.34	May-98	2.66	Sep-01	2.68
7	Mar-01	2.90	Mar-00	3.27	Mar-97	2.63	Mar-99	2.67
8	Mar-97	2.64	Apr-98	2.99	Jan-03	2.63	Jan-04	2.55
9.	May-00	2.64	Oct-99	2.94	Oct-99	2.56	Jan-00	2.53
10	Feb-96	2.59	Mar-97	2.90	Oct-98	2.53	Apr-01	2.53
11	Jul-92	2.56	Sep-00	2.77	Jan-00	2.47	Mar-00	2.38
12	Mar-00	2.55	Mar-98	2.70	Feb-00	2.38	Oct.98	2.36
13	Sep-01	2.52	Sep-01	2.68	Apr-01	2.30	Feb-00	2.34
14.	Dec-92	2.51	Apro-01	2.62	Sep-01	2.30	Oct-99	2.31
15.	Oct-99	2.50	Oct-98	2.58	Mar-98	2.22	Sep-00	2.28
16	Oct-98	2.46	My-98	2.57	Apr-01	2.20	Feb-01	2.18
17	Feb-94	2.44	Jan-04	2.57	Jan-97	2.16	Jul-00	2.17
18	Aug-92	2.33	Feb-00	2.57	Nov-99	2.08	Jan-97	2.12
19	Nov-92	2.33	Oct-97	2.43	May-99	2.05	May-99	2.03
20	Jan-94	2.30	Feb-00	2.41	Feb-00	2.00	May-98	2.02

Source: CMIE Markets Issues, July 2002, August 2003 and June 2004, p. 256-259-278; 248-251, 269-272; 248-251, 270-273.

Table 5.3(b): BSE Indices-Top 20 Volatile Months (Percent)

Rank	BSE Sensex		BSE 100 Index		BSE 200 Index		BSE 500 Index	
	Month	*Volatility*	*Month*	*Volatility*	*Month*	*Volatility*	*Month*	*Volatility*
1	Mar-92	8.28	Apr-98	20.01	Mar-94	6.31	Apro-00	3.59
2	Apr-92	6.16	Mar-92	8.85	May-92	5.75	Mar-01	3.13
3	May-92	5.16	May-92	4.89	Apr-92	3.77	May-00	3.06
4	Apro-00	3.83	Jan-97	4.33	Apro-00	3.70	Apri-99	2.89
5	May-00	3.12	Apr-00	3.89	May-00	3.16	Sep-01	2.73
6	Jun-98	3.09	May-00	3.33	Mar-01	3.16	Apr-01	2.60
7	Apr-99	3.07	Mar-01	3.23	Jun-98	3.02	Jan-04	2.59
8	Ju-92	2.98	Jun-98	3.17	Apr-99	2.92	Mar-00	2.37
9.	Mar-01	2.83	Sep-01	2.82	Sep-01	2.77	Feb-00	2.36
10	Dec-92	2.77	Apr-92	2.80	Apr-01	2.66	Jan-00	2.35
11	Sep-01	2.73	Apr-01	2.77	Jan-04	2.53	Oct-99	2.34
12	Mar-97	2.62	Feb-00	2.70	Jun-92	2.49	Jul-99	2.34
13	Feb-92	2.60	Jan-04	2.56	Mar-97	2.43	Sep-00	2.26
14.	Oct-98	2.59	Oct-98	2.53	Feb-00	2.43	Jul-00	2.08
15.	Jan-00	2.50	Jan-00	2.49	Mar-93	2.41	May-99	2.07
16	Feb-94	2.48	Mar-00	2.48	Oct-98	2.38	Oct-00	1.90
17	Apr-93	2.46	Mar-97	2.42	Jan-00	2.38	Sep-03	1.89
18	Jan-97	2.44	Sep-00	2.36	Jan-94	2.36	dec-00	1.87
19	Feb-00	2.43	Feb-92	2.32	Mar-00	2.36	Nov-99	1.84
20	Apr-01	2.41	July-00	2.32	Jan-94	2.31	Feb-02	1.82

Source: CMIE Markets Issues, July 2002, August 2003 and June 2004, p. 256-259-278; 248-251, 269-272; 248-251, 270-273.

Volatility in number of shares traded daily on NSE and BSE varies between 1.90 to 1.24 and 2.00 to 1.32 respectively. This represents that the volatility rate in BSE is greater than that of NSE. The highest rate of volatility was recorded at NSE in the year 2000-01 but in the case of BSE 1996-97. The pattern of volatility was of these two stock exchanges are nearly similar in the rest of the study period.

Table 5.4: Market Capitalisation (MC) at NSE and BSE

(Rs. Crore)

	NSE		*BSE*	
Year	*MC*	*% of Change*	*MC*	*% of Change*
1991-92	NA	NA	NA	NA
1992-93	NA	NA	NA	NA
1993-94	NA	NA	NA	NA
1994-95	1710115	NA	4761982	NA
1995-96	4492715	162.64	10218708	114.59
1996-97	5131078	14.21	5829416	–42.95
1997-98	5596796	9.08	6370552	9.28
1998-99	5296796	–5.37	5984128	–6.06
1999-00	8718711	64.63	8754348	46.29
2000-01	9247468	6.06	8555791	-2.27
2001-02	6966767	-24.66	6531011	-23.66
2002-03	7398448	6.19	7224801	10.62
2003-04	10661885	44.11	11526163	59.54
Mean	6522127.90		7575690.00	
SD	2622923.64		2137182.56	
CV	40.22		28.21	

NA = Not Available/Applicable.

Source: CMIE, Capital Markets Issues, July 2002, August 2003 and June.

5.7.8. Number of Transactions

The volatility in number of transactions recorded at NSE and BSE are presented in Table-5.9. Volatility at NSE and BSE are varies between 2.00 to 1.29 and 2.00 to 1.28 respectively. The highest and lowest volatilities were recorded at NSE and BSE are nearly similar. So that the responding pattern of NSE and BSE are same in the case of number of transactions

Table 5.5: Turnover of NSE and BSE (Rs. Crore)

	NSE		*BSE*	
Year	*Turnover*	*% of Change*	*Turnover*	*% of Change*
1991-92	NA	NA	NA	NA
1992-93	NA	NA	45,695	NA
1993-94	NA	NA	84,536	85
1994-95	1,806	NA	66,576	-21
1995-96	67,288	3,266	50,054	-25
1996-97	294,503	338	124,284	148
1997-98	370,195	26	196,848	58
1998-99	414,474	12	312,000	58
1999-00	839,050	102	685,032	120
2000-01	2,413,510	188	1,000,030	46
2001-02	513,167	-79	304,898	-70
2002-03	617,988	20	313,584	3
2003-04	1,099,533	78	503,290	61
Mean	663,151		307,236	
SD	698,065		293,709	
CV	95		105	

NA = Not Available/Applicable.

Source: CMIE, Capital Markets Issues, July 2002, August 2003 and June 2004, p. 252-254 and 274-276.

5.7.9. Impact of Budget on Capital Market Volatility

Table-5.10 shows the pre and post budget Sensex movement over a period of thirteen years. Percentage change in pre and post budget ranges between 24.61 to -10.87 and 48.28 to -19.06 respectively. We observed that the year 1992 is the highest volatile year in the pre as well as post budget percentage change on the BSE Sensex.

Table 5.6: Number of New Listings (NNL) On NSE and BSE

	NSE		BSE		
Year	*NNL*	*% to Total*	*NNL*	*% to Total*	*Total*
1991-92	NA	NA	NA	NA	NA
1992-93	NA	NA	NA	NA	NA
1993-94	NA	NA	NA	NA	NA
1994-95	443	28.31	1122	71.69	1565
1995-96	598	32.12	1264	67.88	1862
1996-97	230	30.91	514	69.90	744
1997-98	48	41.10	66	57.90	114
1998-99	24	35.29	44	64.71	68
1999-00	49	42.61	66	57.39	115
2000-01	55	30.90	123	69.10	178
2001-02	16	41.03	23	58.97	39
2002-03	21	28.38	53	71.62	74
2003-04	27	45.76	32	54.24	59
Mean	151.10		330.70		481.80
SD	207.68		478.11		684.88
CV	137.44		144.57		142.15

NA = Not Available/Applicable.

Source: CMIE, Capital Markets Issue, June 2004, p. 266 and 289.

The logic beyond the volatile trend of stock market Index is influenced the expectations of the investors and other players in the stock exchange. These expectations are turned up into scenarios. There are three important scenarios that investors must make a note of them. Firstly, when the positive expectations ahead of the budget are not met in the budget. Secondly, when the expectations are met. In this scenario, investors buy on the pre-budget expectations and book profits when the expectations are met. In the third scenario, when some new positive announcements are made other than expectations already discounted before the budget, the sentiment turns bullish and investors start buying unlike in the previous two scenarios.

Table 5.7: Number of Scrips Traded Daily on NSE and BSE

	NSE			*BSE*		
Year	*Highest*	*Lowest*	*Volatility*	*Highest*	*Lowest*	*Volatility*
1991-92	NA	NA	NA	1457	365	1.20
1992-93	NA	NA	NA	1594	117	1.73
1993-94	NA	NA	NA	1904	731	0.89
1994-95	501	125	1.20	2738	1706	0.46
1995-96	1097	472	0.80	4022	1588	0.87
1996-97	1306	705	0.60	3957	1630	0.83
1997-98	1330	586	0.78	2544	1092	0.80
1998-99	1225	655	0.61	2394	622	1.18
1999-00	1145	886	0.26	2868	1122	0.88
2000-01	1023	88	1.68	2079	757	0.93
2001-02	898	417	0.73	1717	90	1.80
2002-03	804	636	0.23	2188	1096	0.67
2003-04	751	603	0.22	2297	1270	0.58

NA = Not Available/Applicable.

Source: CMIE Capital Markets Issue, June 2004, p. 265 and 288.

However, relevance of the budget effect is diminishing every year because of the critical policy decisions are taken on a regular basis by the government. The government has already taken steps to encourage equity investments earlier like abolition of long-term capital gains tax. Therefore it can be highlighted that the markets are every sensitive and they can react for any negative/ positive implications of budgets.

5.8: MEASURES FOR MINIMIZATION OF STOCK MARKET VOLATILITY

The following measures are suggested for the minimization

Table 5.8: Number of Shares Traded Daily on NSE and BSE

Year	NSE			BSE		
	Highest	Lowest	Volatility	Highest	Lowest	Volatility
1991-92	NA	NA	NA	NA	NA	NA
1992-93	NA	NA	NA	NA	NA	NA
1993-94	NA	NA	NA	NA	NA	NA
1994-95	12,691,990	558,390	2	29,678,820	873,085	2
1995-96	74,342,305	2,012,110	2	57,087,705	1,047,470	2
1996-97	110,353,450	13,647,075	2	63,240,468	8,900	2
1997-98	92,743,575	11,902,055	2	69,143,641	14,180,157	1
1998-99	129,340,266	11,434,020	2	104,142,273	9,463,754	2
1999-00	161,907,709	38,056,521	1	140,653,463	26,150,175	1
2000-01	282,002,526	775,745	2	228,851,064	24,782,046	2
2001-02	216,437;757	3,134,703	2	140,080,913	688,407	2
2002-03	277,677,113	41,535,438	1	206,914,501	24,941,842	2
2003-04	649,247,895	96,030,125	1	396,332,003	51,414,097	2

NA = Not Available/Applicable.

Source: CMIE Capital Markes Issue, June 2004, p. 267 and 290.

of volatility of Stock Price Indices for maintaining stability in the prices of stock market in particular and investors in general. They are: (i) SEBI have to plays an important role for the reduction of volatility of stock price indices in India. The SEBI has rigorously monitor and control by strengthening its pro-active and reactive measures for the control of stock price volatility. SEBI can direct the authorities of stock exchanges to minimize volatility by applying circuit break system from time to time if there are noticeable fluctuations due to price rigging and unwarranted speculation and (ii) Directly and indirectly the Central Government and the Finance Ministry plays a key role in the economy. The controversial announcements are to be avoided in order to eliminate the uncertainties in the minds of the market players about the future.

Table 5.9: Number of Transactions on NSE and BSE

Year	NSE			BSE		
	Highest	*Lowest*	*Volatility*	*Highest*	*Lowest*	*Volatility*
1991-92	NA	NA	NA	NA	NA	NA
1992-93	NA	NA	NA	NA	NA	NA
1993-94	NA	NA	NA	NA	NA	NA
1994-95	NA	NA	NA	121848	4732	1.85
1995-96	NA	NA	NA	235954	5268	1.91
1996-97	216541	27536	1.55	199730	6	2.00
1997-98	244184	35479	1.49	170009	35233	1.31
1998-99	420829	0	2.00	262452	31121	1.58
1999-00	799968	134527	1.42	659657	97098	1.49
2000-01	1378379	5498	1.98	1066457	147194	1.51
2001-02	1257601	35646	1.89	779110	3680	1.98
2002-03	1396840	298567	1.30	783755	170725	1.28
2003-04	2224148	477109	1.29	1289970	271472	1.30

NA = Not Available/Applicable.

Source: CMIE Capital Markets Issue, June 2004, p. 268 and 291.

SECTION-II

RELATIONSHIP BETWEEN VOLATILITY AND LIQUIDITY

5.9: INTRODUCTION

The universe of stock markets is increasing by expanding in the world of finance. Stock market is significant as a source of wealth creation and fuelling real sector growth through equity participation. Volatility in the equity prices became a cause of concern for investors find mobilizers and regulatory bodies. In order to become vigilant on price volatility it is necessary to depend on few reliable indicators which will reflect such volatility. This study looks into the impact of liquidity of equity markets price volatility as one of the measures. For this purpose the movements in BSE SENSEX and NSE S&P CNX NIFTY indices were analyzed from the year 1995-96 to 2003-04 to find out how often the liquidity has consistently influencing the volatility or not.

Table 5.10: Pre & Post Budget Sensex Movement

Budget Year & Month	*% Change Pre Budget*	*% Change Post Budget*
1991, July	8.73	27.02
1992, February	24.61	38.28
1993, February	8.40	-19.06
1994, February	4.51	-12.36
1995, March	-0.57	-0.14
1996, February	22.53	-4.34
1996, July	-4.21	-9.94
1997, February	-4.89	6.87
1998, June	-10.87	-12.36
1999, February	-3.58	13.90
2000, February	10.28	-11.12
2001, February	-3.89	-6.92
2002, February	11.70	-6.38
2003, March	-5.08	-5.78
2004, February	-5.49	2.57
2004, July	-0.13	5.59

The above movement gives a way one month return before and after the budget.

Source: Dalal Street, Feb. 21-March 6, 2005, Vol. xx.No.5, p. 67.

In an uncertain world of capital markets the only certain phenomenon is change. Nowhere, does this oft repeated clich_ stand a greater testimony than in the world of capital markets. Stock market prices are subject to market dynamics. Forces of demand and supply trigger -in variations in price quotes on the bourses. Large degree of price variations can cause uncertainty in future prices. Financial experts proclaim that future being uncertain; the risk-reward equation should carry a justifiable premium on the financial instruments. To be able to arrive at stock valuations commensurate with the risk, an estimation of risk or the uncertainty element is required.

5.10: STAKEHOLDERS IN THE STOCK MARKET VOLATILITY AND LIQUIDITY

Different investor groups have a stake in market volatility. For risk averse investors, when prices fluctuate sharply over a short span of even one trading day, it looks puzzling to justify this on the basis of fundamental economic factors. The speculative investor keeps track of volatility levels to make trading profits through differentials in intra day price swings. If most of investing community is risk averse, sustained levels of high volatility would scarce away investments, affecting thereby, the depth of market. For regulatory agencies, market volatility is an indicator of the degree of instability present in markets. Regulators need to initiate risk containment measures to check possible defaults arising out of volatile swings and ensure that, even in volatile conditions, market are safe to invest in from a liquidity point of view.

Investments are to create surplus wealth through profits. With a given level of investment, profits can be generated by additional value creation. Such value creation may require long term lock-in of investor savings. But investor behavior would be to have control over their savings; implying investments should be as liquid as possible. Liquid stock markets allow investors to acquire the best possible liquid asset -equity shares. In an era of dematerialized shares and electronic trading, equity can be disposed off conveniently if investors want to convert their savings into cash or want to alter their investment portfolio. Companies, too, see equity markets to their advantage as a long term source of capital. Liquidity thus makes equity investments less risky (in terms of easy exit option), improves efficient allocation of capital and enhances long term growth prospects. Liquidity in securities market is meaningful notion only when it results in ease of entry and exit. Entry and exit in stocks are more liquid when there is an increasing trend of traded quantity. Trading quantity is an indicator of the depth of liquidity in this study.

5.11: THEORETICAL RELATIONSHIP BETWEEN VOLATILITY AND LIQUIDITY

The demand- supply paradigm of classical economics finds a place in a circular liquidity-volatility relationship. Let us say, adverse news triggers off a sell pressure in scrip. Markets would be faced with excess sell orders. Higher volumes of sell - side will be offered at gradually declining ask prices. When prices stoop below fair price, contrarian's traders step into the market. They estimate that prices have fallen below justified levels and expect prices to rebound at a later stage. They buy in bear markets. Increasing buy volumes by contrarians absorbs the excessive sell side volumes. Thus volatile prices have enhanced liquidity. Demand for higher volumes with every fall in price, creates a buy pressure. Investors will research for a stage where all excess supply is soaked up and a further demand for purchase of shares will only push up the share price. Panic selling has been neutralized. Now, supply side falling short, contrarians will bid-up prices to entice more supply of shares. Hence demand for more liquidity contains one sided price fall but will cause some degree of volatility in share prices. Prices surge on a buy side demand. Supply of shares by investors is want to exit at rising prices increases till the point that there would be a glut of sellers exceeding the immediate demand. That would turn down prices again, this time in a correction mode. The following Figure-5.1 is shows the relationship between liquidity and volatility.

Figure-5.1: Relationship between Liquidity and Volatility

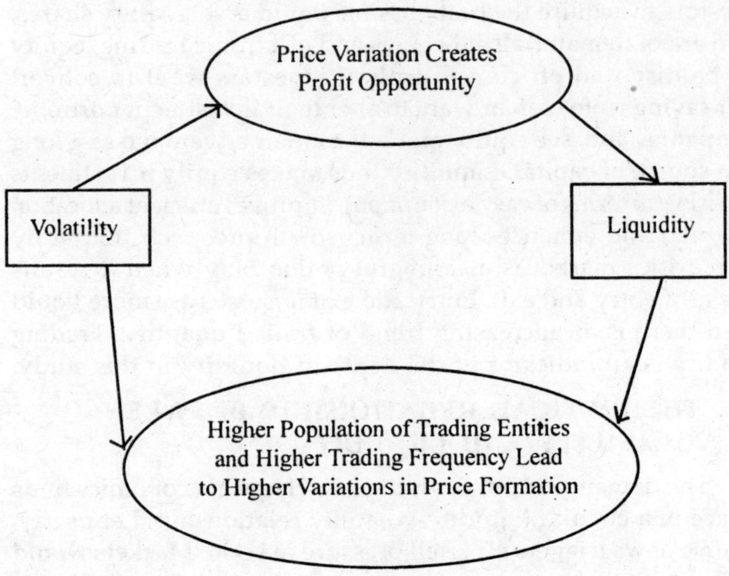

5.12: VOLATILITY IN THE INDIAN STOCK MARKETS

Table-5.11 shows the volatility in the Indian stock market. For the purpose of the study, we have taken the two prominent stock market indices i.e. BSE Sensex and NSE S&P CNX Nifty. The average rate of volatility on the BSE Sensex and NSE Nifty was recorded at 1.58% and 1.57% respectively. Two indices were showing the similar trend i.e. from the year 1995-96 to 2000-01 and 2003-04 also recorded the increasing trend expect in the year 1997-98. However, year 2001-02 to 2002-03 were recorded the decreasing trend. Finally this is also proved by the positive correlation (i.e. +0.97) between the two stock indexes. This positive correlation indicates that there is a strong positive relationship between two indices and reflects the similar pattern and it also proved by the t-test.

Table 5.11: Volatility in the Indian Stock Markets

Year	*BSE Sensex (%)*	*NSE S&P CNX NIFTY (%)*
1995-96	1.32	1.32
1996-97	1.75	1.66
1997-98	1.41	1.52
1998-99	1.93	1.85
1999-00	1.95	1.93
2000-01	2.14	1.98
2001-02	1.50	1.40
2002-03	1.01	0.99
2003-04	1.35	1.43
2004-05	1.48	15.69
Total	15.84	15.69
Average	1.58	1.57
Correlation		0.97
t-Test		11.29
t0.05		2.31

Source: CMIE Capital Markets, June 2005, p. 248, and 272.

5.13: LIQUIDITY IN THE INDIAN STOCK MARKETS

There are various indicators of judging stock market liquidity. Following three ratios are prominently used to measure the liquidity:

One commonly used measure is the Turn Over Ratio (TOR), which is the value of shares traded divided by the market capitalization. It measures the trading of shares relative to the size of the market. The higher the TOR better is the liquidity of the stock market.

The second measure is the Traded Value Ratio (TVR), which is the total value of domestic shares traded divided by the GDP. TVR is a broader concept than TOR because it captures trading relative to the size of the economy rather than the size of the stock market. A liquid market will have a large TVR.

Table 5.12: Liquidity in the Indian Stock Markets

Year	BSE (%)				NSE(%)			
	TOR	TVR	MCAP/ GDP	SINDEX	TOR	TVR	MCAP/ GDP	SINDEX
1995-96	8.88	4.66	52.53	22.02	16.76	6.27	37.41	20.14
1996-97	24.59	9.99	40.62	25.07	70.44	23.75	33.72	42.64
1997-98	32.86	14.90	45.33	31.03	76.88	26.63	34.64	46.05
1998-99	50.16	19.44	38.77	36.12	84.38	25.93	30.73	47.01
1999-00	75.20	38.96	51.81	55.32	82.23	47.62	57.92	62.59
2000-01	174.97	52.55	30.03	85.85	203.62	70.39	34.57	102.86
2001-02	50.19	14.70	29.28	31.39	80.58	24.54	30.46	45.19
2002-03	54.89	13.96	25.44	31.43	115.05	27.47	23.88	55.47
2003-04	41.88	19.93	47.59	36.47	98.09	43.57	44.41	62.02
Total	513.62	189.09	361.40	354.70	828.03	296.17	327.74	483.97
Average	57.07	21.01	40.16	39.41	92.00	32.91	36.42	53.78
Correlaton between BSE Sindex and NSE Sindex								0.93

Source: SEBI, Economic Survey 2002-03 and 2003-04.

The third indicator is the Market capitalization to GDP ratio, which is an indicator of the size of the stock market. As a country's economy develops, the size of its stock market is expected to grow.

Demirgue-Kunt and Levine (1996) in their study that they used to measure the stock market development by taking an aggregate index called SINDEX[1]. Later, in another study Samal (1997) also followed this technique for the period from 1991-92 to 1995-96. Similarly, in the present study a SINDEX is also been constructed and analyzed.

Liquidity of the Indian stock markets as reflected by different ratios is presented in the Table-5.12. It is evident from the data that, TOR and TVR on the two stock exchanges have shown an increasing trend till 2000-01 and exhibited sharp fall in 2001-02. So far Mcap to GDP ratio is concerned it went through a roller coaster ride during the same period. But all these ratios exhibited an upward trend during 2003-04 when that the stock market volatility is very high compared with previous year. This is due to flow of funds from FIIs. They have pumped a maximum of Rs. 4,57,645 Billion in that year. The average TOR and TVR on the two exchanges were recorded at 57.07%, 92.00% and 21.01%, 32.91% respectively. NSE had the higher TOR and TVR when we compare with similar ratios of the BSE. But in the case of Mcap to GDP ratio it is a reversal trend.

The average of the three ratios referred to as SINDEX represents the liquidity of stock exchanges. The higher the rate of SINDEX was observed on the NSE with 53.78% and 39.41% on the BSE. This represents that the NSE is more liquid than that of BSE. The liquidity relationship between the two stock exchange prices was recorded a positive correlation with +0.93. The high degree of positive relationship will reflect the same rate of direction of change in both leading capital markets in India.

5.14: THE RELATIONSHIP BETWEEN VOLATILITY AND LIQUIDITY

The data relevant to the relationship between volatility and liquidity was presented in the Table-5.13. Based on data the following broad trends can be emerged:

5.14.1. Evidences from BSE

- Volatility has been recorded an upward trend from the year 1995-96 to 2000-01 except in the year 1997-98 and the following two years witnessed a declined trend and it was increased in the last year of the study i.e. 2003-04.
- Up to the year 2000-01 liquidity was recorded an upward direction, in the next one year it was declined and in the last two years of the study it was increased.
- From the year 1995-96 to 2000-01 the volatility and liquidity were increased side by side except in the year 1997-98,

Table 5.13: Relationship between Volatility and Liquity

Year	*BSE Sensex (%)*		*NSE S&P CNX Nifty (%)*	
	Volatility	*Liquidity*	*Volatility*	*Liquidity*
1995-96	1.32	22.02	1.32	20.14
1996-97	1.75	25.07	1.66	42.64
1997-98	1.41	31.03	1.52	46.05
1998-99	1.93	36.12	1.85	47.01
1999-00	1.95	55.32	1.93	62.59
2000-01	2.14	85.85	1.98	102.86
2001-02	1.50	31.39	1.40	45.19
2002-03	1.01	31.43	0.99	55.47
2003-04	1.35	36.47	1.43	62.02
Total	14.36	354.70	14.08	483.97
Average	1.60	39.41	1.56	53.78
Correlation	0.66		0.49	
t (calculated)	3.1		1.71	
t0.05 (Table Value)		2.4		

Note: * = SINDEX Value.

Source: CMIE Capital Markets Isse 2004-05, SEBI, Economic Survey.

the volatility has declined. But in the next two years volatility has decreased and in the last year of the study it was recovered. While in the case of liquidity only in the year 2001-02 it has declined and after that has increased.

- Another important observation is that the year 2000-01 has witnessed the higher rate of volatility (2.14%) and liquidity (85.85%).
- The coefficient of correlation between volatility and liquidity is +0.66. The calculated value (3.1) of t is higher than the table value (2.4), the correlation is significant. Hence, the volatility is causing for the liquidity of the stock market prices and vice versa.

5.14.2. Evidences from the NSE

* Volatility has shown an upward trend from the year 1995-96 to 2000-01 except in the year 1997-98. Next two years (from 2000-01) witnessed a declined trend followed by an increase in the last year of the study.
* Up to the year 2000-01 liquidity has recorded an upward direction, in the next one year it has declined and in the last two year of the study it has increased. This indicates a similar pattern like volatility.
* From the year 1995-96 to 2000-01 the volatility and liquidity has increased side by side except in the year 1997-98, whereas in this year with regard volatility has declined. But in the next two years volatility has decreased. In the case of liquidity only in the year 2001-02 it has declined but in the later years it has increased.
* A significant observation is that the year 2000-01 is witnessed the higher volatility (1.98%) and liquidity (102.86%).
* The coefficient of correlation between volatility and liquidity is at +0.49. The calculated value (1.71) of t is less than the table value (2.4), the correlation is not significant. Hence, the volatility is not causing for the liquidity of the stock market prices and vice versa.

SECTION-III

THE IMPACT OF FOREIGN INSTITUTIONAL INVESTMENT ON STOCK MARKET LIQUIDITY AND VOLATILITY

5.15: INTRODUCTION

Stock market liberalization is a decision by a country's Government to allow purchase of shares in that country's stock market (Henry, 2000). The process of economic reforms was initiated to liberalize the Indian economy and to integrate it with the global economy. One of the immediate effects of capital inflows from foreign countries on the stock market is the boom that causes in the stock price indices. In fact, in the nineties, the stock market boom in several emerging economies has coincided by the increase of capital inflows to these countries (Levine, 1996). The external sector reforms in India during the 1990s included a market based exchange rate system, introduction of convertibility of rupee for external transactions on the current account and compositional shift in cross-boarder capital inflows from debt creating to non-debt creating flows. The overall approach of prudence was integrated into the process of growing openness and financial liberalization which were basic elements of the package of structural reforms instituted in the wake of the balance of payments crisis of 1991. In order to strengthen the external sector reforms and to benefit from these measures, complementary reforms were introduced in other segments of the economy as well (Report on Currency and Finance, 2003-04).

As a part of the reform process, the Government of India opened up the Indian capital market to global competition and took measures to initiate structural reforms by putting in place the requisite regulatory and supervisory structure in the form of SEBI. In a move towards current account convertibility and to increase foreign exchange inflows, Foreign Institutional Investors (FIIs) were permitted to invest in the tradable Indian securities such as shares, debentures, bonds, mutual fund units etc. through primary and secondary markets as per guidelines issued by Government of India in September 1992. Financial liberalization improves stock market liquidity on one hand and volatility on the other. This section examines the positive (liquidity) and negative (volatility) impact on the stock market by the investment of FIIs in the country.

5.16: REGULATORY INITIATIVES

The FIIs were allowed to invest in all the securities traded on the primary and secondary markets, including shares, debentures and warrants issued by companies which were listed or were to be listed on the stock exchanges in India and in the schemes floated by domestic mutual funds from September 14, 1992. The sequences of important reforms and regulations related to FIIs were presented as follows:

Chronology of Important Regulations Related to FIIs

Month & Year	*Important Regulations*
Nov. 1995	The Securities and Exchange Board of India Act. 1992 institutionalized the FII Regulations, known as the Securities and Exchange Board of India (Foreign Institutional Investors) Regulations, Nov. 14, 1995, allowing Pension Funds or Investment Trusts, incorporated outside India.
Oct. 1996	(1) University Fund, Endowments, Foundations or Charitable Trust or Charitable Societies were considered eligible for being registered as FIIs.
	(2) FIIs were allowed to invest in unlisted companies.
	(3) Equity share investment on own account and on behalf of sub-accounts increased to 10% from 5%, of total capital issue of a company.
	(4) Custodians asked to become members of the clearing houses/clearing corporations of the stock exchange(s) and participate in the clearing and settlement process through the clearing house/ clearing corporation for all securities.
Feb. 1997	Proprietary FIIs were included as eligible FIIs (for FII and sub-account).
Nov. 1997	SEBI allowed institutional investors, FIIs, Stock Brokers, Stock Exchanges etc., to make use of the facility of ware housing of trades.
Dec. 1997	(1) FIIs mandated to meet certain criteria of proving to be a fit and proper person.

(2) Mandatory for FIIs having securities of Rs. 10 Crore or more, as on the latest balance sheet date, to settle their transactions only through dematerialized securities from Jan. 15, 1998.

Apr. 1998 (1) The Gilts Market was opened up to FII investment.

(2) Investments in Treasury Bills and Dated Government Securities were allowed within the overall approved debt ceilings.

(3) Stock lending permitted through an approved intermediary in accordance with stock lending scheme.

Jun. 1998 (1) FIIs were allowed for investing in unlisted companies through the 100% debt route.

(2) FIIs asked to tender their securities directly in response to an open offer made in terms of the SEBI (Substantial Acquisition of Shares and Takeovers) Regulations, 1997.

(3) FIIs allowed buying and selling derivative (index futures) contracts traded on a stock exchange.

(4) Transactions among FIIs with respect to Indian stocks would no longer require the post facto confirmation from RBI.

(5) Trigger point limit for investments in Indian companies by FIIs/NRIs/OCBs under the portfolio scheme was raised by 2% points.

(6) Authorized Dealers were to be allowed to extend forward cover facility to FIIs to cover the appreciation in the market value of their existing investments in India.

16th Apr. 1999 In respect of investments in the secondary market, FIIs were allowed to participate in open offers in accordance with take over codes; in case of an open offer by a company to buy back its securities, the FIIs may sell the securities held by it to such company in accordance with the SEBI (Buy back of securities) Regulations, 1998.

24th Apr. 1999 Cut-off date for providing forward exchange cover to FIIs in respect of their equity investment was changed from June 11, 1998 to March 31, 1999 and Authorized

Dealers (ADs) were permitted to provide forward exchange cover to FIIs to the extent of 15% of their outstanding equity investment as at the close of business on March 31, 1999, as well as for the entire amount of any additional investment made after March 31, 1999.

29th Feb. 2000

(1) A domestic portfolio or domestic asset management company were made eligible to be registered as a foreign institutional investor to manage the funds of sub-accounts.

(2) In case of foreign corporates or individuals, investing in equity, each of such sub-account (Substituted for all sub-accounts together) shall not invest more than 5% of the total issued capital within the aggregate limit of 24%, of the company in which such investment is made.

(3) Non- resident Indians (NRIs) and Overseas Corporate Bodies (OCBs) registered with RBI shall not be eligible to invest as sub-account or as foreign institutional investor.

28th Mar, 2000

Any person aggrieved by an order of the Board made, on and after the commencement of the Securities Laws (Second Amendment) Act. 1999, (i.e., after 16th Dec, 1999), under these regulations may prefer an appeal to a Securities Appellate Tribunal having jurisdiction in the matter.

24th Apr, 2000

Indian companies (other than banking companies) including those which have already enhanced the aggregate ceiling from the normal level of 24% to 30% were permitted to enhance the aggregate ceiling on FII investment up to 40% of the issued and paid-up capital.

28th Nov, 2000

SEBI simplified the procedures for FIIs permitting them to execute clients' orders immediately and do the registration later within a day or two. The move will help the FIIs to proceed with execution of requests of clients, who are mostly from outside the country without waiting for SEBI clearance for each transaction.

28th Feb, 2001

Increase in the ceiling for investment by FIIs from 40%

to 49% with the approval of the share holders through a special resolution in the General Body Meeting.

20th Sep, 2001 — In consultation with the Government, RBI permitted Indian Companies to increase the FII investment limit up the sectoral capital ceiling.

27th Feb, 2002 — FIIs permitted to trade in all exchange trade derivative contracts; FII portfolio investments will not be subject to the sectoral limits applicable for FDI except in specified sectors.

10th Dec, 2002 — Every applicant eligible for grant of a certificate under Regulation 7 shall pay a registration fee of US $ 5000 (reduced from US $ 10,000).

28th Aug. 2003 — Regulation 7A introduced mandating that a foreign institutional investor holding a certificate shall, at all time, abide by the Code of Conduct as specified in the Third Schedule.

28th Sept. 2004 — SEBI had notified FIIs and their Sub-accounts as 'specified investors' vide notification dated September 28th, 2004. They are required to obtain a Unique Identification Number (UIN) under the SEBI (Central Database of Market Participants) Regulations, 2003 by March 31, 2005.

29th Nov. 2004 —

(1) With reference to SEBI Circular No. IMD/FII/17/2004 dated November 29th, 2004, was informed that the cap of US $ 1.75 billion will be applicable to FII investment in dated Government Securities and T-bills only, both under 100% debt route and general 70:30 route.

(2) It has been further clarified by Ministry of Finance, Government of India that a cumulative sub-ceiling of US $ 500 million outstanding would be fixed on FII investments in corporate debt and this would be over and above the sub-ceiling of US $ 1.75 billion for Government debt under the overall ECB ceiling.

5.17: INVESTMENT TRENDS AND PATTERN OF FIIs

In the context of investing in emerging markets, the FIIs will face the risks such as country risks, regulatory risks, taxation risks, forex risk, etc. which need to be hedged. When FIIs invest in all emerging markets like India, they will have to take all these risks into consideration and decide a minimum level of return to put it on equal footing with what they would have carved by investing in a developed market. Strong risk adjusted returns of Indian market have led FIIs to make more allocations to India. "India is the stock market with the greatest short-term and long-term potential in Asia. Indian economy has progressed significantly over the past 10 years; its corporate sector has experienced a glorious revolution. India has no systemic risk built into its future unlike some other countries" (CLSA Report, of summer 2003).

Investment in stocks by foreign portfolio investors is a signal of global recognition of economic performance of nations. While lack of similar investment destinations elsewhere may rope in FIIs for a short duration, long-term sustenance of inflows hinges upon prospects of real sector growth. FIIs have come to occupy an important role in Indian capital market. Yearly investment by FIIs has gone up substantially. Their stake in some of the bell-weather stocks has also gone up and they have become an important segment of shareholders. Pattern of FII investment and FIIs Registration with SEBI were presented in Table-5.14.

5.18: TRENDS IN PORTFOLIO FLOWS TO INDIA

It can be observed from the table-5.14 that the portfolio investment inflows have always been on the increase. The average investment of FIIs was at US $ 2.3 billion per year. Their cumulative investment till end of the year 2004 was at US $ 25.7 billion. Further, the net investment in capital market securities was around US $ 10 billion. The FIIs investment in Indian securities market as shown a fluctuating trend year after year starting from US $ 1.6 billion in the year 1994-95 and reached US $ 2.0 billion in the year 1995-96. In recent years the interest of FIIs has increased in Indian securities on account of low P/E ratios and high expected ROI coupled with low risk factors. Their net

Table 5.14: Pattern of FII Investment

Year	No. of FIIs	Gross Purchases (Rs. Mn.)	Gross Sales (Rs. Mn.)	Net Investment (Rs. Mn.)	Net Investment* (US $ Mn.)	Cumulative Net Investment* (US $ Mn)
1993-94	158	55,925	4,663	51,262	1,634	1,638
1994-95	308	76,310	28,348	47,963	1,528	3,167
1995-96	367	96,935	27,517	69,420	2,036	5,202
1996-97	439	155,539	69,794	85,745	2,432	7,634
1997-98	496	186,947	127,372	59,575	1,649	9,284
1998-99	450	161,150	176,994	–15,844	–386	8,898
1999-00	506	568,555	467,335	101,219	2,339	11,237
2000-01	527	740,506	641,164	99,340	2,160	13,396
2001-02	490	499,200	411,650	87,552	1,846	15,242
2002-03	502	470,601	443,710	26,889	562	15,804
2003-04	540	1,448,575	990,940	457,645	9,949	25,754
Total		4,460,243	3,389,487	1,070,766	25,749	
Mean		405,477	308,135	97,342	2,341	
SD		416,602	314,225	124,342	2,655	
SV (%)		103	102	128	113	
Correlation Coefficient (r)				0.35		

* Net Inestment in US $ Million at monthly exchange rate.

Source: SEBI Hand Book of Statistics on the Indian Securities Market, 2004, p. 5 and 37.

investment in the year 2003-04 was at US $ 9.9 billion. Further the number of FIIs has also steeply increased from 158 in 1993-94 to 540 in 2003-04 registering 242 percent increase. If we look into the cumulative net investment of FIIs during decade period of study indicates that a steep increase at 1472.3 percent. Their investment was at US $ 1.6 billion in 1993-94 after witnessing a gradual increase year after year reduced a peak at 25.7 billion US $ in 2003-04.

The calendar year 2004 that just concluded has received an historic net inflow from FIIs to the tune of US $ 9.187 billion which is around 28 percent of the total inflows the country has received till December 31, 2004. A huge portion of these flows has been received during the last six months of the year, July-December 2004. This explosive portfolio flows by FIIs brings with them great advantages as they are engines of growth lowering cost of capital in many emerging markets. They facilitate the flow of capital to firms and countries that offer the best investment opportunities breaking the geographical boundaries. They also bring with them the much wanted breadth and depth into the capital markets of the emerging economies. If we analyze the reasons for such enormous enthusiasm of FIIs in Indian capital market may be on account of the following:

* The Indian capital markets are well structured, regulated and matured market.
* The P/E ratios of Indian securities are lowest in the world.
* Relatively low risk associated with investment opportunities.
* Implementation of further capital market reforms along with liberalization of FIIs investment in India in different sectors.
* The overseas investment companies' mutual funds - USA, UK, Japan and other European Countries find India is the safe heaven for investment.
* The optimistic growth rate in the GDP accompanied by low inflationary tendencies.
* Over pricing of securities in all other developed capital markets in the world.

5.19: THE IMPACT OF FIIs INVESTMENT ON STOCK MARKET LIQUIDITY IN INDIA

The Indian stock markets entered into a new bull phase in November 2004. The BSE Sensex crossed the 7700 mark in July, 2005 and further gaining the strength. A major factor that has been driving the Sensex to new highs has been the increasing liquidity in the Indian stock market, with strong inflows from FIIs. In fact, in recent times as the number of FIIs registering with SEBI has gone up sharply, from 637 in 2004 to 733, as on July 14, 2005, it has resulted in a sharp rise in inflows. The net inflows from FIIs during the first seven months have already touched $ 5.42 billion, as on July 14, 2005 (during the 2004, last calendar year, FIIs invested $ 8.5 billion); experts believe that this could see the FII inflows surpassing the previous year's numbers. Their optimism is based on the fact that the Indian economy has been growing at a faster rate and attracting more and more FIIs across the globe. The Japanese investors have also come to India in 2005 for the first time. According to the Economic Times, July 12, 2005 edition, Japan has emerged as one of the biggest investors in recent times. It estimates that Japanese investments in the Indian market have crossed the $ 1.5 billion mark. It further adds that Japanese investors with over $ 10 trillion in savings are looking at newer emerging markets. More so, with the terribly low interest rates in Japan, it adds.

5.19.1. Empirical Analysis

The stock market rally was ignited by the FII inflows into the equity segment. This pattern examined by taking the proportion of FIIs investment in the market capitalization. "Market capitalization refers to the value of the stock multiplied by the total number of shares outstanding". This relation indicates the degree of holding of FIIs over a study period and is presented in the table-5.15.

The impact of FII on stock market liquidity in India is measured by taking three important indicators of liquidity. They are-

5.19.1.1. Turn Over Ratio (TOR)

TOR is the total value of shares traded divided by the market capitalization. It measures the trading of shares relative to the size of the market. A high TOR is used as an indicator of low transaction cost. Therefore, higher the TOR better is the liquidity of the stock market.

5.19.1.2. Traded Value Ratio (TVR)

TVR is the total value of domestic shares traded divided by the GDP. TVR is a broader concept than TOR because it

Table 5.15: Proportion of Cumulative Investment of FIIs with Market Capitalisation

Year	*Cumulative Investment*	*Market Capitalisation #*	*Percentage*
(1)	(2)	(3)	(4)
Mar-95	9,936	435,481	2.28
Mar-96	16,878	526,476	3.21
Mar-97	25,362	463,915	5.47
Mar-98	30,238	560,325	5.40
Mar-99	29,053	545,361	5.33
Mar-00	39,271	912,642	4.30
Mar-01	48,856	625,553	7.81
Mar-02	57,603	612,224	9.41
Mar-03	60,189	572,197	10.52
Mar-04	109,158	1,201,207	9.09

: Market Capitalisation figures are takenfrom the BSE

Source: CMIE: Capital Markets Special Issue, June 2004, p. 274-276 & 296.

captures trading relative to the size of the economy rather than the size of the stock market. A liquid market will have a large TVR.

5.19.1.3. Market Capitalization to GDP Ratio

Market capitalization to GDP is an indicator of the size of the stock market. As a country develops, the size of its stock market is expected to grow. The correlation among FII to TOR, TVR and Mcap/GDP ratio is presented in the Table-5.16.

5.19.2. Remarks from the above analysis are as follows

* From the data of Table-5.15, it is observed that there has been steady growth in investment by FIIs in India over the years; yet their cumulative investment continues to be a small fraction of the market capitalization of securities traded in Indian markets, i.e., the cumulative investment of FIIs as percentage of market capitalization has remained below 10.52 percent during the period of study. The holding of the FIIs is increasing from 2.28 percent over

Table 5.16: Indicators of Liquidity

Year	% Change in Cumulative FII	TOR (%) BSE Sensex	TOR (%) NSE NIFTY	TVR (%) BSE Sensex	TVR (%) NSE NIFTY	Mcap/GDP (%) BSE Sensex	Mcap/GDP (%) NSE NIFTY
1995-96	69.90	8.88	16.76	4.66	6.27	52.53	37.41
1996-97	50.30	24.59	70.44	9.99	23.75	40.62	33.72
1997-98	19.20	32.86	76.88	14.90	26.63	45.33	34.64
1998-99	-3.90	50.16	84.38	19.44	25.93	38.77	30.73
1999-00	35.20	75.20	82.23	38.96	47.62	51.81	57.92
2000-01	24.40	174.97	203.62	52.55	70.39	30.03	34.57
2001-02 P	17.90	50.19	80.58	14.70	24.54	29.28	30.46
2002-03 QE	4.50	54.89	115.05	13.96	27.47	25.44	23.88
2003-04 RE	81.40	41.88	98.09	19.93	43.57	47.59	44.41
Correlation Coefficient		-0.30	-0.33	-0.18	-0.07	0.65	0.50
Coefficient of Determination (%)		9.00	10.89	3.24	0.49	42.25	25.00
t-Test		-0.83	-0.92	--.48	-0.19	1.57	1.53
t0.05 Table Value)		2.40	2.40	2.40	2.40	2.40	2.40

P= Provision; QE = Quarterly Estimate: RE = Revised Estimate

the study period. The FII investment has increased three folds in the last four years of the study compared to the first year of the study. Thus, we can conclude that the FIIs share is increasing from time to time in terms of liberalization of the Indian stock market regulations.

* From the Table-5.16 we find that the Turnover Ratio on BSE Sensex and NSE Nifty recorded the upward trend. Further, the liquidity of the NSE Nifty is more than doubled over the BSE Sensex. The percentage change in cumulative FII shows the downward movement. From the negative correlation, we can say that the FIIs investing their funds when the turnover ratio is lower and withdrawing investments when the turnover ratio is higher. This indicates that the active participation from the FIIs leads to the stock market liquidity in India. The coefficient of determination is at 9 and 10.89 percent on BSE Sensex and NSE Nifty respectively. According to

the above, we can suggest that FIIs investment affects the stock market liquidity to the maximum extent of 11 percent only and it is not a significant factor influencing for liquidity of Indian capital market, because there are 89 percent of other than FIIs which have been showing major impact on the liquidity.

* On the basis of the data of Table-5.16, the Traded Value Ratio on BSE Sensex and the NSE Nifty shows the upward movement. NSE Nifty recorded the higher traded value ratio over the BSE Sensex in all the years of the study period. Therefore, NSE Nifty is actively engaged in the stock market liquidity as compared to BSE Sensex. The relationship between percentage change in cumulative FII with BSE Sensex and NSE Nifty is recorded the negative trend. The higher the traded value ratio the higher is the size of the economy. According to this statement the relation between FII with Traded Value Ratio on BSE Sensex and NSE Nifty was recorded at low rate. This view is also supported by the coefficient of determination, since it is very low at3.24 and 0.49 percent of BSE Sensex and NSE Nifty respectively. Hence, it can be pointed out that the impact of FIIs on stock market liquidity is not much significant.

* The Indian economy has been one of the fastest growing economies in the world, next only to China. According to the strong growth rate of GDP, India now ranks 10th among the largest economies in the world (World Bank Report). The country's GDP has been growing at a faster rate in the recent years. In fact, in Financial Year 2004 it clocked a growth rate of 8.5 percent and is expected to grow well over 6 percent. Market Capitalization to GDP Ratio indicates the size of the stock market. We observed from table-5.16 that the size of the BSE Sensex is higher than the NSE Nifty. The FII to Mcap/GDP ratio on BSE Sensex and NSE Nifty showed the positive relation. This relation explains the impact of FII on stock market liquidity is up to the extent of 42.25 and 25 percent.

* Thus, it is evident that FII flows have not significantly influenced the liquidity of the Indian stock market. There could be two important reasons for this. One reason could be the sheer volume of FII investment in the stock markets. FIIs have invested $4.7 billion in Indian equities in 2005 so far. Where as it was at $8.4 billion in 2004 and $ 6.7 billion in 2003. Over the past six months, 100 new FIIs have registered with SEBI to take the total number to 733. If the market estimates are any thing to go by, an increased investor interest in Japan, Taiwan, South Korea and the new economic co-operation treaty with Singapore is likely to trigger even more registrations. In addition to that the liberalized policies relating to FIIs implemented by the SEBI is also increasing the stock market liquidity. Second reason could be that FIIs are active traders in the Indian stock market. Hence, both quantum of investment and active trading, have possibly helped to increase the liquidity of the Indian stock market.

5.20: THE IMPACT OF FIIs INVESTMENT ON STOCK MARKET VOLATILITY IN INDIA

The impact of global financial integration and the associated rise in capital inflows on stock market volatility is in general, investors' decision of buying/selling of shares depends on the price earning ratios of the companies. But FIIs influencing the stock market are very high even though their cumulative investment as a percentage of total market capitalization is relatively lower. They completely changed the pattern and psychology of the capital market and they have become the market movers. We examine the impact of FII's investment on stock market volatility by comparing the market index movements of BSE Sensex and NSE Nifty.

5.20.1: Empirical Analysis

Stock market volatility and FIIs investment is measured by using standard deviation. In simple terms, standard deviation measures the deviation of the returns of equity from its mean return. It is an absolute measure i.e. standard deviation of stock returns in one period can be compared with standard deviation of another period to understand which period has been more

Table 5.17: Investment Behaviour of FIIs and Market Index Movements

Months	*Net Investment (Rs. Crore)*	*Cumulative Investment (Rs. Crore)* x	*BSE Sensex* y	*NSE S&P CNX* z
2002				
April	-446	57,157	3,338	1,084
May	122	57,279	3,126	1,029
June	-671	56,608	3,245	1,058
July	190	56,798	2,988	959
August	191	56,989	3,181	1,011
September	222	57,211	2,991	963
October	-698	56,513	2,949	951
November	605	57,118	3,229	1,050
December	550	57,668	3,377	1,094
2003				
January	1,163	58,831	3,250	1,042
February	482	59,313	3,284	1,063
March	877	60,190	3,049	978
April	1,012	61,202	2,960	934
May	3,102	64,304	3,181	1,007
June	3,438	67,742	3,607	1,134
July	2,243	69,985	3,793	1,186
August	2,163	72,148	4,245	1,357
September	4,293	76,441	4,453	1,417
October	6,565	83,006	4,907	1,556
November	3,773	86,779	5,045	1,615
December	6,407	93,186	5,839	1,880
2004				
January	3,161	96,347	5,696	1,810
February	3,329	99,676	5,668	1,800
March	9,483	109,159	5,591	1,772
Correlation (Rxy and Rxz)			0.968	0.861
Coefficient of determination (%)			93.70	92.35
t-Test			18.160	16.331
to.05 (Table Value)			2.074	2.074

Source: CMIE: Capital Markets Special Issue June 204, p. 248, 270 and 296.

Table 5.18: Relative Movement of FII's Investment with Market Index

Months	*Cumulative Investment*	*BSE Sensex*	*NSE S&P CNX NIFTY*
2002			
April	100.0	100.0	100.0
May	100.2	93.0	94.9
June	98.8	103.8	102.8
July	100.3	92.1	90.6
August	100.3	106.5	105.4
September	100.4	94.0	95.3
October	98.8	98.6	98.8
November	101.1	109.5	110.4
December	101.0	104.6	104.2
2003			
January	102.0	96.2	95.2
February	100.8	101.0	102.0
March	101.5	92.8	92.0
April	101.7	129.9	95.5
May	105.1	107.5	107.8
June	105.4	113.4	112.6
July	103.3	105.2	104.5
August	103.1	111.9	114.4
September	106.0	104.9	104.4
October	108.6	110.2	109.8
November	104.5	102.8	103.8
December	107.4	115.7	116.4
2004			
January	103.4	97.6	96.3
February	103.4	99.5	99.4
March	109.5	98.6	98.4

Source: Compiled from Table 5.17.

volatile. Volatility is calculated as the standard deviation of the rates of return. The rate of return is the change in price during the period, divided by the price of the investment at the beginning of the period. We compared the FIIs investment with the volatility of BSE SENSEX and NSE S&P CNX NIFTY indices by taking correlation and tests of hypothesis.

5.20.2. Following observations are made on the basis of the above data

- We observed from the Table-5.17 that the cumulative investment by FIIs shows the increasing trend and some of the downwards are also witnessed. The BSE Sensex and NSE Nifty have been moving in cycle with investment behavior of FIIs over the period of two years (compared on month to month basis) from April 2002 to March 2004. The positive net investments by FIIs have resulted into appreciation in both BSE Sensex and NSE Nifty and negative net investment is followed by decline in both. This trend is recorded reverse in some of the months because of the other capital market reforms like online trading, dematerialized trading, etc. The high positive values of Coefficient of Correlation at 0.968 and 0.961 between cumulative investment and BSE Sensex and NSE Nifty indicate that the market indices are highly influenced by the FIIs flows.
- However, it will also pertinent to note that the entire volatility in stock market is not due to investment behavior of FIIs. It is also evident from Table-5.18, the relative movement in BSE Sensex and NSE Nifty compared to FIIs investment is not of the same magnitude, rather some what greater both on upward and downward side. Thus, there are several other factors which also add to volatility in stock market. However, the effect of all of these together is quite lesser than that of the FIIs investment pattern. Hence, FIIs have emerged as the market movers.

REFERENCES

1. The BSE Sensex crossed over 6930 points in the first week of March 2005 in view of positive budget implications presented on February 28th 2005 by the Finance Minister for the Financial Year 2005-06. This is the highest Sensex in the Indian Capital Market history.
2. Sindex= (TOR + TVR + Mcap to GDP)/3.

CHAPTER-VI

FINANCIAL DERIVATIVES

6.1: INTRODUCTION

An uncertain future and uncertainty leads to risk. Everyone, irrespective of nature and form of existence is subject to risk and uncertainty. This is caused by changes in economic, social and political scenarios. Adverse changes tend to threaten the survival of otherwise successful institutions / individuals / businesses. Thus, a need was felt to develop financial instruments for the management of such risk. These instruments are known as derivatives. By providing commitments to prices or rates for future dates, or by giving protection against adverse movements, derivatives can be used to reduce the extent of risk, which is or may be subject too. Conversely they also provide profit opportunities for those prepared to accept risk. To some extent, they involve the transfer of risk from those who wish to avoid it, to those who are willing to accept.

6.2: MEANING

Derivatives are financial contracts whose values are derived from the value of an underlying primary financial instrument, commodity or index, such as: interest rates, exchange rates, commodities and equities. In a common man's language, derivatives are a kind of insurance instruments, which can be traded in the stock markets. Although insurance products are the simplest forms of derivative instruments, these are in fact are non-tradable derivative instruments. In technical terms, these are risk hedging tradable and non-tradable instruments / products. We personally view the term derivative as being an umbrella covering insurance and all risk, hedge related instruments with trading / non-trading possibilities falling under it as the derivative instruments.

6.3: DEFINITIONS

Some of the important definitions are presented below:

The US Security and Exchange Commission defines "derivatives" as financial instruments whose performance is derived, at least in part, from the performance of an underlying asset, security or index. In other words, a derivative (or a derivative security) is a financial instrument whose value depends on the values of other, more basic underlying variables.

The Securities Contracts (Regulation) Act, 1956 in India defines "derivative" to include a security derived from a debt instrument, share, loan whether secured or unsecured, risk instrument or contract for differences or any other form of security and a contract which derives its value from the prices, or index of prices, of underlying securities.

The International Monetary Fund defines "derivatives" are financial instruments that are linked to a specific financial instrument or indicator or commodity and through which specific financial risks can be traded in financial markets in their own right. The value of a financial derivative derives from the price of an underlying item, such as an asset index. Unlike debt securities, no principal is advanced to be repaid and no investment income accrues.

6.4: FEATURES OF FINANCIAL DERIVATIVES

Some of the important features of financial derivatives are presented below:

* The derivatives are those financial instrument whose value changes in response to the change in the value of variable from which it is derived.
* The variable from which it is derived should be objectively observable.
* The basic elements of definition are risk, futurity and origination.
* The futurity element of derivatives (settlement of contract

or transaction at some future date) makes it more risky as its value changes with the future change in the value of variable from which it is derived.

* Transactions such as insurance contract, bank guarantees etc., are having the element of risk and futurity but are excluded from the definition of derivatives because it originates from the past events.
* Generally derivatives require very little initial investment as compared to the other kind of financial instruments.
* The classification of a financial instrument as derivatives should be according to the nature and intention of the transaction or contract not by their name or specific class. For example convertible warrants issued with shares or bond. The conversion of warrant will take place at some future date and conversion ratio will depend on the market value of shares or bonds on conversion date. The convertible warrant issued with shares and bonds are derivatives as it possess all elements of derivatives.
* Like other financial instrument some derivatives are traded on the organized market while other is on over the counter (OTC). The organized market traded, derivatives has standardized features whereas OTC traded derivatives are non-standardized and customized to meet specific requirements.
* The value of derivatives, which are traded in the organized market, can be measured accurately on particular day by its quotation in free and active market on that particular day.
* The values of derivatives, which are not traded in the organized market, are measured by adopting some model of valuation. The model of valuation will contain certain factors by which value of derivatives can be measured reliably. The value of those factors can be gathered from the organized, free and active markets.
* The derivatives can be divided into two categories Viz. Derivative held for trading / speculation and Derivative held for heading.

* The point of difference between investment in financial instrument and investment in derivatives are presented in the Table-6.1.

Table 6.1: Differences between Investment in Financial Instrument and Investment in Derivatives

Particulars	*Financial Instruments*	*Derivatives*
Intention	Financial Instruments are held for earning income by way of interest, dividend, and capital appreciation or for other benefits.	Derivatives are held for trading/speculation of hedging.
Period	Short or Long-term	Trading/Speculation purpose derivatives are generally short-term but for hedging may be for short-term or long-term.
Initial Investment	Acquisition cost plus cost of financial instruments	Acquisition cost plus margin money if any.
Origin and Valuation	Independent	It takes it origin from other objectively observable variables. Its valuation is dependent on such variable.

6.5: OBJECTIVES

The Chapter "Financial Derivatives" is based on the following objectives:

* To explain the concepts of financial derivatives like meaning, definition, features and historical background.
* To know the need for financial derivatives market in India.
* To study the components, players and policy initiatives

initiated in the financial derivatives market in India.

* To understand the trading, clearing and settlement mechanism in the financial derivatives market in India.
* To examine the trends and pattern of financial derivatives market in India.

6.6: HISTORICAL DEVELOPMENT OF FINANCIAL DERIVATIVES

The historical development of financial derivatives is presented in the Table-6.2.

Table-6.2: Financial Derivatives Timeline

Period	*Events*
12th Century	In European trade fairs sellers sign contracts promising future delivery of the items they sold.
Early 17th Century 1634-1637	Tulip Mania in Holland- Fortunes is lost in after a speculative boom in tulip futures burst.
Late 17th Century	Dojima Rice Futures - A futures market in rice gets developed to protect sellers from bad weather or warfare in Japan at Dojima, near Osaka.
19th Century 1868	Trading in wheat, pork belly and copper futures starts at Chicago Board of Trade.
20th Century Late 1960s	Black and Scholes begin collaboration- Fischer Black and Myron Scholes tackle the problem of determining how much an option is worth. Robert Merton joins them in 1970.
April 1973	The Chicago Board Options Exchange opens.
May/June 1973	The Black-Scholes Model is Published, after having been previously rejected by a number of journals. The paper was published in the Journal of Political Economy, which was one of the journals that had rejected it earlier.
1994	Metallgesellshaft loses $1.5 billion on oil futures.
1995	Barings Bank goes bust. Nick Leeson loses $1.4 billion

	by gambling that the Nikkei 225 index of leading Japanese company shares would not move materially from its normal trading range. That assumption was shattered by the Kobe earthquake on the 17th January 1995 after which Lesson attempted to conceal his losses.
1997	Nobel Prize in Economics awarded to Robert Merton and Myron Scholes.
1998	Long Term Credit Management Bailout - The hedge fund is rescued at a cost of $3.5 billion because of worries that its collapse would have severe repercussions for the world financial system.
1999	The Flaming Ferraris- Some traders at CSFB are sacked following allegations of illegal trades in an attempt to manipulate the Swedish stock market index.
21st Century	
2001	Enron goes Bankrupt - The 7th largest company in the US and the world's largest energy trader made extensive use of energy and credit derivatives but becomes the biggest firm to go bankrupt in American history after systematically attempting to conceal huge losses.
2002	AIB loses $750 million - John Rusnak uses fictitious options contracts to cover loses on spot and forward foreign exchange contracts.
2003	Terrorism Futures Plan Dropped - The US Defense Department had thought that such a market would improve the prediction and prevention of terrorist outrages.
2004	NAB loses a $ 180 million - Four foreign currency dealers at the National Australia Bank are said to have run up the losses in three months of unauthorized trades.
2004	Citigroup bear raid- Citigroup traders led by Spiros Skordos made 15 million by suddenly selling 11 billion worth of European bonds and bond derivatives, and buying many of them back at a lower price.

Source: Gambling on Derivatives, Hedging Risk or Courting Disaster?

www.ex.ac.uk/Rdavies/arian/ scandals.derivatives.html

6.7: NEED FOR FINANCIAL DERIVATIVES

The following are some of the important aspects required to consider for the financial derivatives in the derivatives market:

- Help in discovery of future as well as current prices.
- Help to transfer the risk from risk averse people to risk oriented people.
- Encourage for the savings and investment in the long run.
- Increase managing, monitoring and surveillance of the activities of various participants.
- Provide lower transact costs.
- Increase the volume of transactions.
- Provide hedge for the investors.
- Facilitate to liquidity for investors.
- Enhance the price discovery process.

6.8: PLAYERS IN FINANCIAL DERIVATIVES TRADING

There are three broad categories of participants/Players who trade in the derivatives market. They are discussed below:

6.8.1. *Hedgers*: They use futures or options markets to reduce or eliminate the risk associated with price of an asset.

6.8.2. *Speculators*: They use futures and options contracts to get extra leverage in betting on future movements in the price of an asset. They can increase both the potential gains and potential losses by usage of derivatives in a speculative venture.

6.8.3. *Arbitrageurs*: They are in business to take advantage of a discrepancy between prices in two different markets. For example, they see the futures price of an asset getting out of line with the cash price; they will take off setting positions in the two markets to lock in a profit.

6.9: COMPONENTS OF FINANCIAL DERIVATIVES

Derivative contracts have several components/variants. Some of them have been described herewith:

6.9.1. *Forward* contract is a customized contract between two entities, where settlement takes place on a specific date in the future at today's pre-agreed price.

6.9.2. *Futures* contract is an agreement between two parties to buy or sell an asset at a certain time in the future at a certain price. Futures contracts are special types of forwards contracts in the sense that the former are standardized exchange-traded contracts.

6.9.3. *Option* contracts are of two types- calls and puts. Call option gives the buyer the right but not the obligation to buy a given quantity of the underlying asset, at a given price on or before future date. Whereas, put option give the buyer the right, but not the obligation to sell a given quantity of the underlying asset at a given price on or before given date.

6.9.4. *Swaps* are the agreements between two parties to exchange cash flows in the future according to a pre-arranged formula. The two commonly used swaps are: Interest Rate Swaps: These entail swapping only the interest related cash flows between the parties in the same currency. Currency Swaps: These entails swapping both principal and interest between the parties, with the cash flows in one direction being in a different currency than those in the opposite direction.

Warrants: All options having maturity above one year are called warrants. These are generally treaded over- the -counter.

Table-6.3 presents the comparative differences among forwards, futures and options.

6.10: EXCHANGE-TRADED VS. OTC MARKETS

The OTC market for derivative contracts has existed in some form or other since many years. It is a negotiated and client specific market. The features of this market are as follows:

(a) The management of counter-party (credit) risk is decentralized and located within individual institutions;

(b) There are no formal centralized limits on individual positions or leverage;

(c) There are no formal rules for risk and burden-sharing;

Table 6.3: COMPARISION AMONG FORWARDS, FUTURES AND OPTIONS

PARAMETERS	FORWARDS	FUTURES	OPTIONS	
			OTC	ORGANIZED
Market	OTC	Organized	OTC	Organized
Nature of Contract	Customized	Standardized	Customized	Standardized
Margin	No margin	Margin	Upfront Premium payment payable by Buyer	
Counter Party	Known Bank or Client	Clearing House	Known Bank or Client	Clearing House
Valuation	No special method of valuation	Marked to market everyday	No special method of valuation	Marked to market everyday
Regulation	Self Regulation	By organized market	Self Regulation	By organized market
Counter Party Risk	Depend on counter party	Absent	Depend on counter party	Absent
Settlement	Dependent on terms contract	Clearing House	Dependent on terms of contract	Clearing House
Gain/Loss	Unlimited	Unlimited	Gain-unlimited/Loss to the extent premium paid upfront	

(d) There are no formal rules or mechanisms for ensuring market stability and integrity, and for safeguarding the collective interests of market participants; and

(e) OTC contracts are generally not regulated by a regulatory authority although they are affected indirectly by national legal systems, banking supervision and market surveillance.

Some of the features of OTC derivatives markets can give rise to financial instability affecting not only institutions but also the overall domestic financial markets. Thus it poses to be a threat to the stability of the entire international financial system. Few of them are: (i) the dynamic nature of gross credit exposures; (ii) information asymmetries; (iii) the effects of OTC derivative activities on available aggregate credit; (iv) the high concentration of OTC derivative activities in major institutions: and (v) the central role of OTC derivatives markets in the global financial system. Sharp movements in underlying asset prices and counter-party defaults five rise to instability, which apart from significantly altering the perceptions of current, also alters potential future credit exposures. If the asset prices change rapidly, the size and configuration of counter-party exposures may become unsustainably large and provoke a rapid unwinding of positions.

There has been some progress in addressing these risks and perceptions. However, the progress has been limited in implementing reforms in risk management, including counterparty, liquidity and operational risks as they are outside the regulatory purview. In view of the inherent risk associated with OTC derivatives, Indian law considers them illegal except for specific contracts under FRAs/IRS on domestic currency as allowed by RBI.

6.11: DEVELOPMENT OF DERIVATIVES MARKET IN INDIA

The prohibition on options in securities was withdrawn with the promulgation of the Securities Law (Amendment) Ordinance, 1995. This paved the way for introduction of derivatives in the Indian financial markets. On November 18th, 1996, SEBI set up a 24-member Committee under the Chairmanship of Dr. L.C. Gupta to develop appropriate regulatory framework for derivatives trading in India. The Committee was of the view that derivatives should be declared as 'securities' so that regulatory framework applicable to trading of 'securities' could be extended to govern derivatives. SEBI has set up a Committee under the Chairmanship of Prof. J.R. Varma, in June 1998 to recommend measures for risk containment in derivatives market. The Report worked out the operational details of margin system, methodology for charging initial margins, broker net worth, deposit requirement and real-time monitoring requirements.

In December 1999, the Securities Contracts (Regulation) Act was amended to include derivatives within the ambit of 'securities'. Thereafter, a regulatory framework was developed for governing the trading in derivatives. Derivatives were formally defined to include: (a) a security derived from a debt instrument, share, loan whether secured or unsecured, risk instrument or contract for differences of any other form of security, and (b) a contract which derives its value from the prices, or index of prices, or underlying securities. The Act also made it clear that derivatives are legal and valid, but only if such contracts are traded on a recognized stock exchange. The Government also rescinded in March 2000 the three-decade old notification, which prohibited forward trading in securities. Derivatives trading commenced in India after SEBI granted the final approval to commence trading and settlement in approved derivatives contracts on the NSE and BSE.

6.12: POLICY INITIATIVES

Following are some of the important policy initiatives initiated by the Regulators and the Government of India:

6.12.1. Introduction of Exchange Traded Interest Rate Derivatives

A scheme for introduction of futures contracts on dated Government Security and Treasury Bills and its risk containment measures have been framed by the SEBI in consultation with the Government and the RBI.

6.12.2. Investments by FIIs/NRIs in Exchange Traded Derivative Contracts

The Foreign Exchange Management (Transfer or Issue of security by a Person Resident outside India) Regulations 2000 have been amended to include that (i) a registered FII having a valid account under FERA 1973 or under FEMA 1999 may trade in all SEBI approved exchange traded derivative contracts (ii) a Non-Resident Indian (NRI) may also invest in exchange traded derivative contracts out of NRI funds held in India on non-repatriable basis. These investments will however not be eligible for repatriation benefits. On 16th July, 2004, SEBI modified FII position limit in all index derivative contracts (Futures or Options) on a particular underlying index would be Rs. 250 crore or 15 percent of the total open interest of the market per exchange, whichever was higher, in that index derivative.

6.12.3. Interest Rate Future Contracts

As per the recommendations of the SEBI Advisory Committee on Derivatives and Market Risk Management, SEBI has also decided to permit interest rate futures contracts on a "10 year coupon bearing notional bond" which would be priced off a basket of bonds.

6.12.4. Issuance of Offshore Derivative Instruments by Registered FIIs

In February 2004, SEBI amended the SEBI (FII) Regulations, 1995 to include a new regulation which states that "a FII or sub-account may issue, deal in or hold, offshore derivative instruments such as Participatory Notes (P-Notes), Equity Linked Notes (ELN) or any other similar instruments against underlying securities, listed or proposed to be listed on any stock exchange in India, only in favor of those entities which are regulated by any relevant authority in the countries of their incorporation or establishment, subject to compliance of "Know Your Client" requirement, provided that if any such instrument has already been issued, prior to February 2004, to a person other than a regulated entity, contract for such transaction should expire on maturity of the instrument or within a period of five years from February 3rd, 2004 whichever is earlier".

6.12.5. Minimum Contract Size for Exchange Traded Derivative Contracts

At the time of introduction of derivatives, SEBI stipulated the lot size at 100 and in multiples thereof and the derivative contract value at not less than Rs. 2 lakh. However, with the changes in the prices of underlying stock, while the contract value of most derivative contracts had exceeded the stipulated value of Rs. 2 lakh, in the case of some, the contract size/value had fallen below Rs. 2 lakh. With a view to aligning the contract size to Rs. 2 lakh, SEBI vide its circular dated February 2004, reduced/increased the lot size and multiplier. It had also revoked its earlier stipulation on the lot size/multiplier of 100.

6.13: TRADING MECHANISM

Only the NSE and the BSE offer a platform for trading in derivatives contracts. The derivatives trading system at NSE is called NEAT-F&O system, which provides a fully automated screen-based, anonymous order driven trading system for derivatives on a nationwide basis. It provides tremendous flexibility by allowing users to place orders with their own time and price related conditions. Nevertheless, trading in derivatives segment is essentially similar to that of capital market segment. There are four entities in the trading system. They are:

6.13.1. Trading Members

Trading Members can trade either on their own account or on behalf of their clients including participants. They are registered as members with NSE/BSE and are assigned an exclusive Trading Member ID.

6.13.2. Clearing Members

Clearing Members are members of NSCCL. They carry out risk management activities and confirmation/inquiry of trades through the trading system. These clearing members are also trading members and clear trades for themselves and/or others.

6.13.3. Professional clearing Members

A professional clearing member (PCM) is a clearing member who is not a trading member. Typically, banks and custodians become PCMs and clear and settle for their trading members.

6.13.4. Participants

A Participant is a client of trading members like financial institutions. These clients may trade through multiple trading members, but settle their trades through a single clearing member only.

6.14: CLEARING AND SETTLEMENT MECHANISM

National Securities Clearing Corporation Limited (NSCCL) undertakes clearing and settlement of all trades executed on the futures and options (F&O) segment of the NSE. It also acts as legal counterparty to all the trades on the F&O segment and guarantees their settlement. The Clearing and Settlement process comprises of three main activities viz., Clearing, Settlement and Risk Management.

6.14.1. Clearing Mechanism

The first step in clearing process is working out open positions and obligations of clearing (self-clearing / trading-cum-clearing/ professional clearing) members. The open positions in the contracts traded of capital markets are arrived at by aggregating the open positions of all the trading members and all custodial participants clearing through him. The open position of a trading member is arrived at by summing up his proprietary open position and his clients' open positions.

6.14.2. Settlement Mechanism

The underlying for index futures/options on the index cannot be delivered; therefore, they have to be settled in cash. Futures and options on individual securities can be delivered as in the spot market. However, it has been currently mandated that stock options and futures would also be cash settled. The settlement amount for a clearing member is netted across all their trading members/clients, across various settlements. For the purpose of settlement, all capital markets are required to open a separate bank account with NSCCL designated clearing banks for F&O segment.

6.15: CONTRACT SPECIFICATION FOR F&O

Contract specification for the derivative products are presented in the following pages and its summary is exhibited in the Table-6.4.

6.15.1. Settlement of Futures Contracts on Index or Individual Securities

Futures contracts have two types of settlements, the Mark-to-Market (MTM) settlement which is done on a daily basis, and the final settlement, which is on the last trading day of the futures contracts.

6.15.2. Settlement of Options Contracts on Index or Individual Securities

Options contracts have three types of settlements, daily premium settlement, interim exercise settlement in case of option contracts on securities and final settlement.

6.15.3. Settlement of Interest Rate Futures

Daily and Final Mark to Market settlement of interest rate futures contracts are also cash settled. All positions (brought forward, created during the day, closed out during the day) in futures contracts, at the end of trading hours, should be marked to market at the Daily Settlement Price. And on the last trading it should be marked to market at Final Settlement Price for settlement. Daily settlement price should be the closing price of the relevant futures contract for the trading day. Final settlement price should be based on the value of the notional bond determined using the ZCYC computed by the Exchange.

Table-6.4: Contract Specification for Futures and Options

Particulars	*Index Futures*	*Stock Futures*	*Index Options*	*Stock Options*	*Interest Rate Futures*
Security Description	N FUTIDX	N FUTSTK	N OPTIDX	N OPTSTK	N FUTINT
Underlying	S&P CNX Nifty Index/ CNX IT Index	Individual Securities	S&P CNX Nifty Index/ CNX IT Index	Individual Securities	Notional 10 year bond (6% coupon). Notional 10 year zero coupon bond and Notional 91 day T-Bill
Style of Option	NA	NA	European	American	NA
Contract Size	200 or multiples thereof	Multiples of 100, as may be specified	200 or multiples thereof	Multiples of 100, as may be specified	Permitted lot size is 2000

	(minimum value of Rs. 2 lakh)	by NSE	(minimum value of Rs. 2 lakh)	by NSE	
Price Steps	Rs. 0.05				Rs. 0.01
Expiration Months	3 near months				One year
Trading Cycle	A maximum of three months trading cycle- the near month (one), the next month (two) and the far month (three). New contract is introduced on the next trading following the expiry of near month contract.				The Concern shall be for a period of a muturity of one year with three months continuous contracts for the first three months and fixed quarterly contracts for the entire year.
Last Trading / Expiration Day	Last Thursday of the expiry month or the preceding trading day, if last Thursday is a trading holiday.				Last Thursday of the expiry month. If last Thursday is a trading holiday, the contract shall expire on previous trading day. Further, where the last Thursday falls on the annual or half yearly closing dates of the bank, the contract shall expire on previous trading day.
Price Bonds	Operating range of 10% of the base price	Operating range of 20% of the base price	Operating range of 99% of the base price	Operating range of 99% of the base price	NA

No. of Strike Prices	NA	NA	Minimum of 5 (two 'in the money', one 'at the money' and two 'out of the money') for every option type (i.e. call and put)	Minimum of 5 (two 'in the money', on 'at the money' and two 'out of the money') for every option type (i.e. call and put)	NA
Strike Price Interval (in Rs.)	NA	NA	10	Between 2.5 and 50 depending on the price of underlying	NA
Settlement	In cash on T+1 basis	In cash on T+1 basis	In cash on T+1 basis	Daily settlement on T+1 basis and final settlement on T+2 basis	Daily Mark-to- Market settlement and Final Scttlement will be on T+1 basis
Daily Settlement Price	Closing price of futures contracts on the trading day	Closing price of futures contracts on the trading day	Premium Value (net)	Premium Value (net)	As may be stipulated by NSCCL in this regard from time to time
Final Settlement Price	Closing value underlying index / security on the last trading day of the futures contract	Closing value underlying Index/ security on the last trading day of the future contract	Closing value of such underlying security (index) on the last trading day of the options contracts	Closing value of such underlying security (index) on the last trading day of the options contracts	As may be stipulated by NSCCL in this regard from time to time
Settlement Day			Last trading day		
Margins			Up-front initial margin on daily basis.		

NA: Not Applicable.

6.16: TRENDS AND PATTERN OF DERIVATIVES MARKET IN INDIA

Derivatives trading began with the launch of index futures in June 2000 followed by index options, single stock options and single stock futures in 2001. Interest rate futures were launched in June 2003. There is hardly any secondary market trading in interest rate futures. The derivative products have a monthly maturity cycle. From September 13th 2004 onwards, weekly stock and index options cycle was launched on the derivative segment of BSE. Trends and pattern of financial derivatives on NSE and BSE were analyzed in this section.

6.16.1. Evaluation of Trends and Pattern of Turnover on Cash Market Segment and Derivatives Market Segment

From the data of the Table-6.5, we observe the following trends and patterns:

(a) The combined derivatives turnover recorded at Rs. 4,038 crore in the year 2000-01 and Rs. 25,63,165 crore in the year 2004-05. This shows that the increase of 634 times over the study period. Second year witnessed the highest annual growth rate of 2,471.1 percent. The least growth rate was observed in the last year with 19.6 percent.

(b) The combined turnover on the cash market segment in the year 2000-01 was Rs. 23,39,542 crore and in the last year it was recorded at Rs. 73,53,438 crore. The highest and lowest annual growth rate was recorded at 71.9 percent and -64.9 percent in the year 2003-04 and 2001-02 respectively. The over all decline in the rate from the first year to the last year of the study was -0.29 times.

(c) When we compare the overall growth rate of turnover on derivatives market segment and cash market segment, the increase in derivatives market is much higher than the cash market. This amount of increase in the last two years of the study is much higher. The important reasons for this growth are: (i) On 27th February 2002, SEBI permitted FIIs and NRIs to trade in all exchange traded derivative contracts and their revised position limits were materialized from October 31, 2003; (ii) The new products such as interest rate futures contracts were introduced in June 2003 and futures and options contracts on sectoral indices have been introduced in August 2003; (iii) Exchange traded derivatives contracts on a notional 10 year government bond have been allowed for trading; and (iv) improved risk management mechanism in the F&O segment.

6.16.2. Comparative Analysis of Derivatives Turnover at NSE and BSE

From the same Table 6.5, 6.6 and 6.7, we pointed out the following lines on derivatives turnover at NSE and BSE:

(a) Derivatives turnover on the NSE was recorded at Rs. 2,365 crore in the first year and Rs. 25,47,053 crore in the last year. The overall growth rate on the NSE derivatives market was recorded at 1,076 times. The annual growth rate was ranging in between 19.5 percent to 4,209.7 percent. The highest annual growth rate was recorded in 2001-02. The average turnover is above 98 percent in all the years except in the first year of the study.

(b) Derivatives turnover on the BSE was recorded at Rs. 1,673 crore in very first year and Rs. 16,112 crore in the year 2004-05. The overall growth rate on the BSE segment was stood at 8.6 times. The highest annual growth rate was recorded in the year 2003-04. This increase was recorded because of the revised settlement period from one month to one week.

(c) Number of trading days on the NSE was recorded at 211, 247, 251, 254 and 253 from the year 2000-01 to 2004-05. The similar days of trading was observed on the BSE excepting in the year 2000-1 it traded 207 instead of 211 days on the NSE. The number of trading days on both the exchanges were recorded the increasing trend except in the last year.

(d) The total average daily turnover on NSE and BSE were Rs. 4,294.29 crore and 28.58 crore. This points out that the average daily turnover on the NSE was greater than

149 times over the BSE.

(e) The total number of contracts on NSE and BSE were 15,50,80,600 and 12,35,284 respectively. On both the stock exchanges the number of contracts was showed the increasing trend from the first year to the last year. The lowest and highest number of contracts was observed at the first and last year of the study on the two exchanges. But the share of contribution was differs. NSE was contributing 99.2 percent and BSE was contributing a meager of 0.8 percent.

Table-6.5: Derivatives Turnover VS. Cash Market Turnover

Year	*NSE*		*BSE*		*Total*	
	TCS	*TDS*	*TCS*	*TDS*	*TCS*	*TDS*
2000-01	13,39,510 (–) [57.3]	2,365 (–) [58.6]	10,00,032 (–) [42.7]	1,673 (–) [41.4]	23,39,542 (–) [100.0]	4,038 (–) [100.0]
2001-02	5,13,167 (-61.7) [62.5]	1,01,925 (4,209.7) [98.1]	3,07,292 (-69.3) [37.5]	1,922 (14.9) [1.9]	8,20,459 (-64.9) [100.0]	1,03,847 (2,471.7) [100.0]
2002-03	6,17,989 (20.4) [66.3]	4,39,865 (331.6) [99.4]	3,14,073 (2.2) [33.7]	2,478 (28.9) [0.6]	9,32,062 (13.6) [100.0]	4,42,343 (325.9) [100.0]
2003-04	10,99,534 (77.9) [68.6]	21,30,649 (384.4) [99.4]	5,03,053 (60.2) [31.4]	12,452 (402.5) [0.6]	16,02,587 (71.9) [100.0]	21,43,101 (384.5) [100.0]
2004-05	11,40,072 (03.7) [68.7]	25,47,053 (19.5) [99.4]	5,18,716 (03.1) [31.3]	16,112 (29.4) [0.6]	16,58,788 (03.5) [100.0]	25,63,165 (19.6) [100.0]
Total	47,10,272 [64.0]	52,21,857 [99.3]	26,43,166 [36.0]	34,637 [0.7]	73,53,438 [100.0]	5256494 [100.0]

Note: (1) TCS: Trading on Cash Segment;
(2) TDS: Trading on Derivative Segment;
(3) Trading on Derivatives Segment is started from June, 2000;
(4) Turnover figures are in crore;
(5) Figures in (...) indicates Annual Growth Rate; and
(6) Figures in [...] indicates Average to Total.

Source: Various Annual Reports of SEBI, NSE and BSE Web Sites.

Fig. 6.1: Derivatives Turnover VS. Cash Market Turnover

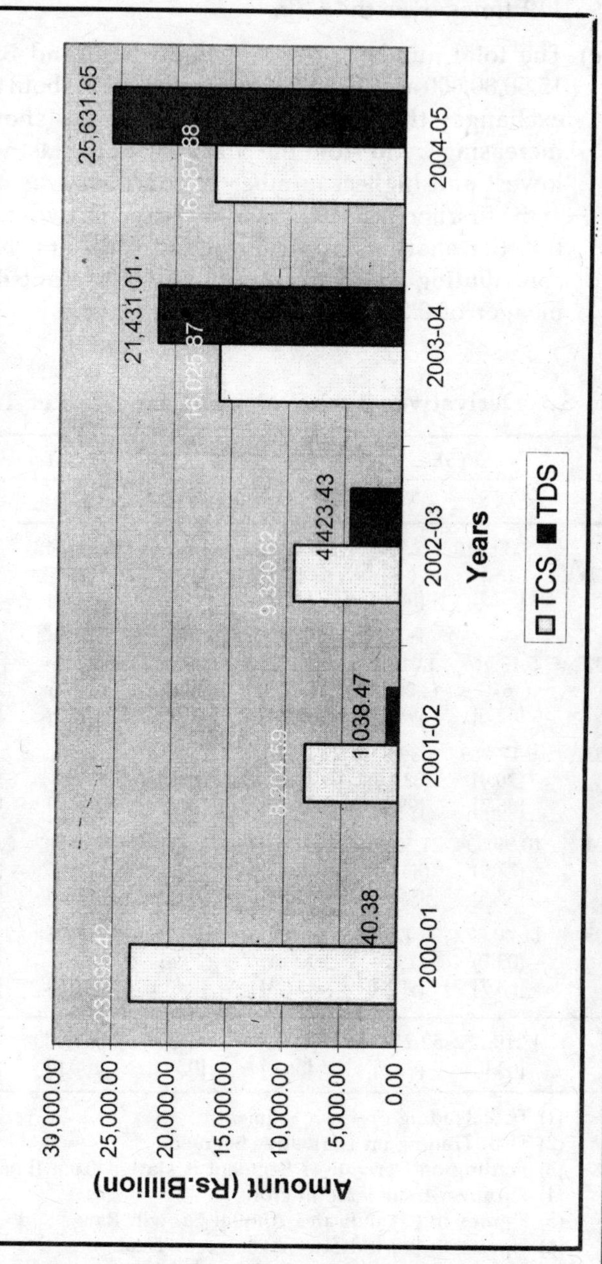

(f) The overall turnover per contract was identified at Rs. 0.034 crore and Rs. 0.028 crore on the NSE and BSE respectively. In this area is also the NSE contributing higher (55%) share of turnover per contract over the BSE (45%).

(g) Finally, we can conclude that the NSE contributing a lion's share in the form of total turnover, average daily turnover, total number of contracts and turnover per contract. Above all NSE emerged as a target market for the derivatives in India and it also competing with the global derivative markets. NSE occupied 20th position in the top 20 exchanges offering options and futures and 14th rank among the top 40 exchanges trading in futures.

Table-6.6: Derivatives Turnover per Day at NSE and BSE

Year	*NSE*			*BSE*		
	Total Turn over	*No. of Trading Days*	*Avg. Daily Turn over*	*Total Turn over*	*No. of Trading Days*	*Avg. Daily Turn over*
2000-01	2,365	211	11.21	1,673	207	8.08
2001-02	1,01,925	247	412.65	1,922	247	7.78
2002-03	4,39,865	251	1,752.45	2,478	251	9.87
2003-04	21,30,649	254	8,388.38	12,452	254	49.02
2004-05	25,47,053	253	10,067.40	16,112	253	63.68
Total	52,21,857	1,216	4,294.29	34,637	1,212	28.58

Note: (1) Total Turnover and Average Daily Turnover is in Rs. Crore.
(2) First Year of the study is beginning from the June 2000.

Source: Various Annual Reports of SEBI, NSE and BSE Web Sites.

6.16.3. Analysis of Trends and Pattern of Product- wise Derivatives Turnover at NSE and BSE

Table-6.8 and 6.9 were presents the product-wise derivatives turnover at NSE and BSE respectively. From the table-6.8, we observed the following trends:

Table-6.7: Derivatives Turnover per Contract at NSE and BSE

Year	NSE			BSE		
	Total Turn over	*No. of Contracts*	*Turn over per Contract*	*Total Turn over*	*No. of Contracts*	*Turn over per Contract*
2000 -01	2,365	90,580	0.026	1,673	7,7743	0.022
2001 -02	1,01,925	41,96,873	0.024	1,922	1,05,527	0.018
2002 -03	4,39,865	1,67,67,852	0.026	2,478	1,38,037	0.018
2003 -04	21,30,649	5,70,08,110	0.037	12,452	3,82,258	0.033
2004 -05	25,47,053	7,70,17,185	0.033	16,112	5,31,719	0.030
Total	52,21,857	15,50,80,600	0.034	34,637	12,35,284	0.028

Note: (1) Total Turnover and Turnover per Contract is in Rs. Crore.
(2) First Year of the study is beginning from the June 2000.
Source: Various Annual Reports of SEBI, NSE and BSE Web Sites.

(a) The total turnover on the Index Futures of NSE was observed with Rs.13,94,434 crore and its overall contribution to the total turnover was 26.7 percent. The overall growth rate in that derivative is 325.5 times. The highest amount (Rs. 7,72,174 crore) of turnover was placed in the year 2004-05 and the lowest amount (Rs.2,365 crore) of turnover was recorded in 2000-01.

(b) The total amount of turnover on the Stock Futures at NSE was recorded at Rs.31,28,064 crore and its overall contribution to total turnover is 60.0 percent. The overall growth rate is 27.8 times. The highest (456.2%) and lowest (13.4%) annual growth rate was recorded in the year 2002-03 and 2004-05 respectively.

(c) The total amount of turnover on the Stock Futures was identified with Rs.1,87,791 crore and its overall contribution to total turnover was 3.5 percent. The overall growth rate is 31.4 times. The highest (471.2%) and lowest (130.9%) annual growth was highlighted in the year 2003-04 and 2004-05 respectively.

(d) The total amount of turnover on the Stock Options was recorded at Rs.5,11,368 crore and its overall contribution to total turnover was 9.8 percent. The overall growth rate is 5.7 times. The highest (298%) and lowest (-22.3%) annual growth rate was observed in the year 2002-03 and 2004-05 respectively.

(e) The total amount of Interest Rate Futures was recorded at Rs. 202 crore and its contribution to the total turnover is negligible. This amount of turnover is recorded only in the year 2003-04.

(f) Finally, we can conclude that the highest amount of contribution to the total amount of turnover has come from the Stock Futures. The annual growth rate is more in the case of Index Futures. Index Futures and Stock Futures jointly contributed to the total amount of turnover above 86 percent and the remaining amount is contributed by the Index and Stock Options.

(g) From the data of the Table-6.9, it is evident that the productive-wise derivatives turnover of BSE on the Index Futures was at Rs.24,932 crore and its overall contribution to total turnover was 72 percent. The overall annual growth rate is 7.1 times. The highest (262.9%) and lowest (-23.7%) annual growth rate was recorded in the year 2003-04 and 2001-02 respectively.

(h) The total amount of turnover on the Stock Futures was recorded at Rs. 6,481 crore and its overall contribution to total turnover is 18.7 percent. The highest (703.1%) and lowest (-96.0%) annual growth rate was given in the year 2003-04 and 2004-05 respectively.

(i) The total amount of turnover on the Index Options was at Rs.2,382 crore and its contribution to total turnover was 6.8 percent. Out of the total amount of Rs.2,382 crore Rs. 2,297 crore was traded only in the year 2004-05. The reason for this significant increase is that the BSE introduced weekly options for trading in Sensex and three selected stocks.

(j) The total amount of contribution on the Stock Options

was Rs. 470 crore and its overall contribution to total turnover is 1.4 percent. The business through Stock Options was significant in the year 2001-02 and 2003-04.

(k) Interest Rate Futures trading is not taken place on BSE.

(l) Finally, we can conclude that the Index futures and Stock Futures have been jointly contributing above 90 percent and remaining 10 percent was contributed by other products.

(m) At the end, we can draw the following conclusions about turnover of individual products and its contribution to the total turnover on the NSE and BSE:

* Large amount of turnover is contributed by Index Futures and Stock Futures on the NSE as well as BSE.

* Higher annual growth rate is also observed on the same products on the two exchanges.

* Individual product's contribution to the total turnover gives a controversial result. Stock Futures on NSE and Index Futures on BSE were playing a dominant role in the form of turnover contribution. Hence, we combine the Index Futures of NSE & BSE and Stock Futures of NSE & BSE, the Stock Futures playing a dominant role in the Indian derivatives market.

* We can differentiate Indian derivative market from the rest of the world in the relative share of options and futures. While the world over, options are more popular, in the India futures are more popular.

* Interest Rate Futures were not taking off in India. Several reasons are attributed to this position. The use of Zero Coupon Yield Curve (ZCYC), while the market trades on Yield to Maturity (YTM) concept is one. Limiting the participation of Banks in the market is another. Limiting the futures to only 10-year notional Government Security futures and 91 day Treasury Bills, while the actual trading takes place in varying maturities is yet another. The dual regulation - RBI regulating transactions by banks in these instruments and SEBI regulating the transactions

Table-6.8: Product-wise Derivatives Turnover at NSE

(Rs. Crore)

Year	*Index Futures*	*Stock Futures*	*Index Options*	*Stock Options*	*Int. Rate Futures*	*Total*
2000-01	2,365 (–) (100.0)	NA (–) (0.0)	NA (–) (0.0)	NA (–) (0.0)	NA (–) (0.0)	2,365 (–) (100.0)
2001-02	21,482 (808.3) [21.1]	51,516 (–) [50.5]	3,766 (–) [3.7]	25,163 (–) [24.7]	NA (–) [0.0]	1,01,925 (4,209.7) [100.0]
2002-03	43,951 (104.6) [10.0]	2,86,532 (456.2) [65.1]	9,248 (145.6) [2.1]	1,00,135 (298.0) [22.8]	NA (–) [0.0]	4,39,865 (331.6) [100.0]
2003-04	5,54,462 (1,161.5) [26.0]	13,05,949 (355.8) [61.3]	52,823 (471.2) [2.5]	2,17,212 (117.0) [10.2]	202 (–) [0.0]	21,30,649 (384.4) [100.0]
2004-05	7,72,174 (39.3) [30.3]	14,84,067 (13.4) [58.3]	1,21,954 (130.9) [4.8]	1,68,858 (-22.3) [6.6]	NA (–) [0.0]	25,47,053 (19.5) [100.0]
Total	13,94,434 [26.7]	31,28,064 [60.0]	1,87,791 [3.5]	5,11,368 [9.8]	202 [0.0]	52,21,857 [100.0]

Note: (1) Figures in (–) indicates Annual Growth Rate;
(2) Figures in [–] indicates Individual items percentage to Total.
(3) NA: Not Applicable / Not Available.

Source: Various Annual Reports of SEBI and NSE Web Site.

as exchange traded product- could also have contributed its mite to the failure.

6.16.4: Analysis of Settlement System in F&O Segment at NSE and BSE

The detailed information on settlement system in F&O segment at NSE and BSE were presented in the Table-6.10 and 6.11. The following observations are made in this regard:

(a) All derivative contracts are currently cash settled. The Index / Stock Futures Settlement were made through the MTM and Final Settlement and the Index / Stock

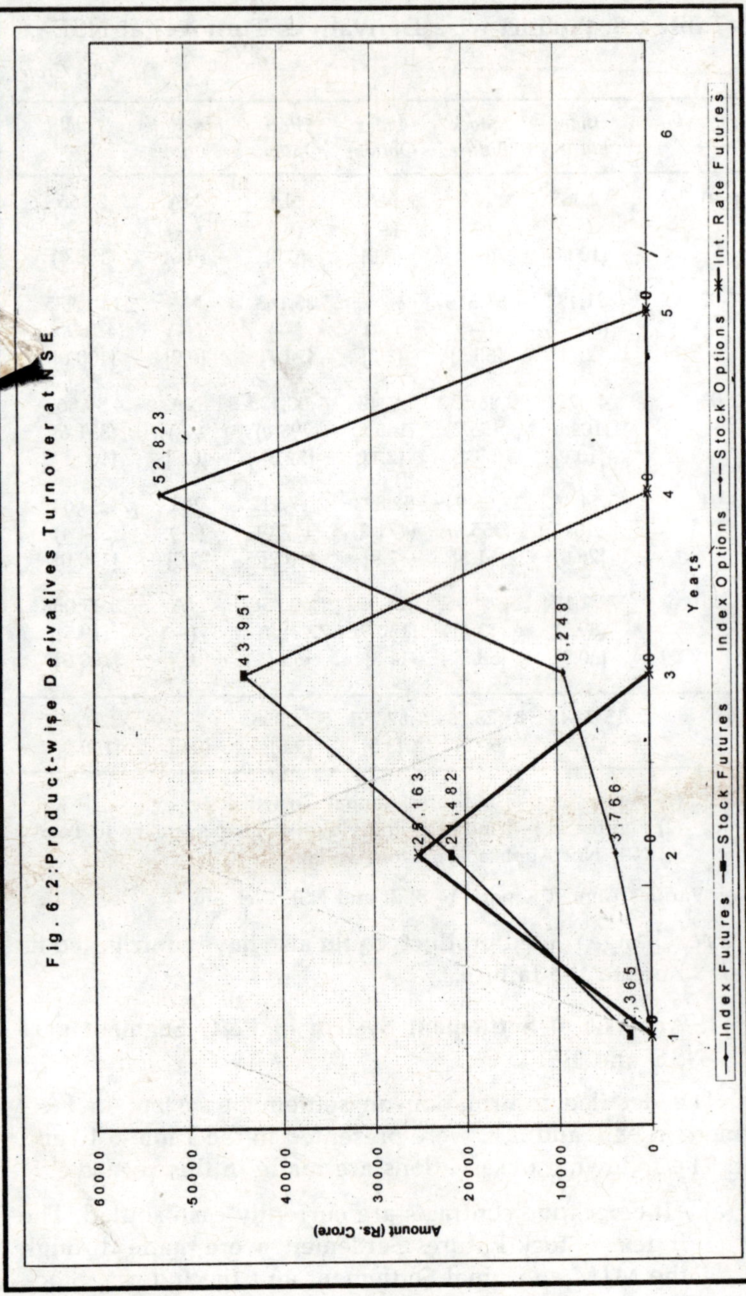

Fig. 6.2: Product-wise Derivatives Turnover at NSE

Table-6.9: Product-wise Derivatives Turnover at BSE

(Rs. Crore)

Year	*Index Futures*	*Stock Futures*	*Index Options*	*Stock Options*	*Int. Rate Futures*	*Total*
2000-01	1,673 (–) [100.0]	NA (–) [0.0]	NA (–) [0.0]	NA (–) [0.0]	NA (–) [0.0]	1,673 (–) [100.0]
2001-02	1,276 (-23.7) [66.4]	452 (–) [23.5]	84 (–) [4.4]	114 (–) [5.9]	NA (–) [0.0]	1,922 (14.9) [100.0]
2002-03	1,811 (42.0) [73.1]	644 (42.5) [26.0]	1 (-98.8) [0.0]	21 (-81.6) [0.8]	NA (–) [0.0]	2,478 (28.9) [100.0]
2003-04	6,572 (262.9) [52.8]	5,172 (703.1) [41.5]	1 (0.0) [0.0]	332 (1,481.0) [2.1]	NA (–) [0.0]	12,452 (402.5) [100.0]
2004-05	13,600 (106.9) [84.4]	213 (-96.0) [1.3]	2,297 (2,296T) [14.3]	3 (-98.8) [0.0]	NA (–) [0.0]	16,112 (29.4) [100.0]
Total	24,932 [72.0]	6,481 [18.7]	2,382 [6.8]	470 [1.4]	00 [0.0]	34,637 [100.0]

Note: (1) Figures in (–) indicates Annual Growth Rate;
(2) Figures in [–] indicates Individual items percentage to Total.
(3) NA: Not Applicable/Not Available.

Source: Various Annual Reports of SEBI and BSE Web Site.

Options were made through Premium and Exercise Settlement.

(b) The total amount of cash settlement over the study was Rs. 30,125.6 crore at NSE and Rs. 332.02 crore at BSE.

Out of the total amount of cash settlement, Index / Stock Futures accounting Rs. 26,609.5 crore and Rs. 169.5 crore at NSE and BSE respectively. Cash settlement on the Futures market is higher than the Options market at NSE (88.3%) as well as BSE (51.0%).

(c) In the case of Index / Stock Futures, MTM settlement was recorded higher proportion at 86.9 percent and 48.4 percent at NSE and BSE respectively.

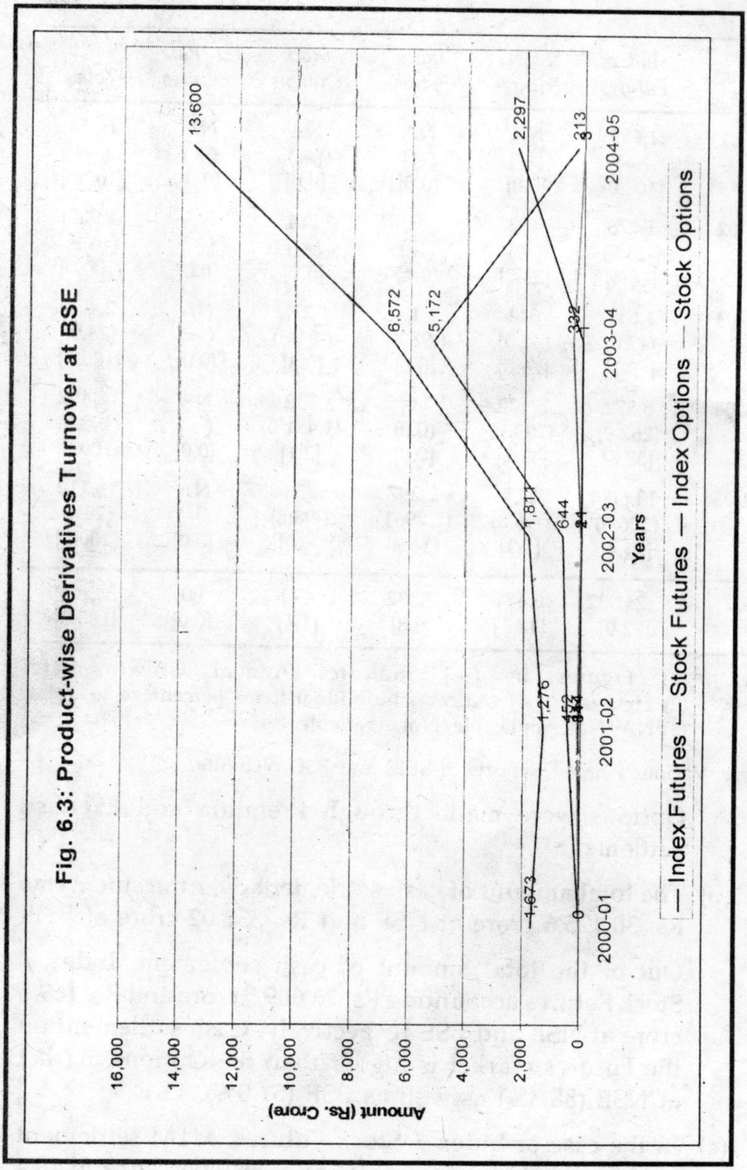

Fig. 6.3: Product-wise Derivatives Turnover at BSE

(d) The Premium Settlement in the point of view of Index/Stock Options was witnessed at 7.6% and 48.4% at NSE and BSE respectively. Another important observation is that the MTM and Premium settlement at BSE recorded the same proportion (48.4%) of cash settlement.

Table-6.10: Settlement System in F&O Segment at NSE

(Rs. Crore)

Year	*Index/Stock Futures*		*Index/Stock Options*		Total
	MTM Settlement	*Final Settlement*	*Premium Settlement*	*Exercise Settlement*	
2000 -01	84.1 (–) [97.8]	1.9 (–) [2.2]	NA (–) [0.0]	NA (–) [0.0]	86.0 (–) [100.0]
2001 -02	505.2 (500.7) [64.3]	21.9 (1,052.6) [2.8]	164.8 (–) [21.0]	93.9 (–) [11.9]	785.8 (813.7) [100.0]
2002 -03	1,737.9 (244.0) [75.2]	45.8 (109.1) [2.0]	331.2 (101.0) [14.3]	195.9 (08.6) [8.5]	2,310.8 (194.1) [100.0]
2003 -04	10,822.1 (522.7) [88.0]	138.9 (203.3) [1.1]	858.9 (159.3) [7.0]	476.1 (143.0) [3.9]	12,296.0 (432.1) [100.0]
2004 -05	13,024.2 (1,103.3) [89.0]	227.5 (63.8) [1.6]	941.1 (9.6) [6.4]	455.9 (-4.2) [3.1]	14,648.6 (19.1) [100.0]
Total	26,173.5 [86.9]	436.0 [1.4]	2,296.0 [7.6]	1,221.8 [4.1]	30,125.6 [100.0]

Note: (1) NA: Not Available/Not Applicable.

(2) Figures in (–) indicates Annual Growth Rate.

(3) Figures in [–] indicates Individual items percentage to Total.

Source: NSE Web Site.

Table-6.11: Settlement System in F&O Segment at BSE

(Rs. Crore)

Year	*Index/Stock Futures*		*Index/Stock Options*		Total
	MTM Settlement	*Final Settlement*	*Premium Settlement*	*Exercise Settlement*	
2000 -01	50.5 (–) [97.9]	1.1 (–) [2.1]	NA (–) [0.0]	NA (–) [0.0]	51.6 (–) [100.0]
2001 -02	25.8 (-48.9) [73.7]	1.5 (36.4) [4.3]	5.1 (–) [14.6]	2.6 (–) [7.4]	3.5 -32.2) [100.0]
2002 -03	12.2 (-52.7) [93.0]	0.6 (-60.0) [4.6]	0.3 (-94.1) [2.3]	0.02 -99.1) [0.1]	13.12 -62.9) [100.0]
2003 -04	53.3 (336.9) [85.0]	1.0 (66.7) [1.6]	8.2 (2,633.3) [13.1]	0.2 (900.0) [0.3]	62.7 (377.9) [100.0]
2004 -05	19.0 (-64.4) [11.2]	0.9 (-10.0) [0.5]	147.0 (1,692.7) [86.7]	2.7 (1,250.0) [1.6]	169.6 (170.5) [100.0]
Total	160.8 [48.4]	5.1 [1.5]	160.0 [48.4]	5.52 [1.7]	332.02 [100.0]

Note: (1) NA: Not Available/Not Applicable.
(2) Figures in (–) indicates Annual Growth Rate.
(3) Figures in [–] indicates Individual items percentage to Total.

Source: BSE Web Site.

CHAPTER-VII

EMERGING PATTERN OF COMMODITY FUTURES MARKET

7.1: INTRODUCTION

Traditionally, developing countries are known to depend heavily on export of commodities for income generation. One study estimates that primary commodities account for 68 percent of exports of low-income developing countries, while it is 44 percent in case of high income developing countries. In the recent past, the share of commodity exports from developing countries has declined, but it is still quite high. Such dependency on a few commodities for income generation evidently exposes the traders and producers to commodity price uncertainties in the global markets.

The changes in commodity prices affect even the traders who are otherwise known to operate on tight margins. For instance, a trader who purchased tobacco or coffee from local farmers with an intention to export faces enormous risk if the international prices collapse before he sells his stock of tobacco / coffee. Uncertainty in commodity prices also affects the debt servicing capacity of the traders as well as the producer- farmers of the commodity. This indirectly makes the cost of their debt prohibitively high, leading to increased cost of production. Even the availability of credit may at times become difficult, particularly for farmers whose earlier debts remained outstanding owing to a previous year's price disaster. The price-risk associated with commodities is also known to impact government revenues.

Uncertainty associated with national revenues ultimately makes the planning exercise of the government puzzled. Such risk even impacts the government's debt-servicing ability.

The ongoing liberalization process across the globe and the shift of countries towards market-driven economies has only worsened the situation further. Liberalization of commodity markets has resulted in drastic changes. One, the prices of commodities are hitting "multi-year-heights", and two, the style of managing price-risks associated with commodity trading has undergone a drastic changes. The governments of developing countries are finding it increasingly difficult to intervene in the markets with support prices, etc., and stabilize commodity prices, owing to increased focus on mounting fiscal deficits.

7.2: COMMODITY PRICES: NATURE OF THE PROBLEM

Primary commodity prices and their markets are known to behave differently from those of the manufactured goods or services. Theoretical analysis suggests that commodity prices will fall relative to others because of the relatively inelastic demand. Thus, the real income of the commodity producers falls because inelastic demand prevents them from offsetting price movements with volume changes. The prime reason for extra volatility in commodity prices is the presence of natural shocks that are not predictable and mostly relate to the previous year's production or consumption decisions. A reduction in supply that can result in shocks, will lead to a sharp increase in price, followed by a slow or rapid reduction depending on the nature of the commodity. Commodity price cycles mostly have flat bottoms with occasional sharp peaks.

There are four important commodity price problems. They are: (i) Short-term fluctuations- common among the agriculture products, either within a year due to seasonal variations or from year to year because of normal weather variations; (ii) Medium-term changes- as seen often in oil or other mineral markets, responding to multi-year business cycles in the world economy; (iii) permanent changes effecting one or a few countries- owing to technological changes or the discovery of new technology which alters competitiveness; and (iv) Long-term declining commodity prices. Normally, the behavior of commodity prices will be shorter periods of rises than falls and this asymmetric behavior tends to impose costs on any scheme meant for balancing price fluctuations. All these expose producers to the dual problem of lower returns and higher risks.

7.3: TRADITIONAL METHODS FOR MANAGING COMMODITY PRICE-RISK

Governments are known to intervene in commodities markets essentially- (i) to make the price distribution less variable; (ii) to make prices and relatives more predictable; and (iii) to smoothening expenditure, given income flows. Against these theoretical underpinnings, developing countries are known to manage commodity price risks essentially in three ways- (a) Governments implement domestic and international price stabilization schemes; (b) Reserve management; and (c) Contingent finance.

Domestic price stabilization scheme involves purchase of commodities and creation of buffer stock when commodity prices fall below a certain predetermined price and sell it when the prices recover. Some countries like India are known to prescribe minimum support prices for various commodities produced by farmers to protect them from the falling prices and thereby enable them to at least recover their cost of production. Some other countries maintain a "stabilization fund" with an objective of compensating producers when prices fall and accumulating reserves when prices increase. However, large commodity stabilization schemes are known to inflict high costs on national economy by demanding large capital outlay. Secondly, they are often found to be ineffective during the periods of crisis. Thirdly, most of such schemes in the developing countries were found to be used more for achieving social objectives rather than for price stabilization. The net result is huge corruption and mismanagement of the scare capital.

As against this, the international commodities stabilization schemes involve agreements between export / import countries. These agreements essentially float around quota systems, buffers stocks, compensatory financing schemes, etc. They provide financial assistance to cope with external price or volumes shocks. Historically and theoretically, it is observed that:

(a) Benefits out of such agreements were not distributed among all the producers equally. It was often the major producers who were benefited by not joining a commodity agreement;

(b) Buffer stock operations were used under several international commodity stabilization agreements to influence world prices of the commodities rather than help the real producers;

(c) The agreements being defined by the prevailing market condition are often found to be less than sufficiently adaptable to changing markets in a dynamic world;

(d) At times, the success of agreements to raise international prices often lead to their ultimate failure, since it is the farmers who decide how much to produce and what to invest. For instance, it was reported that Tobacco growers in India are known to often cultivate more tobacco than what the National Tobacco Board authorizes, and the result is an excess in the market. The international agreements failures were presented in the Table-7.1.

Table-7.1: International Agreements: Failure

	Sugar	*Tin*	*Coffee*	*Cocoa*	*Rubber*
Initial Agreement Dates	1954	1954	1962	1972	1980
Status of Economic Clauses	Lapsed in 1963 and 1983	Collapsed in 1985	Suspended in 1989	Suspended in 1988	Suspended in 1996
Number of Agreements	4	6	4	4	3

Source: Gilbert, 1995, and World Bank.

Either the traditional methods of governmental intervention in the commodity markets for stabilization have failed to deliver results or the governments are finding it increasingly difficult to allocate such huge capital at the cost of growing fiscal deficits, more so under the evolving market dynamics. The result is that most of the governments have withdrawn from market stabilization programs, shifting a part or all of commodity price risks from the government to the private sector.

7.4: MANAGING PRICE RISK BY COMMODITY DERIVATIVES

The slow withdrawal of governments from market stabilization activities resulted in a search for new alternatives, and thus derivatives entered into the commodity markets. Commodity derivative instruments aim at making commodity prices and revenues more predictable, rather than stabilizing them. They simply remove price uncertainty for commercial transactions and thereby reduce uncertainty in revenues. Commodity derivative markets have several advantages over price stabilization schemes hitherto operated by governments:

(a) Trading in commodity derivatives may result in transfer of risk from domestic markets to global markets;

(b) Trading in commodity derivatives increases credit worthiness of a borrower by insuring this revenue from future price fluctuations and thus, his loan repaying capacity is increases;

(c) Derivatives are market neutral and the premiums are determined by markets.

(d) Comparatively operating commodity derivatives were less expensive; and

(e) Secured prices help the farmers to make appropriate decisions about allocation of resources.

7.5: MEANING

A futures contract is an agreement to purchase/sell the commodity at a specific price and on a specific future date. These are traded in commodity futures exchanges where the counterparty risk is taken over by the exchange itself. Unlike in the stock market derivatives, the settlement in the commodity derivative markets is often accomplished through physical delivery of the underlying asset. Secondly, to meet the margin requirements either under "initial margin" or "mark-to-market-margin", farmers can as well lodge the title pertaining to the underlying commodity with the exchange/clearing corporation.

7.6: OBJECTIVES

The Chapter "Emerging Pattern of Commodity Futures Market" is based on the following objectives:

* To introduce the nature of commodity price problems and the problems with the use of traditional methods for managing commodity price risk.
* To know the importance of commodity derivative markets in India.
* To examine the role of commodity futures trading in India.
* To study the impediments for the development of commodity futures trading in India.
* To suggest the measures for the development commodity futures trading in India.

7.7: EVOLUTION OF COMMODITY FUTURES MARKETS IN INDIA

India has a long history of trade in commodity derivatives; this sector remained underdeveloped due to government intervention in many commodity markets to control prices. The production, supply and distribution of many agricultural commodities are still governed by the state and forwards & futures trading are selectively introduced with stringent controls. Free trade in many commodity items is restricted under the Essential Commodities Act, 1955 and Agriculture Productive Marketing Committees Acts of various state governments.

The Bombay Cotton Trade Association has set up the first commodity exchange in India and formal organized futures trading started in cotton in 1875. Subsequently, many exchanges came up in different parts of the country for futures trade in various commodities. The Gujrati Vyapari Mandali came into existence in 1900, which undertook futures trade in oilseeds for the first time in the country. The Calcutta Hessian Exchange Ltd and East India Jute Association Ltd were set up in 1919 and 1927 respectively for futures trade in raw jute. In 1921, futures in cotton were organized in Mumbai under the auspices of East India Cotton Association. Many exchanges were set up in major agricultural centres in north India before the World War broke out and they were mostly engaged in wheat futures until it was prohibited. The existing exchanges in Hapur, Muzaffarnagar, Meerut, Bhatinda, etc., were established during this period. During and in the aftermath of Second World War, futures trading in most of the agro-commodities were banned allegedly to curb hoarding and inflation.

However, the government withdrew the ban on futures with passage of Forward Contract Regulation Act in 1952. The Act also provided for the establishment and constitution of Forward Markets Commission (FMC) for the purpose of exercising the regulatory powers assigned to it by the Act. Later, futures trade was altogether banned by the government in 1966 in order to have control on the movement of prices of many agricultural and essential commodities. After the ban of futures trade, all the exchanges went out of business and many traders started resorting to unofficial and informal trade in futures. On the recommendation of the Khusro Committee in 1980, government reintroduced futures on some selected commodities including cotton, jute, potatoes, etc. As part of economic liberalization of the 1990s, the government of India in 1993 appointed an expert committee on forward markets under the chairmanship of KN Kabra. Its report submitted in 1994 and recommended the reintroduction of futures, which were banned in 1966 and also to widen its coverage to many more agriculture commodities. In order to give more thrust on agricultural sector, the National Agricultural Policy 2000 envisaged external and domestic market reforms and dismantling of all controls and regulations in agricultural commodity markets. It also proposed enlargement of coverage of futures markets to reduce the wide fluctuations in commodity prices and for hedging the risk arising from price fluctuations.

7.8: PRESENT STATUS OF COMMODITY FUTURES MARKET

In the Budget speech delivered on 28th February 2002, the then Finance Minister announced expansion of futures and forward trading to cover all agricultural commodities. This was followed by the removal of prohibition of futures trading on 27 (out of 81 items) of oilseeds, oils and their cake in August 2002. Subsequently, in February 2003, the Government removed the prohibition on the remaining 54 commodities also under the

Forward Contract (Regulation) Act, 1952, thus removing the statutory hurdles on futures trading in general and the agricultural sector in particular. The Securities Contracts (Regulation) Act 1956 was also amended in August 2003 to provide for commodity derivatives. Soon thereafter, the FMC granted permission to three national multi commodity exchanges, viz., National Multi-Commodity Exchange of India Ltd. (NMCE), Ahmedabad, National Commodity & Derivatives Exchange (NCDEX), Mumbai, and Multi Commodity Exchange (MCX), Mumbai. The 'national status' given to these exchanges implied that they would be automatically permitted to conduct futures trading in all commodities subject to clearance of bye-laws and contract specifications by the FMC. While the NMCE, Ahmedabad commenced futures trading in November 2002, MCX and NCDEX, Mumbai commenced operations in October/December 2003 respectively.

Table-7.2: Exchanges and Commodities

S.No.	*Exchange*	*Commodity*
1.	India Pepper & Spices Trade Association, (IPSTA) Kochi	Pepper (both domestic and international contracts)
2.	Vijai Beopar Chambers Ltd., Muzaffarnagar	Gur, Mustard seed
3.	Rajdhani Oils & Oilseeds Exchange Ltd., Delhi	Gur, Mustard seed, its oil & oil cake
4.	Bhatinda Om & Oil Exchange Ltd., Bhatinda	Gur
5.	The Chamber of Commerce, Hapur	Gur, Potatoes and Mustard seed
6.	The Meerut Agro Commodities Exchange Ltd., Meerut	Gur
7.	The Bombay Commodity Exchange Ltd., Mumbai	Oilseed Complex (Castor oil international contracts)
8.	Rajkot Seeds, Oil & Bullion Merchants Association, Rajkot	Castor seed, Groundnut, its oil & cake, cottonseed, its oil & cake, cotton (kapas) and RBD palmolein
9.	The Ahmedabad Commodity Exchange, Ahmedabad	Castor seed, Cottonseed, its oil and oilcake

10.	The East India Jute & Hessian Exchange Ltd., Calcutta	Hessian & Sacking
11.	The East India Cotton Association Ltd., Mumbai	Cotton
12.	The Spices & Oilseeds Exchange Ltd., Sangli	Turmeric
13.	National Board of Trade, Indore	Soya seed, Soya oil and Soya meals. Rape seed/Mustard seed its oil cake and RBD Palmolien
14.	The First Commodities Exchange of India Ltd., Kochi	Copra/Coconut, its oil & oil cake
15.	Central India Commercial Exchange Ltd., Gwalior	Gur and Mustard seed
16.	E-sugar India Ltd., Mumbai	Sugar
17.	National Multi-Commodity Exchange of India Ltd., Ahmedabad	Several Commodities
18.	Coffee Futures Exchange India Ltd., Bangalore	Coffee
19.	Surendranagar Cotton Oil & Oilseeds, Surendranagar	Cotton, Cottonseed, Kapas
20.	E-Commodities Ltd., New Delhi	Sugar
21.	National Commodity & Derivatives Exchange Ltd., Mumbai	Several Commodities
22.	Multi Commodity Exchange Ltd., Mumbai	Several Commodities
23.	Bikaner Commodity Ltd., Bikaner	Mustard seed its oil & oilcake, Gram, Guar seed, Guar Gum
24.	Haryana Commodities Ltd., Hissar	Mustard seed complex
25.	Bullion Association Ltd., Jaipur	Mustard seed Complex

Presently futures trading (options trading is still prohibited in the country) permitted in all the commodities. Trading takes place in about 78 commodities through 25 Exchanges/Associations (Table-7.2). Besides, FMC has also given in principle approval to NSC InfoTech Ltd., Hyderabad, United Planters Association of South India, Connoor (Tamil Nadu), and SGI Commodity Exchanges, Mumbai. While the first two exchanges will trade in Sugar and Tea respectively, the SGI commodity Exchange will deal with Soya Bean, Groundnut, their oils and oil cakes.

Out of 25 exchanges, which were functional as on March 31, 2004, three, viz., National Multi-Commodity Exchange of India Ltd., Ahmedabad, National Commodity & Derivatives Exchange Ltd., Mumbai and Multi Commodity Exchange Ltd., Mumbai are national exchanges. All other exchanges are regional exchanges. All the national exchanges are demutualized, managed by a Board comprising independent directors, adopt screen based trading system and daily mark to market margining.

Table-7.3: Turnover on Commodity Futures Markets

(Rs. Crore)

Year	*NCDEX*	*NBOT*	*MCX*	*NMCE*	*Total*
2001-02	0	14,278	0	0	14,278
	(–)	(–)	(–)	(–)	(–)
	[0.0]	[100.0]	[0.0]	[0.0]	[100.0]
2002-03	0	34,376	0	4,572	38,948
	(–)	(140.8)	(–)	(–)	(172.8)
	[0.0]	[88.3]	[0.0]	[11.7]	[100.0]
2003-04	1,490	53,014	2,456	23,842	80,802
	(–)	(54.2)	(–)	(421.4)	(107.5)
	[1.8]	[65.6]	[3.0]	[29.5]	[100.0]
2004-05*	54,011	51,038	30,695	7,943	1,43,687
	(3,524.9)	(-3.7)	(1,150.0)	(-66.7)	(77.8)
	[37.6]	[35.5]	[21.4]	[5.5]	[100.0]
Total	55,501	1,52,706	33,151	36,357	2,77,715
	[20.0]	[55.0]	[12.0]	[13.0]	[100.0]

Note: (1) NCDEX= National Commodity and Derivatives Exchange, Mumbai.
(2) NBOT= National Board of Trade, Indore.
(3) MCX= Multi Commodity Exchange, Mumbai.
(4) NMCE= National Multi Commodity Exchange, Ahmedabad.
(5) * =Indicates figures taken from first half of the year.
(6) Figures in (–) indicates the percentage of annual growth rate.
(7) Figures in [–] indicates the percentage to total.

Source: Economic Survey 2004-05, p.84.

7.9: COMMODITY FUTURES TRADING IN INDIA

The third component of organized trading of standardized products in the country is in the commodity futures markets. In recent years, these markets have drawn upon the success of nationwide electronic trading on the equity market, and three new exchanges have come about: NCDEX, MCX and NMCE. The NCDEX has setup 505 terminals in 138 centers, MEX has setup 763 terminals in 132 centers and NMCE has setup 346 terminals at 96 centers. These terminals facilitate pooling up of orders from across the country and feed them to the computerized order system to match them. This has offered transparency in price discovery.

We observed the following trends and patterns of commodity derivatives trading in India over a short period of its introduction (Table-7.3):

(a) *NCDEX*: It was commenced operations only in December 2003 and in the four months ended March 2004, the exchange achieved a turnover of Rs. 1,490 crore and in the first half of 2004-05 its turnover is increased to Rs. 54,011 crore. Its contribution to total turnover is 1.8 percent and 37.6 percent in the year 2003-04 and the first half of 2004-05 respectively.

(b) *NBOT*: The commodity turnover on this exchange is commenced before the commencement of three national exchanges. Its proportion to total turnover is 100%, 88.3%, 65.6% and 35.5% from the first year of the study to the first half of the last year. This downward trend witnessed the importance of national exchanges in the commodity derivatives market.

(c) *MCX*: This exchange commenced operations in November 2003, during the first four months the exchange achieved a turnover of Rs. 2,456 crore and it increased to Rs. 30,695 crore in the first half of 2004-05. The exchange contribution is increased from 3.0% to 21.4% for its ten months period of commencement.

(d) *NMCE*: It is the first to commence operations among the national exchanges. This exchange is reported to be the

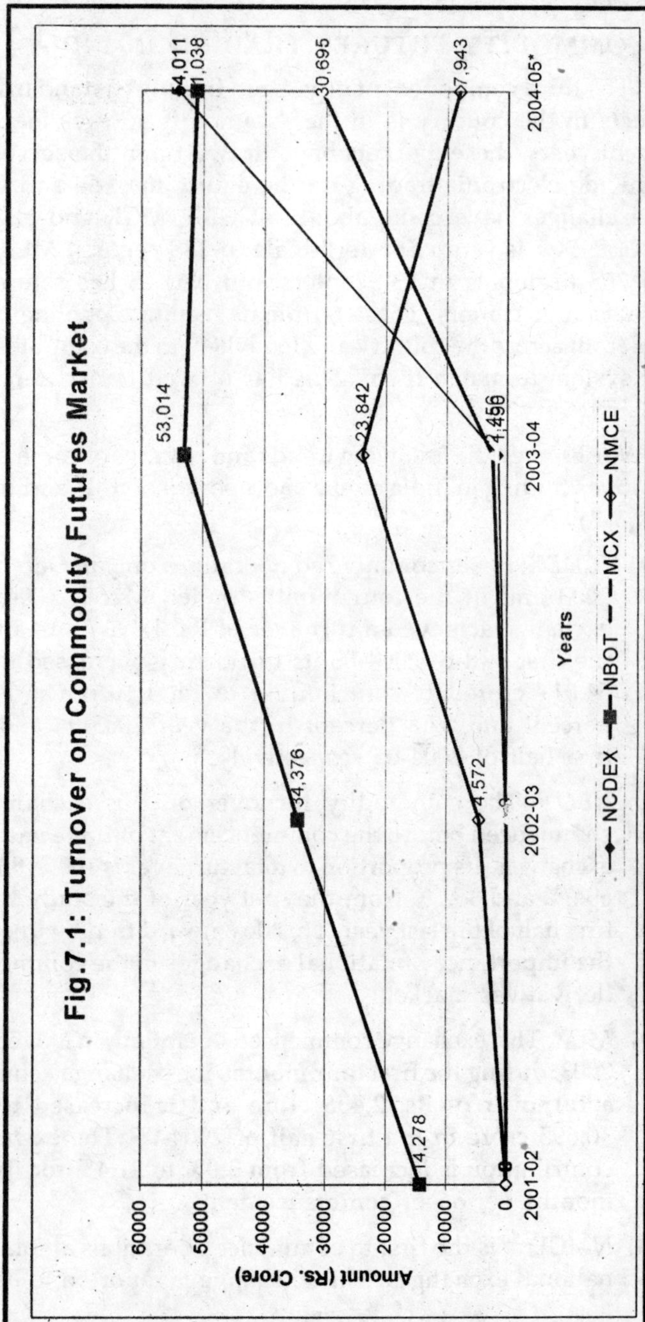
Fig.7.1: Turnover on Commodity Futures Market
Amount (Rs. Crore)
60000
50000
40000
30000
20000
10000
0
2001-02
2002-03
2003-04
2004-05*
Years
14,278
34,376
53,014
51,038
54,011
4,572
23,842
7,943
30,695
4,456
1,490
NCDEX
NBOT
MCX
NMCE

only commodity exchange in the world to have received ISO 9001:2000 certification from British Standard Institutions (BSI). It commenced futures trading in 24 commodities on 26th November, 2002. Turnover is increased from Rs. 4,572 crore to Rs. 23,842 crore and it decreased to Rs. 7,943 over the study period of its commencement of operations.

(e) In the first half of 2004-05, all commodity (national as well as regional) futures exchanges clocked trading volume of Rs. 1.7 lakh crore. This works out to roughly one third of the Government of India Bond market and one-tenth of exchange trading on the equity market.

7.10: IMPEDIMENTS FOR THE DEVELOPMENT OF COMMODITY FUTURES TRADING IN INDIA

Commodity futures markets in India are still not developed as compared to other countries. The dominant political ideology during early years after independence dealt a severe blow to development of futures markets in India. It is only after the onset of liberalization during 1990s, that attitude towards futures trading has changed and its potential benefits are now being acknowledged in the policy circles. The major problems afflicting the commodity markets are: (a) Poor infrastructure in the exchanges, (b) Lack of on-line trading facilities in the large number of exchanges, (c) Low level of awareness among various stakeholders including farmers, (d) Strong presence of unofficial "havala" trading, (e) High operational costs, (f) Unfavorable/ stringent trading parameters, (g) Single commodity focus, and (h) Poor transparency in transactions.

7.11: SUGGESTIONS FOR THE DEVELOPMENT OF COMMODITY FUTURES TRADING IN INDIA

The following prerequisites are certain to give a big boost to commodity futures trading in India:

(a) A negotiable document that furnishes the full details of the underlying asset of the futures being traded so that the title of the goods can be transferred from one individual to another without undertaking the physical delivery of stocks.

(b) An agency that can help the seller and buyer by grading the stocks being offered by the seller for sale and certify its quality, grade so that the buyer can be sure of what grade of commodity he is trading on.

(c) There must be an agency that takes care of the stock that is being traded in the derivative exchanges and ensures that quality is maintained till the stock under the traded contact is delivered to the ultimate buyer, at a reasonable cost.

(d) Commodities trading have settlements in dematerialized form so that traders from across the country can trade on futures being certain of the underlying commodity in terms of its quality, grade, quantity and its maintenance during the intervening period.

(e) Banks come forward to sanction agriculture produce loans to farmers against the pledge of warehouse receipts and futures contracts of national derivative exchanges. They should also explore the possibility of offering hedge prospects to farmers on a pooled basis, with banks as intermediaries between exchanges and farmers and thus pave the way for active futures trading on agriculture commodities so that farmers can enjoy the benefit of dependable price discovery well in advance to their planting and sowing season.

(f) As of now, the Forward Contracts Regulations Act (FCRA) 1952 doesn't permit index based products and these are traded on the commodity exchanges. But this may soon as the FCRA 1952 is in the process of undergoing considerable changes, subject to parliament clearance.

(g) The market must mature with widespread awareness amongst various market players, liquidity would increase further with a well-diversified basket of commodities.

(h) The FMC does not have similar powers as enjoyed by the CFTC in the US. The FCRA 1952 is under the scanner of the present Government and its amendment is likely to bestow more powers on the FMC to regulate this market.

(i) The Union Finance Minister, in his Budget-2005, has quoted for a single regulatory regime. It will find very difficult to tackle complexities in the socio-economic dimensions of this fledging commodity futures.

(j) Healthy competition is always beneficial to catalyze the growth in any market. In this case too, the Government has to take necessary steps for the implementation of online commodity trading on the regional exchanges also.

(k) Mutual Funds should be allowed to enter into commodity futures market as it will enable them to diversify their portfolio risk with commodities like gold, silver, crude oil, soya oil etc. the risk and returns for the investors in these funds will depend on the nature of the fund itself, such as Growth, Balanced or Safe funds.

(l) The market should be made more broad-based by allowing banks and FIIs to participate in commodity futures. Options should be allowed to be traded, as that will give one more efficient tool to the participants to apply various hedging strategies for averting their price risks.

CHAPTER-VIII

SUMMARY OF FINDINGS CONCLUSIONS AND SUGGESTIONS

8.1: INTRODUCTION

The present study on "THE CHANGING PATTERN OF CAPITAL MARKETS IN INDIA -AN ANALYTICAL STUDY" has been broadly divided into four major parts. The first part of the study deals with the trends in domestic savings, changing pattern of primary capital issues including the Euro and Book -Building System. Second part covers the secondary market analysis through its indicators like P/E ratio, Turnover Ratio, stock market volatility & liquidity and its relationship, the impact of FIIs investment on stock market volatility & liquidity, and the performance of regional stock exchanges, and investors' protection in India. Third part examines the trends and pattern of financial derivatives at NSE and BSE. Fourth part evaluates the commodity futures trading in India.

8.2: FINDINGS

The important findings from all the chapters of the study are presented in the following four parts:

Part-I: Primary Market:

- The primary and secondary markets are an integral part of the capital market of a country. The organic development of the security's markets as well as the scope for higher productive capacity of industry and social welfare of the people depend upon the efficiency of the capital market.

- The number of intermediaries has gone down substantially. Their number fell by 65 from 143 to 78 and in terms of percentage, it declined by 45 percent. The next category in this class includes bankers to an issue, whose number has come down to 55 from 67, a decline of 12. The other two categories-merchant bankers and debenture trustees also registered a decline of one percent to stand at 123 and 34 respectively.
- Only two categories of intermediaries; portfolio managers and underwriters showed positive growth of six and four at 60 and 47 respectively. The overall decline can be attributed to the excessive increase, i.e., the large number of intermediaries who have entered the market. Compared to many of the international markets, the number of intermediaries registered in India, in certain categories, still continues to be on the high side.
- Between 1990-91 and 2003-04, the primary market has witnessed introduction of variety of financial instruments with a varying maturity, return and other features in tune with that of new liberalized economic policies. Not only had there been a flush of financial instruments, but also a variety of tax incentive schemes were extended to promote savings and investments.
- Annual growth rate of GDP and GDS ranges in between 7.9 percent to 17.9 percent and 5.8 percent to 29.9 percent respectively. The average annual growth rate of GDP and GDS are recorded at 13 percent and 15 percent respectively. According to this trend we can say that the growth rate in GDS is higher than that of GDP. The ratio of GDS to GDP is increased from 23.10 percent (1990-91) to 28.13 percent (2003-04) with a net increase of 5.03 percent barring ups and downs in a couple of years.
- In the above background, it can be concluded that the array of financial instruments and incentive schemes had improved the savings rate. Further, they have also helped to prevent decline in savings rate.

- The gross domestic savings during 2003-04 amounted to Rs. 7,76,420 crore. A bulk of the savings amounting to Rs. 7,31,387 crore (94.20%) was contributed by the household sector. Private corporate sector accounted for Rs.1,10,484 crore, while the public sector's share has negative at Rs. -65,451 crore. What is relevant to note is that over the years, the proportion of savings by household sector has been going up with a slight variations. While the household sector accounted for about 83.67 percent of the savings in 1990-91, it went up to 94 percent of the savings in 2003-04. Therefore, it is the savings of the household sector have fuelled for encouraging trend in the primary market.
- The average number of capital issues was at 904 and their amount was at Rs.49703 crore. The numbers of issues were highest at 2122 indicating 311.2 percent of growth rate. The year 2000-01 claimed highest position with an amount of Rs.77,383 crore.
- The decline in the number of public issues in recent years did not influence the decline in their amount due to the fact that number of companies tapped the capital market have come with the mega issues of IPO's.
- The impact of scams such as Harshad Mehta, Kethan Parekh and doubtful quality issues such as MS Shoes East, CRB Capital Market and Usha Rectifier Corporation have shown greater negative influence on household sector investors and they have abstained from the primary issues in the later half of the post Economic Reforms period and which has contributed for under subscription of several IPO's.
- The amount of capital issues steeply declined to -38.7 percent in the year 2001-02 due to adverse capital market conditions, price volatility, attack on World Trade Centre on September 11th 2001 etc.
- The years of highest rate of growth in number and amount of capital issues of public sector have accompanied a negative growth in the private sector capital issues indicating a negative relationship. This may be due to

the fact that if both the sectors are tapping the capital market with mega issues, the market may not absorb such huge amount and issues may be under subscribed. Hence, the issues were planned in such a way that in the years of mega issues of public sector were associated with lower number of private sector capital issues.

- The second year of the post Economic Reforms period has shown greater impact on the private sector to come out with mega issues offering huge amount for the public. This trend was caught by the public sector capital issues in the year 1993-94. This indicates that there is a lag and lead relationship between public and private sector capital issues.
- The growth rate of capital issues in both the sectors has declined significantly from 1993-94 on wards in view of depressed market conditions, different scams and political instability along with September 11, 2001 event.
- The average growth rate of amount of capital issues of the public sector was at 30.4 percent and that of the private sector was at 37.1 percent.
- The manufacturing sector has accounted for 73 to 82.3 percent, capital issues from this sector during 1991-92 to 1994-95, has claimed significantly highest number of issues. The number of issues in service sector have accounted for highest position ranging between 61.7 percent and 74.5 percent from the year 1996-97 to 2002-03. This reflects that in the first four years of post liberalization the manufacturing sector has come out with large number of public issues, whereas in the rest of the period due to encourage given to the service sector more specifically telecommunications, transportation, treasury sector, growth of mutual funds have contributed for maximum number of capital issues. The mining industry's number of issues moved among 1.3 percent to 5.0 percent reflecting very insignificant role in the total capital issues.
- On an average the services industry has accounted for major share with 59.0 percent of total capital issues,

while the manufacturing sectors 32.0 percent, giving very meager share to mining industry. This went to highlight that the service sector including irrigation and construction has gained highest proportion of total capital issues during the study period.

- The second half of the post liberalization period was dominated by the service sector companies to mobilize highest amount of capital from the public issues. This may be on account of the fact that on the basis of Narsimham Committee Recommendations, the banking sector reforms were introduced and many banks have come out with the mega public issues, on the other hand have launched variety of innovative schemes by public sector and private sector mutual funds in order to mobilize resources from the primary capital market.
- In the first six years of post liberalization period number of public issues have accounted for highest proportion ranging between 42.4 percent in 1991-92 to 68.1 percent in 1996-97. Whereas, the private placements claimed more than 76 percent of total number of issues from 1997-98 to 2004-05. The share of number of Euro issues was moved between 0.40 to 4.1 percent. Whereas rights issues varied between 45.7 percent and 3.8 percent. The right issues were very prominent in first three years of post liberalization period.
- This trend highlights that the first half of the post liberalized period was dominated by IPO's and right issues. When the secondary capital markets were unstable with price volatility, scams and various events, the companies that have preferred private placements as the safe root for mobilization of funds.
- The average number of capital issues was 63.4 percent in the size group of below Rs.10 crore, 18.0 percent in the size group of Rs.10 to Rs.50 crore, 6.1 percent in the size group of Rs. 50 crore to Rs. 100 crore and 12.6 percent in the size group of Rs. 100 crore and above.
- The mega issues which were accounting for on an average 12.6 percent of total number of issues have claimed 81.4

percent of total amount of capital issues, and it was 90.1 percent in the year 2000-01.

- The capital issues size group of below Rs.10 crore has claimed highest number, however its share in total amount of capital issues was very insignificant and moved between 0.3 percent and 18.9 percent during the period under review. The size group of Rs. 10 crore to Rs. 50 crore has mobilized 8.6 percent of total amount of capital issues. Whereas the size group of Rs. 50 to 100 crore has claimed 7.7 percent.
- Thus we conclude that with regard to number of capital issues the size group below Rs.10 crore with 63.4 percent claimed major share, whereas in respect of amount of capital issues the mega size group of Rs. 100 crore and above has mobilized 81.4 percent of total capital issues.
- The average number of capital issues was 42.0 percent in the Western Region, 24.7 percent in the Northern Region, 23.0 percent in the Southern Region and only 10.3 percent in the Eastern Region.
- The average amount of capital issues was 53.3 percent in the Western Region, 26.7 percent in the Northern Region, 14.2 percent in the Southern Region and only 5.8 percent in the Eastern Region.
- The average number and amount of capital issues were shown the dissimilar proportion of contribution from the four regions. Hence, we conclude that the Western Region contributes above 50 percent of the total capital issues and the remaining was contributed by the other three regions.
- The annual growth rate in number and amount of Euro Issues were witnessed greater fluctuations. These fluctuations were influenced by various reasons like, steps taken by the Government from the time to time, rate of growth / expansion of individual companies and their ambition to raise funds from overseas, etc.
- The last two years of the study witnessed the positive growth rate in number as well as amount of Euro Issues.

This is because; the companies were permitted to make Euro Issues by the Government of India.

- The foreign investment is encouraging, with the majority of equity participation in its portfolio. The Indian companies have been encouraged to access global capital market through the Euro issues GDRs and ADRs. The Euro issues have a brighter scope to access more foreign funds from Global Markets. There should be a national policy on Euro issues to monitor the various government agencies like SEBI, DEA, and RBI etc.
- The spirit beyond the introduction of book-building mechanism in India is to discover the right price for a public issue which in turn would eliminate unreasonable issue pricing by greedy promoters.

Part-II: Secondary Market:

* The number of new benchmarks are: online screen based trading, cent percent dematerialized trading, shortening of settlement cycle from T+5 to T+1, risk mitigating prudential norms of capital adequacy and exposure limits, value at risk based margining, real-time monitoring of positions and margins, automatic disablement of the terminals, a central counterparty, and trade / settlement guarantee fund, index based market wide circuit breakers, segregation of cash and derivative markets, enhancement of Governance standards among corportes and stock exchanges, continual disclosure requirements, registration and regulation of intermediaries - are already in place to manage and mitigate the risks in secondary market.
* There are only 7 stock exchanges in 1946, 9 in 1980 and 11 in 1990. As on March 31st 2005, 23 stock exchanges were operating in India.
* Over the time, number of brokers-proprietor firms and partnership firms has converted themselves into corporates. Out of 9,128 brokers registered with SEBI at the end of March 2005, 3,773 brokers, accounting for 41.33 percent of total, were corporate entities. At the end of March 2005, there were 13,684 sub-brokers

registered with the SEBI.

* At the end of March 2003, the primary listing of companies on stock exchanges was 9,413. The number of companies listed on the NSE was increased from 415 to 970 over a period of study. But in the case of BSE first six years showed the increasing trend and last six years showed the decreasing trend due to enormous response to the listings in NSE.

* The total number of FIIs registered with SEBI went up from 540 as on March 31st, 2004 to 685 as on March 31st, 2005, recording an increase of 145 over the year. The FIIs continued to remain bullish on the Indian securities for the second year in succession. The net FII investment in 2004-05 was Rs. 45,881 crore which was marginally higher than Rs. 45,764.5 crore in 2003-04.

* The stock market in India gradually gathered momentum with benchmark BSE Sensex crossing 6000-mark on November 17th, 2004 and reached an all time high of 6,915.05 on March 8th, 2005 before closing at 6,492.82 on March 31st, 2005. The market reached a crescendo when the Sensex zoomed past 7000-mark for the first time in its history in June 2005, then reached to all time high of 9300 points in December, 2005. The similar trend is observed on the NSE S&P CNX Nifty.

* The P/E ratio on the NSE S&P CNX Nifty shows the continuous up and down trend from 1998-99 to 2004-05. The BSE Sensex is also recorded the fluctuating trends by taking more time than the NSE S&P CNX Nifty.

* Change is an essential ingredient of any organization. Change may be voluntary or forced. RSEs and their pathetic conditions are a result of failure to adopt voluntary changes and thus getting left behind. While the world moved on to better technology and innovations, RSEs continued to live in their cocoon and closed their eyes to the emerging market realities, which brought their doom.

* This attitude, coupled with dynamic regulatory changes

led to a total collapse of the RSEs. They continued to think that their age-old supremacy as a stock exchange would continue till eternity. But, with credit to NSE, post 1994 even a stock exchange is now considered more of a service provider and not as an extension of regulatory machinery.

* At a point of time even the colossal BSE also felt this threat but it realized the tide and decided to change voluntarily while RSEs continued to clamor for protection and crib around on every possible platform - which yielded no results. Finally it is time for RSEs to adopt changes, which are essential for survival.
* They are out of business and will become extinct in no time, if do not act fastly and take the suggested steps with all sincerity. Even when they may decide to use their strengths for educating the people about investing in stock and its nitty-gritty they will be doing yeoman service to the nation and also earn suitable revenues in this process. It will add to the market, new and informed investors and also the overall depth of market shall expand. Banks, who are presently bleeding due to excessive deposits, will get relieved, as a good amount of money may get absorbed in the stock exchanges.
* As new money moves in, undoubtedly it shall boost the morale of the entire market and stock valuations shall rise due to increased demand for stocks, created by this new breed of investors. An overall sentiment booster is that the capital market in India needs changed RSEs.
* The SEBI has playing an important role for the redressal of investor grievances in the Indian capital market. Its rate of redressal is around 95 percent. It is organizing various investors' awareness programmes throughout the country by covering different towns and cities. In the era of liberalization, privatization and globalization it has improved its efficiency to meet the global standards.
* The volatility of stock Indices is measured by using Standard Deviation and Co-efficient of Variation, based on these measures we find that Nifty is highly consistent

and less volatile followed by S&P CNX 500, whereas Nifty Junior was highly volatile followed CNX Midcap 200. Thus it shows that there was volatility in the stock Indices of Nifty.

* The volatility of BSE stock prices is highest in the case of BSE Sensex followed by BSE 100 Index with 745.0 and 496.2 respectively. On the other hand the BSE 200 Index has shown more consistent and less volatile since its Co-efficient of Variation is 66.5 percent. We find that BSE 200 Index followed by BSE Sensex were less volatile as compared to BSE 500 Index and BSE 100 Index.

* A comparative analysis of stock Indices volatility of BSE Sensex and NSE Nifty followed by other Indices reveals that the volatility of BSE Sensex and NSE Nifty have shown similar pattern because, the Co-efficient of Variations of them were 21.37 and 21.80 respectively.

* It is observed that the April month of every year has experienced the highest average volatility of 2.17, 2.43, 2.09, 2.05, 2.22, 3.23, 1.98 and 2.28 on S&P CNX Nifty, CNX Nifty Junior, CNX Midcap 200, S&P CNX 500, BSE Sensex, BSE 100 Index, BSE 200 Index and BSE 500 Index respectively.

* NSE CNX Nifty and BSE Sensex have indicated the highest volatile year was the 1992. The Indices other than S&P CNX Nifty and BSE Sensex have shown that the year 2000 is the highest volatility year.

* The Capitalization of stock market is influenced by price movements in the market. The market capitalization of NSE has increased by 6.32 times in 2003-04 when compared to 1994-95. Whereas the market capitalization of BSE has increased by 2.4 times for the same period. The increased market capitalization in NSE may be on account of greater volatility of stock prices.

* The Turnover of stock exchange transactions will also indicate depth of the market. There was greater crash in the market prices in 2001-02 and caused for lowest turnover indicating a decline of -78.7 and -69.7 respectively

of NSE and BSE.

* The number of companies listed has declined abnormally over a decade and the share of NSE has increased significantly and equating with that of BSE listed companies.
* Volatility in number of shares traded daily on NSE and BSE varies among 1.90 to 1.24 and 2.00 to 1.32 times respectively. This represents that the volatility in BSE is greater than that of NSE.
* The volatility in number of transactions recorded at NSE and BSE is varied between 2.00 to 1.29 and 2.00 to 1.28 respectively. The highest and lowest volatilities were recorded at NSE and BSE are nearly similar.
* Percentage change in pre and post budget ranges between 24.61 to -10.87 and 48.28 to -19.06 respectively. We observed that the year 1992 is the highest volatile year in the pre as well as post budget percentage change on the BSE Sensex.
* Relevance of the budget effect is diminishing every year because of the critical policy decisions are taken on a regular basis by the government. The government has already taken steps to encourage equity investments earlier like abolition of long-term capital gains tax. Therefore it can react for any negative or positive implications of budgets.
* Higher volatility exhibits the higher liquidity and in turn the higher liquidity is leads to the higher volatility. In this process we have drawn the following findings:
* The average rate of volatility of the BSE Sensex and NSE Nifty was recorded at 1.60% and 1.56% respectively.
* The volatility correlation on the stock exchanges was recorded at +0.98. This indicates that the two stock indices were changing in the similar direction and pattern throughout the study.
* The average TOR and TVR on the two exchanges were recorded at 57.07%, 92.00% and 21.01%, 32.91%

respectively. NSE had the higher TOR and TVR by comparing with the BSE.

* The higher the rate of SINDEX was observed on the NSE and BSE with 53.78% and 39.41% respectively. This represents that the NSE is more liquid than that of BSE.

* The coefficient of correlation between volatility and liquidity in the BSE is at +0.66. The calculated value (3.1) of t is higher than the table value (2.4), the correlation is significant. Hence, the volatility is causing the liquidity of the stock market prices and vice versa.

* The coefficient of correlation between volatility and liquidity in the NSE is +0.49. The calculated value (1.71) of t is less than the table value (2.4), the correlation is not significant. Hence, the volatility is not causing the liquidity of the stock market prices and vice versa.

* This study points out a paradoxical situation with regard to the relationship between volatility and liquidity on the BSE and NSE stock market indices.

* The impact of Foreign Institutional Investment on Stock Market Liquidity and Volatility in India has revealed the following broad findings:

* The FIIs investment in Indian securities market has shown fluctuating trends year after year. It was at US $ 1.6 billion in the year 1994-95 and reached to US $ 2.0 billion in the year 19995-96, then reached to US $ 9.9 billion in 2003-04.

* The number of FIIs has also steeply increased from 158 in 1993-94 to 540 in 2003-04 registering an increase at 242 percent and it was further, steeply gone up to 733 as on July 14th, 2005, registering a record high growth of 364 percent during the period of study.

The reasons for enormous enthusiasm of FIIs in Indian capital market may be on account of the following:

* The Indian capital market is well structured, regulated and matured.

* The P/E ratios of Indian securities are lowest among world capital markets.
* Relatively low risk associated with moderate rate of return and investment opportunities.
* Implementation of further capital market reforms along with liberalization of FIIs investment in India in different sectors.
* The optimistic growth rate in the GDP accompanied by low inflationary tendencies.
* Over pricing of securities in all other developed capital markets in the world.
* According to the Turn Over Ratio, FIIs investment affects the stock market liquidity to the maximum extent of 11 percent only and it is not significant factor influencing the liquidity of Indian capital market, because the other factors other than FIIs have shown greater impact at 89 percent on the stock market liquidity in India.
* The relationship between FII with Traded Value Ratio on BSE Sensex and NSE Nifty was recorded at low rate. This view is also supported by the co-efficient of determination, since it is very low at 3.24 and 0.49 percent of BSE Sensex and NSE Nifty respectively. Hence, it can be pointed out that the impact of FIIs on stock market liquidity is not at all significant.
* The FIIs to Mcap/GDP Ratio on BSE Sensex and NSE Nifty showed the positive relationship. This explains the impact of FII on stock market liquidity is up to the extent of only 42.25 and 25 percent.
* The high positive values of co-efficient of correlation at 0.968 between cumulative investment and BSE Sensex and NSE Nifty indicate that the market indices are highly influenced by the FIIs flows. However, there are several other factors which have not significantly influenced than FIIs. Hence, FIIs have emerged as the market movers in India.

Part-III: Financial Derivatives Market:

* The overall growth rate of turnover on derivatives market segment was recorded at 633.8 times and on the cash market segment was at -0.29 times. The increase in the growth rate of derivatives market is much higher than the cash market.

* NSE contributing a lion's share in the form of total turnover, average daily turnover, total number of contracts and turnover per contract. Above all, NSE emerged as a big market for the derivatives in India and it also competing with the global derivative markets. NSE occupied 20th position in the top 20 exchanges offering options and futures and 14th rank among the top 40 exchanges trading in futures.

* The Index futures and Stock Futures have been jointly contributing above 90 percent and remaining 10 percent was contributed by other products.

* We can differentiate Indian derivative market from the rest of the world in the relative share of options and futures. While in the rest of the world, options are more popular, contrary to it in India futures are more popular.

* All derivative contracts are currently on cash settlement basis. Cash settlement on the Futures market is higher than the Options market at NSE (88.3%) as well as BSE (51.0%).

* In the case of Index / Stock Futures, MTM settlement was recorded higher proportion at 86.9 percent and 48.4 percent at NSE and BSE respectively. The Premium Settlement in the point of view of Index / Stock Options was witnessed at 7.6% and 48.4% at NSE and BSE respectively.

Part-IV: Commodity Futures Market:

* The third component of organized trading of standardized products in the country is in the commodity futures markets. In recent years, these markets have drawn upon the success of nationwide electronic trading on the equity market, and three new exchanges have come about:

NCDEX, MCX and NMCE. The NCDEX has setup 505 terminals in 138 centers, MEX has setup 763 terminals in 132 centers and NMCE has setup 346 terminals at 96 centers. These terminals facilitate pooling up of orders from across the country and feed them to the computerized order system to match them. This has offered transparency in price discovery.

* The following are trends and pattern of commodity derivatives trading in India over a short period of its introduction:

* *NCDEX*: It was commenced operations only in December 2003 and in the four months ended March 2004, the exchange achieved a turnover of Rs. 1,490 crore and in the first half of 2004-05 its turnover has increased to Rs. 54,011 crore. Its contribution to total turnover is 1.8 percent and 37.6 percent in the year 2003-04 and the first half of 2004-05 respectively.

* *NBOT*: The commodity turnover on this exchange is commenced before the commencement of three national exchanges. Its proportion to total turnover is 100%, 88.3%, 65.6% and 35.5% from the first year of the study on wards. This downward trend indicates the importance of national exchanges in the commodity derivatives market.

* *MCX*: This exchange commenced operations in November 2003, during the first four months the exchange achieved a turnover of Rs. 2,456 crore and it increased to Rs. 30,695 crore in the first half of 2004-05. The exchange contribution is increased from 3.0% to 21.4% for its ten months period of commencement.

* *NMCE*: It is the first to commence operations among the national exchanges. This exchange is reported to be the only commodity exchange in the world to have received ISO 9001:2000 certification from British Standard Institutions (BSI). It commenced futures trading in 24 commodities on 26th November, 2002. Turnover is increased from Rs. 4,572 crore to Rs. 23,842 crore and it decreased to Rs. 7,943 over the study period of its

commencement of operations.

* In the first half of 2004-05, all commodity (national as well as regional) futures exchanges clocked trading volume of Rs. 1.7 lakh crore. This works out to be roughly one third of the Government of India Bond market and one-tenth of exchange trading on the equity market.

8.3: TESTING OF HYPOTHESES

A selected number of hypotheses are stated in Chapter-I, based on the review of various studies. They are tested here by taking the empirical analysis of the study into consideration.

HYPOTHESIS-I

Whether the performance of primary market is fairly satisfactory for mobilizing savings from various sections of investors?

The above hypothesis was examined in the present study by analyzing the average amount and percentage of savings according to gross domestic sector and household sector (for details refer Chapter-II). It was evident from the analysis that the gross domestic savings amount was increased from Rs. 1,31,340 crore to Rs. 7,76,420 crore over the study period and the financial savings of household sector was also increased from Rs. 49,640 crore to Rs. 3,48,799 crore over the same period. The percentage of Euro Issues was increased from 2.7 to 20.1 percent over the study period. From the above findings, it may be inferred that the performance of primary market is fairly satisfactory for mobilizing savings from various sectors of the investors. Hence, the above hypothesis stands valid.

HYPOTHESIS-II

The sector-wise, region-wise, industry-wise, and size-wise public issues do not have major diversities.

The above hypothesis is examined in the present study by analyzing trend and pattern of public issues over the study period (Chapter-III). It is clearly observed that the highest amount of contribution came from service sector (59%), Private placement (43%), Mega issues (78.3%), and Western-region (61.6%). Thus, it can be concluded that there were major diversities in the public issues. Hence, this hypothesis not stands valid.

HYPOTHESIS-III

Whether the pre-pricing of public issues has created confidence in the investing public and helped for mobilization of the capital?

This hypothesis is examined in the present study by taking Book-Building process for the initial public offer (Chapter-III). The share of mega issues in total capital mobilized was increased from 45.25 percent to 92.30 percent over the study period. It is prominent to note that the mega issues have flooded the capital market to capitalize the positive sentiment of the investors due bullish trend in the capital market followed by heavy inflow of funds from FIIs. This trend is also observed by the oversubscription of number of companies. Some of the prominent them are Bharat Shipyard Ltd. (72 times), Indoco Remedies Ltd. (68 times), Power Trading Corporation of India (38 times), Dishman Pharmaceuticals & Chemicals Ltd. (38 times), NDTV (37 times) and Biocon Ltd. (32 times). Therefore, the pre-pricing of public issues has created confidence in the investing public and helped for mobilization of the capital.

HYPOTHESIS-IV

The performance of secondary market will not affect the investors as well as its players.

The hypothesis is analyzed in the present study by taking the NSE and BSE indices (Chapter-V). The increasing or decreasing tendencies of indices in the secondary market, the amount of investment by both Indian as well as foreign institutional investors are also changing such fluctuations have also affected the earnings pattern of the players in the stock market like merchant bankers, under-writers, brokers to issues, debenture trustees, portfolio managers, lead managers etc. Therefore, the hypothesis is not valid. Hence, the performance of secondary market will affect the investors as well as its players.

HYPOTHESIS-V

SEBI through its regulatory measures has controlled the price rigging and price volatility and ensured safety to the investors.

This hypothesis has been tested by examining the correlation and t-test results for the number of cases investigated and completed, type of regulatory actions taken, prosecutions launched, and redressal of investor grievances by SEBI (Chapter-IV). The correlation between number of cases investigated and completed by SEBI is 0.774 and the calculated value of t at 5 percent level of significance is much higher than the table, hence, the correlation is significant. The relationship between redressal of investor grievances by SEBI is 0.84 and the calculated value of t is much higher than the table, hence, the correlation is significant. Therefore, the SEBI has been redressing the grievances of the investors from the time to time as well as it also controlling the price rigging, price volatility and introduced many investor awareness programmes. Hence, the above hypothesis stands valid.

HYPOTHESIS-VI

Whether financial derivatives in the secondary market enabled to minimize speculative tendencies and price volatility?

This hypothesis is examined in the present study by comparing stock market volatility on BSE and NSE (Chapter-V). BSE Sensex and NSE Nifty have shown the volatility of stock prices around 21%, the BSE 500 Index, S&P CNX 500 were around 22% and have similar pattern of stock price volatility. On account of introduction of futures and options trading has also not controlled the speculative tendencies and price volatility (Chapter-VI). Therefore, the financial derivative in the secondary market is not minimizing the speculative tendencies and price volatility.

HYPOTHESIS-VII

Whether the introduction of commodity futures exchanges in India has minimized the commodity price fluctuations in the economy?

This hypothesis has been tested by examining the results of commodity futures trading on the National Commodity & Derivatives Exchange Mumbai, Multi Commodity Exchange Mumbai, National Board of Trade Indore, and National Multi Commodity Exchange Ahmedabad and found that these exchanges are still not enough developed as compared to other exchanges in the abroad (Chapter-VII). The major problems afflicting the commodity markers are: poor infrastructure in the exchanges, lack of on-line trading facilities in the large number of exchanges, low level of awareness among various stakeholders including farmers, strong presence of unofficial 'havala' trading, high operational costs, unfavorable trading parameters, single commodity focus, and poor transparency in transactions. Therefore, the introduction of commodity futures exchanges in India is not minimizing the commodity price fluctuations in the economy.

8.4: CONCLUSIONS

The important conclusions of the study on "CHANGING PATTERN OF CAPITAL MARKETS IN INDIA - AN ANALYTICAL STUDY" are presented below:

* The growth rate in GDS was at 15%, is higher than that of GDP at 13%. The array of financial instruments and incentives had influenced for improved savings rate.
* The average growth rate of amount of capital issues of the public sector was at 30.4 percent and that of the private sector was at 37.1 percent.
* On an average the services industry has accounted for major share with 59 percent of total capital issues, while the manufacturing sector 32 percent; giving very meager share to mining industry. This went to highlight that the service sector including irrigation and construction has gained highest proportion of total capital issues during the study period.
* Private placements claimed more than 76 percent of total number of issues from 1997-98 to 2004-05. The share of number of Euro issues was moved between 0.40 to 4.1 percent. Whereas rights issues varied between 45.7 percent and 3.8 percent.
* The number of capital issues as per capital size group below Rs.10 crore was at 63.4 percent claimed major share, whereas in respect of amount of capital issues of mega size group of Rs.100 crore and above has mobilized 81.4 percent of total capital issues.

* Western Region contributes above 50 percent of the total capital issues and the remaining was contributed by the other three regions.

* The spirit beyond the introduction of book-building mechanism in India is to discover the right price for a public issue which in turn would eliminate unreasonable issue pricing by greedy promoters.

* There are only 7 stock exchanges in 1946, 9 in 1980 and 11 in 1990. As on March 31st 2005, 23 stock exchanges have been operating in India.

* RSEs and their pathetic conditions are on account of failure to adopt voluntary changes and thus, getting left behind. While the world moved on to better technology and innovations, RSEs continued to live in their cocoon and closed their eyes to the emerging market realities, which brought their doom.

* SEBI has been playing an important role for the redressal of investor's grievances in the Indian capital market. Its rate of redressal is around 95 percent. It has been organizing various investors' awareness programmes throughout the country by covering various towns and cities. In the era of liberalization, privatization and globalization it has to improve its efficiency to meet the global standards.

* A comparative analysis of stock Indices volatility of BSE Sensex and NSE Nifty followed by other Indices reveals that the volatility of BSE Sensex and NSE Nifty similar pattern because the Co-efficient of Variations of them was 21.37 and 21.80 respectively.

* It is found that the April month in every year has experienced the highest average volatility of 2.17, 2.43, 2.09, 2.05, 2.22, 3.23, 1.98 and 2.28 on S&P CNX Nifty, CNX Nifty Junior, CNX Midcap 200, S&P CNX 500, BSE Sensex, BSE 100 Index, BSE 200 Index and BSE 500 Index respectively. NSE CNX Nifty and BSE Sensex have identified 1992 as the highest volatile year.

* The relationship between volatility and liquidity on the

BSE is significant but on the NSE it is not significant. This study points out a paradoxical situation with regard to the relationship between volatility and liquidity on the BSE and NSE stock market indices.

* The impact of FIIs investment on stock market liquidity and volatility in India points out a paradoxical situation i.e. FIIs investment influences the stock market volatility but it does not true in the case of liquidity.

* NSE contributing a lion's share in the form of total turnover, average daily turnover, total number of contracts and turnover per contract. Above all NSE emerged as a big market for the derivatives in India and it is also competing with the global derivative markets. NSE occupied 20th position in the top 20 exchanges offering options and futures and 14th rank among the top 40 exchanges trading in futures. The Index futures and Stock Futures have been jointly contributing above 90 percent and remaining 10 percent was contributed by other products.

* Commodity futures markets in India are still not developed as compared to other countries. The dominant political ideology during early years after independence dealt a severe blow to development of futures markets in India. It is only after the onset of liberalization during 1990s, that attitude towards futures trading has changed and its potential benefits are now being acknowledged in the policy circles.

8.5: SUGGESTIONS

Keeping in view the findings and conclusion of the study on "THE CHANGING PATTERN OF CAPITAL MARKETS IN INDIA - AN ANALYTICAL STUDY", the following suggestions have been made:

* In order to develop efficient capital market, there is big challenge before the new issue market and stock exchange to bring changes in the pattern of the investment of the household sector savings in favor of the industrial securities. It will be possible through motivating the

masses for such investments. Government has also been taking certain steps in promoting the savings towards investing in capital market instrument.

* SEBI needs to bring some discipline into the enormous issues of private placements, which have displaced public issues. It is commonly believed that private placements have grown, because they are not subject to the discipline imposed on public issues by SEBI. SEBI's idea of restricting private placements to "qualified institutional investors" is also not appreciated.

* The foreign investment is encouraging, with the majority of equity participation in its portfolio. The Indian companies have been encouraged to access global capital market through the Euro issues, GDRs and ADRs. The Euro issues have a brighter scope to access more foreign funds from Global Markets. There should be a national policy on Euro issues to monitor the various government agencies like SEBI, DEA, and RBI etc.

* The spirit beyond the introduction of book-building mechanism in India is to discover the right price for a public issue which in turn would eliminate unreasonable issue pricing by greedy promoters. This mechanism is not reached the expected heights of the investors in Indian capital market. The success of the book-building system is depending on the co-operation among the Book Runners, Lead Managers, Issuing Company, Securities and Exchange Board of India (Regulator), and Investors.

* There is a need to strengthen the RSEs to promote the investment attitude in the people throughout the country by taking the various steps like, float the membership, convince the management of unlisted companies, disseminate the information, educate the investors, upgrade the skills of market operators, monitor the compliance, etc.

* A sound system of continuous review and follow-up on disclosure to protection of individual investors should

be developed demarking clear cut areas where regulatory authorities including SEBI, Governments, RBI, Company Law Board, Department of Company Affairs and Standard Setting Institutes. There is a need for better and healthy investment-environment, through rigorous and quick actions against law-breakers in the financial system.

* SEBI has to play an important role for the reduction of volatility of stock price indices in India. The SEBI has to rigorously monitor and control by strengthening its pro-active and reactive measures for the control of stock price volatility. SEBI can direct the authorities of stock exchanges to minimize volatility by applying circuit break system from time to time if there are noticeable fluctuations due to price rigging and unwarranted speculation. Directly and indirectly the Central Government and the Finance Ministry plays a key role in the economy. The controversial announcements are to be avoided in order to eliminate the uncertainties in the minds of the market players about the future.

* Derivative instruments came into existence to mitigate risk in financial markets. However, in India only high net worth individuals and financial institutions could hedge the risks because of the enormous contract sizes and subsequent high margins demanded by the exchanges. These state of affairs must be changed by the SEBI and stock exchanges by reducing the lot size of contracts, adopting spread strategies, reducing margins on spread strategies, abolishing monthly options and introducing the quarterly contracts in general and developing the options and interest rate futures market in particular.

* The following prerequisites are certain to give a big boost to commodity futures trading in India:

* A negotiable document that furnishes the full details of the underlying asset of the futures being traded so that the title of the goods can be transferred from one individual to another without undertaking the physical delivery of stocks.

* An agency that can help the seller and buyer by grading

the stocks being offered by the seller for sale and certify its quality, grade so that the buyer can know what grade of commodity he is trading on.

* There must be an agency that must take care of the securities prices that is being traded in the derivative exchanges and ensures that quality is maintained till the stock under the traded contact is delivered to the ultimate buyer, at a reasonable price.
* Commodities trading have settlements in dematerialized form so that traders from across the country can trade on futures being certain of the underlying commodity in terms of its quality, grade, quantity and its maintenance during the intervening period.
* Banks come forward to sanction agriculture produce loans to farmers against the pledge of warehouse receipts and futures contracts of national derivative exchanges. They should also explore the possibility of offering hedge prospects to farmers on a pooled basis, with banks as intermediaries between exchanges and farmers and thus pave the way for active futures trading on agriculture commodities so that farmers can enjoy the benefit of dependable price discovery well in advance to their planting and sowing season.
* As of now, the Forward Contracts Regulations Act (FCRA) 1952 doesn't permit index based products and these are traded on the commodity exchanges. There is need to amend the Act.
* The capital market must become efficient with widespread awareness amongst various market players, liquidity would increase further with a well-diversified basket of commodities.
* The FMC does not have similar powers as enjoyed by the CFTC in the US. The FCRA 1952 is under the scanner of the present Government and its amendment is likely to bestow more powers on the FMC to regulate this market.
* The Union Finance Minister, in his Budget-2005, has

quoted for a single regulatory regime. It will find very difficult to tackle complexities in the socio-economic dimensions of this flooding commodity futures.

* Healthy competition is always beneficial to catalyze the growth in any market. In this case too, the Government has to take necessary steps for the implementation of online commodity trading on the regional exchanges also.
* Mutual Funds should be allowed to enter into commodity futures market as it will enable them to diversify their portfolio risk with commodities like gold, silver, crude oil, Soya oil etc. the risk and returns for the investors in these funds will depend on the nature of the fund itself, such as Growth, Balanced or Safe funds.
* The market should be made more broad-based by allowing banks and FIIs to participate in commodity futures. Options should be allowed to be traded, as that will give one more efficient tool to the participants to apply various hedging strategies for averting their price risks.

8.6: PRACTICAL UTILITY OF THE STUDY

The present exercise as a whole is a fact-finding research work to predict and monitor the position of Indian stock market after the post liberalized period. The study has been carried out to judge the changing pattern of Indian capital market by evaluating trends and pattern of primary market, secondary market, derivatives market and commodity futures market. For this purpose, different statistical tools have been applied as to derive at the empirical results.

Since, the topic itself is a contemporarily relevant; the findings of this study assume a greater significance and are quite useful to various individual, organizations and institutions.

This study has been potentially relevant to a number of authorities such Banks, Financial Institutions, Investors, Government, Public and Private Industrial Corporations and Research Organizations. The Government/SEBI can use the findings of the study for taking major policy initiations like protection of investors by implementing various measures, reduction of volatility, improvement of performance of regional stock exchanges, for widening the scope of financial and commodity derivatives, etc. For the scholars who are presently working in this area, can make use this study as an ideal reference. On the whole, the findings of this study if properly considered by the concerned authorities can go a long way in bringing a fruitful results and high degree of industrial development in general and capital mobilization in particular in India.

8.7: FURTHER AREAS OF STUDY

Every attempt has been made to make the study more intensive. Still there are some limitations in this study due to lack of time and coverage of data. To overcome these limitations and to enhance the scope of the study, further research may be undertaken in the following areas:

- The Impact of FIIs Investment on the Performance of Indian Companies.
- Stock Market Development and its Impact on the Financing Pattern of the Indian Corporate Sector.
- Is the Futures and Options Market Control the Stock Market Volatility?
- The Impact of International Listings on the Liquidity of Indian Stock Market.
- Role of Commodity Futures Market in Production and Inventory Decisions in India.
- Commodity Futures Market in India Are They Rising to Challenge the Global Derivative Exchanges?

BIBLIOGRAPHY

BOOKS

* Aggarwal A.N: Indian Economy, Current Developments, Willey Eastern Limited, New Delhi.
* Aggarwal & Chowdhary: Indian Economy Crisis and Reforms, Shipra Publications.
* Aggarwal A N & Chowdhary: "Indian Economy, Crisis and Reforms", Shirpa Publications, 1991.
* Aggarwal A N: "Indian Economy, Current Development", Willey Eastern Limited, New Delhi, 1992.
* Ajit Kumar Sinha: New Economic Policy of India, Deep & Deep Publications, New Delhi.
* Arun K. Datta: Government, Finance and Capital Market, P.G. Book Market, Calcutta.
* Avadhani V. A: Capital Market Management, Himalaya Publishing House, Mumbai, India.
* Avadhani V. A: Investment and Securities Markets in India, Himalaya Publishing House, Mumbai, India.
* Bhata: Indian Economy, Issues and Policies, Vikas Publishing House, New Delhi.
* Bhole L M: Financial Institutions and Markets, Tata McGraw-Hill Publishing Company Limited, New Delhi, India.
* Bhuleshkar & Desai: Indian Economy Under Liberalized
* Fischer D. E. & Jordan R. J: Security Analysis and Portfolio Management, Prentice Hall India, New Delhi.
* Gangadhar V. Prof: Investment Management, Anmol Publications

Pvt. Ltd., New Delhi, 2003.

* Gangadhar V. Prof: Securities Analysis and Portfolio Management, Anmol Publication, New Delhi, 2003.
* Gupta Shashi K. & Others: Financial Institutions and Markets, Kalyani Publishers, New Delhi, India.
* Gupta. K.R: Liberalization and Globalization of Indian Economy, Atlantic Publishers and Distributors, New Delhi, India.
* Gupta. S.P: Liberalization: It's Impact on the Indian Economy, Macmillan India, Delhi.
* Guruswamy S. Dr: Financial Markets and Institutions, Vijay Nicole Imprint, Chennai, India.
* Hari Shanker Singhania: "Economic Issues Global & National", Vikas Publishing House Pvt. Ltd., New Delhi, 1995.
* James C. Van Horne: Fundamentals of Financial Management, Prentice Hall of India, p. 526, 1997.
* Khan M Y: Indian Financial System, Tata McGraw-Hill Publishing Company Limited, New Delhi, India.
* Livingston F: The English Capital Market, Methuen, London, 1929.
* N.K.P. Sinha & M.B. Singh: "Industrial Development in India", Rawat Publications, New Delhi, 1993.
* Pandey I. M: Financial Management, Vikas Publishing House Pvt. Ltd. New Delhi, India.
* R.K. Sinha: "Indian Economy in Transition", Deep & Deep Publications, New Delhi, 1994.
* Ravi M. Kishore: Financial Management, Taxmann Allied Services (P.) Ltd., New Delhi, India.
* Robert J. Shiller: Market Volatility, The MIT Press, Massachusetts Institute of Technology, Cambridge, Massachusetts.
* Ruddar Datta & Sundaram: Indian Economy, Sultan Chand & Sons Company Ltd., New Delhi.
* S.K. Misra & V.K. Puri: Indian Economy - Its Development Experience, Himalaya Publishing House.
* S.P. Gupta: Statistical Methods, Sultan Chand & Sons, Educational Publishers, New Delhi, India.

* UmaKapila: Indian Economy Since Independence: The Ongoing Economic Reforms, Delhi Academic Foundation.

* V.S. Mahajan: "Manmohan's India", Deep & Deep Publications, New Delhi, 1994.

* Varghese: Indian Economy Problems & Prospects, Ashish Publishing House, New Delhi.

* Venkata Subramanian. K: Policy and Performance of Indian Economy, Manoj Prakasham Publications, Bangalore, India.

* Vinod Vyasulu Hemalata Rao: Indian Economy: Emerging Challenges, Printwell, Jaipur, India.

ARTICLES:

* Agarwal R N: Capital Market Development, Corporate Financing Pattern and Economic Growth in India, The Asian Economic Review, April, 2003, Vol.45, No.1, P.23.

* Alan Blaylock and Edwin H. Duett: The Declining Market Reaction to ADR Issuers in Emerging Markets, Global Business and Finance Review Fall 2004, p. 1 to 12.

* Alexander G J Eun C S & Janakiramanan S: International Listings and Stock Returns: Some Empirical Evidence, Journal of Financial and Quantitative Analysis, 23 (2) 839-55.

* Amanulla S. & M. Thiripalraju: Week-end Effect: New Evidence from the Indian Stock Market, Vikalpa, Vol. 26, No. 2, April - June 2001, p.33 to 50.

* Amilan S: Consistency of Equity Returns with Corporate Fundamentals in India, Indian Journal of Commerce, Vol.57, No.4, Oct-Dec.2004, P. 31.

* Antoniou A and P Holmes: Futures trading, information and spot price volatility: evidence for the FTSE 100 stock Index and futures contract using GARCH, Journal of Banking and Finance, Vol. 19, 1995, p. 117- 129.

* Basab Dasgupta: Role of Commodity Futures Markets in Spot Price Stabilization, Production and Inventory Decisions with Reference to India, Indian Economic Review, Vol. XXXIX, No. 2, 2004, p. 315 to 325.

* Bharati Pathak: The Government Securities Market-Post Reforms

Scenario & Policy Issues, Finance India, Vol. XVII No.2, June2003, P.535.

* Bhatia. B.: New Issue Market in India, Vora Publications, Bombay, 1976, p. 9.

* Briston. R.J. and Liversidge. J: Practical Approach to Business Investment Decision, London, Mac million, 1979, p.75.

* Chan K, K C Chan and G A Karolyi: Intra day volatility in the stock Index and stock Index futures markets, Review of Financial Studies, Vol. 4, 1991, p. 657-683.

* Chandra: The Impact of Stock Market Liberalization on Liquidity and Efficiency in Emerging Equity Markets, Paper presented at the Annual Conference of the Columbia Business School, September 2002.

* Chuppe & Atkin: Regulation of Securities Markets; Some Recent Trends for Emerging Markets, Washington, D.C., World Bank, 1992.

* Edwards F R: Does futures trading increase stock market volatility? Financial Analysis Journal, Jan/Feb 1988, p. 63-69.

* Gangadhar V. Prof. & Yadagiri: Capital Market Reforms in India, The Indian Journal of Commerce, December, 1993.

* Gangadhar V. Prof. & Arifa Begum: Critical Analysis of Pattern of Capital Issues in India, The Management Accountant, April, 2004, P.324.

* Gangadhar V. Prof. & Mr. G. Naresh Reddy: Book-Building Process: An Efficient Mechanism for Management of Mega Public Issues in India, Research Bulletin of the Institute of Cost and Works Accountants of India, Vol. XXVII, July, 2005, p.31 to 45.

* Gokarm.S: Indian Capital Market Reforms, 1992-96, Economic and Political Weekly, April13, 1996, p.956.

* Gregory K and T Michael: Temporal relationships and dynamic interactions between spot and futures markets, The Journal of Futures Markets, Vol.16, No.1, 1996, p. 55-69.

* Gupta. L.C.: The Changing Structure of Industrial Finance in India, Clarendon Press, Oxford, 1969, p. 200.

* Gurucharan Singh: Illiquidity in Stock Exchanges: Some Issues, The Indian Journal of Commerce, Vol.57, No.4, Oct-Dec.2004, P.71.

* Harris L H: The October 1987 S&P 500 stock futures basis', Journal of Finance, Vol. 44, 1989, p. 77-99.

* Harvinder Kaur: Stock Market Volatility in India, The Indian Journal of Commerce, Vol.57, No.4, Oct-Dec.2004, P.55.

* Henderson. R.F.: New Issues Market and Finance for Industry, Bower and Cambridge, New York, 1951, p.24.

* Joydeep Biswas: Foreign Portfolios Investments and Stock Market Behavior in a Liberalized Economy: An Indian Experience, Asian Economic Review, August Issue 2005, Volume 47, No.2 p. 221 to 232.

* Kalyan Mukherjee: Seasonality Pattern of Stock Indices Volatility: A Study of Selected Indices, Vitta Shodh, The Journal of Finance, Vol.1, No.2, July-December, 2003, p.7-15.

* Kamara A, T Miller and A Siegel: The effects of futures trading on the stability of the S&P 500 returns, The Journal of Futures Markets, Vol.12, 1992, p. 645-658.

* Kamlesh Vikamsey: Capital Market-Future in India, Monthly Public Opinion Surveys, September, 2002, P.14.

* Kim and Singal: Stock Market Openings: Experience of Emerging Issues, Journal of Business, Vol. 73, #1, 2000.

* Krishan Bal: Industrial Securities Market in India, Common Wealth Publishers, New Delhi, 1989, p.53.

* Kulkarni. P.V: Corporation Finance, Himalaya Publishing House, New Delhi, 1987, p. 317.

* L.M. Bhole and Shreeya Pattanaik: The State of Indian Stock Market Under Liberalization, Finance India, Vol. XVI No.1, March 2002, P.159.

* Levine and Zervos: Capital Control Liberalization and Stock Market Development, World Development, Vol. 26, 1998, p. 1169-1183.

* M.T. Raju and Kiran Karande: rice Discovery and Volatility on NSE Futures Market, SEBI Working Paper Series No.7, March 2003, p. 7.

* M.T. Raju, Anirban Ghosh: Stock Market Volatility - An International Comparison, SEBI Working Paper Series No.8, April 2004, p. 8.

* M.T. Raju: Capital Market Reforms in India An Evaluation, The Indian Journal of Commerce, Vol.57, No.4, Oct-Dec.2004, and P.1.

* Madhu Kalimipalli Dr. & Dr. Latha Ramchand: Changes in Liquidity Following Exposure to Foreign Shareholders: The Effect of Foreign Listing and Issues of American Depository Receipts by Indian Firms, NSE Working Paper No. 7, 2002.

* Majumdar N. A: Financial Sector Reform an Exercise in Introspection, Economic and Political Weekly, March 23, 1996, p.727.

* Malodia G. L: Rules and Regulations to Curb Insider Trading in Indian Stock Market, The Indian Journal of Commerce, October-December 2001, Vol.54, No.4, P.48.

* Manas Pandey: Contribution of Domestic Saving in the Growth of New Issue Market, The Indian Journal of Commerce, Vol.57, No.4, Oct-Dec.2004, P.93.

* Manas Pandey: Contribution of Domestic Saving in the Growth of New Issue Market, The Indian Journal of Commerce, Vol. 57, No. 4, October-December 2004, p. 93.

* Manoj Kumar et al: The Impact of International Listings on Liquidity: Evidence from the Indian Stock Market, Vikalpa, Vol. 26, No.4, October - December 2001, p. 35 to 50.

* Merrent. Howe and New Bould: Equity Issue and London Capital Market, 1967, p.4.

* Mukherjee D N & George P: Corporate India in the Age of Reform, Business World, 6-19 September, 1995, p. 34.

* Nagaraj R: India's Capital Market Growth: Trends, Explanations and Evidence, Economic and Political Weekly, September, 1996.

* Parthapratim Pal: Volatility in the Stock Market in India and Foreign Institutional Investors -A Study of the Post-election

Crash, Economic and Political Weekly, February 19th 2005, p. 765 to 772.

* Pasricha J.S and Umesh C. Singh: Foreign Institutional Investors and Stock Market Volatility, The Indian Journal of Commerce, Vol. 54, No.3, July-September, 2001.

* Patro and Wald: Firm Characteristics and the Impact of Emerging Market Liberalizations, Rutgers University Working Paper, 2003.

* Philip Maiyo & Subash Chander: Testing Stock Market Efficiency: A Study of Non-Specified Shares, The Indian Journal of Commerce, October-December 2001, Vol.54, No.4, P.14.

* Prakash Nath Bhargava: Using VARs to Assess Share Price Movements Some Hypotheses and Tests, The Indian Journal of Commerce, Vol.57, No.4, Oct-Dec.2004, P.41.

* Premalata Shenbagaraman: Do Futures and Options Trading Increase Stock Market Volatility? NSE Working Paper, 2004.

* S N Sarma: Stock Market Seasonality in an Emerging Market, Viklpa, Volume-29, July-September 2004, No.3, p.35 to 41.

* Sanjay K. Hansda & Partha Ray: Stock Market Integration and Dually Listed Stocks Indian ADR and Domestic Stock Prices, Economic and Political Weekly, February 22nd 2003, Vol. XXXVIII, No.8, p. 741 to 754.

* Seth A.K. & Saloni Gupta: Understanding Volatility at BSE: A Quality Control Approach Implications for Investors", Decision, Vol.32, No.1, January - June, 2005, p. 1 to 37.

* Siddhartha Sankar Sharma: The Book Building Mechanism of IPOs, The Chartered Account, August 2004, Vol. 53, No. 2, p. 198

* Singh.K.K: The Times of India, Bombay, November11, 1995.

* Suchismita Bose & Dipankor Coondoo: The Impact of FII Regulations in India: Time Series Intervention Analysis of Equity Flows: ICRA Bulletin, Money & Finance Vol.2 Nos. 18-19, July-December 2004, p.54 to 83.

* Sunil Kumar: Price Discovery and Market Efficiency: Evidence

from Agricultural Commodities Futures Markets, South Asian Journal of Management, Vol. 11, Issue No. 2, April -June 2004, p. 12 to 47.

* Tamboli R L: Analysis of Accounting Disclosure and Investor Protection, The Indian Journal of Commerce, Vol.57, No.4, Oct -Dec.2004, P. 108.

* Vashist B. K. & Ashutosh Vashist: Agricultural Futures Markets: Analysis of Equilibrium conditions and Inter-Market Relations, Finance India, Vol. XVI, No. 1, March 2002, P. 121 to 146.

* World Bank: Private Capital Flows to Developing Countries: The Road to Financial Integration, World Bank Policy Research Report, Oxford University Press, New York, 1997.

REPORTS AND OFFICIAL PUBLICATIONS:

* BSE Annual Report 2004-05 and previous issues.

* Budgets, the Government of India: 2000-01 to 2004-05.

* Capital Market Chronicle, A Monthly Bulletin on Capital Market News published by Stock Holding Corporation of India.

* Centre for Monitoring Indian Economy (CMIE) Reports.

* Finance India, Volume XVII, December 2003, 2004 and 2005.

* Government of India, Ministry of Finance & Company Affairs, Economic Division, ECONOMIC SURVEY, 2004-05 and previous reports.

* Hand Book of Statistics on the Indian Securities Market, SEBI 2004.

* Indian Share Owners- A Survey Society for Capital Market Research and Development, New Delhi, 1991.

* NSE Annual Report 2004-05 and previous issues.

* NSE Fact Book 2005.

* Organization for Economic Co-operation and Development (OECD), Working Papers.

* Press Releases, Ministry of Commerce & Industry, Government of India, August 2004.

* Reserve Bank of India Annual Report 2004-05 and previous

issues.

* Reserve Bank of India Bulletin, various issues.
* Reserve Bank of India Reports on Currency and Finance.
* SEBI Annual Report 2004-05 and previous issues.
* SEBI Bulletin various issues.
* SEBI working papers.
* The Hindu Survey of Indian Industry 2005 and previous issues.
* Working Papers of Indian Institute of Management Bangalore.

Web Sites:

* BSE: www.bseindia.com
* Business Line: www.blonet.com
* Business World: www.businessworldindia.com
* Economic & Political Weekly: www.epw.org.in
* Economic Times: www.economictimes.com
* Finance Ministry: www.finmin.nic.in
* London Stock Exchange: www.londonstockexchange.com
* NASDAQ Stock Exchange: www.nasdaq.com
* NSE: www.nseindia.com
* RBI: www.rbi.org.in
* SEBI: www.sebi.gov.in
* Stock Holding Corporation of India: www.shcil.com
* The Hindu: www.thehindu.com
* The Hindustan Times: www.hindustantimes.com
* The Times of India: www.timesofindia.com
* Yahoo Business: www.in.biz.yahoo.co